Record, Mix and Master

Simon Duggal

Record, Mix and Master

A Beginner's Guide to Audio Production

Edited and with Contributions by Paul J Rogers

Simon Duggal
Birmingham, UK

ISBN 978-3-031-40066-7   ISBN 978-3-031-40067-4 (eBook)
https://doi.org/10.1007/978-3-031-40067-4

© The Editor(s) (if applicable) and The Author(s), under exclusive licence to Springer Nature Switzerland AG 2024

This work is subject to copyright. All rights are solely and exclusively licensed by the Publisher, whether the whole or part of the material is concerned, specifically the rights of translation, reprinting, reuse of illustrations, recitation, broadcasting, reproduction on microfilms or in any other physical way, and transmission or information storage and retrieval, electronic adaptation, computer software, or by similar or dissimilar methodology now known or hereafter developed.

The use of general descriptive names, registered names, trademarks, service marks, etc. in this publication does not imply, even in the absence of a specific statement, that such names are exempt from the relevant protective laws and regulations and therefore free for general use.

The publisher, the authors, and the editors are safe to assume that the advice and information in this book are believed to be true and accurate at the date of publication. Neither the publisher nor the authors or the editors give a warranty, expressed or implied, with respect to the material contained herein or for any errors or omissions that may have been made. The publisher remains neutral with regard to jurisdictional claims in published maps and institutional affiliations.

This Palgrave Macmillan imprint is published by the registered company Springer Nature Switzerland AG.
The registered company address is: Gewerbestrasse 11, 6330 Cham, Switzerland

Paper in this product is recyclable.

This work contains media enhancements, which are displayed with a "play" icon. Material in the print book can be viewed on a mobile device by downloading the Springer Nature "More Media" app available in the major app stores. The media enhancements in the online version of the work can be accessed directly by authorized users.

What Makes a Great Recording?

Professional recordings sound great in your car, on your mp3 player, streaming device, Hi-Fi, in a store or just about anywhere else. They contain multiple tracks that are well balanced in level and frequency and include effects such as reverb, delay and modulation. Individual audio tracks are free from noise, hums, hisses, clicks, pops and unwanted ambience, equalised to bring out desired tones, compressed to reduce the difference between the quiet parts and the loud parts, and the volume level of each instrument and voice are set relative to all the other tracks contained within the recording.

A great sound will make you want to listen. If a recording sounds unpleasant, your instinct might be to turn it off or skip to another song. The sonic character of a recording is as important as the components that make up the song.

For film and Television, a great sound can enhance the viewer's experience and make the visual message more direct and emotive. Imagine watching a tense thriller at the movies where the underlying soundtrack lacks bass. It would of course reduce the dynamic impact of the visual, thereby making the scene feel weak and anticlimactic.

I have written this book to help you achieve great recordings, mixes and masters. It is written in a way that is easy to understand, and wherever possible, I have avoided complicated jargon. Recording, mixing and mastering music to a high standard requires technical knowledge and lots of practice. This book will teach you about the audio tools available and how to use them, the science of digital audio as well as how to create an acoustically accurate listening environment where you can trust what you are hearing. This book is also full of handy tips and tricks, including lots from world class mix engineers and producers.

Whether you are just starting out on your journey into the world of audio reproduction, or whether you have some experience under your belt, this book is for you.

Good luck with your music projects.

Birmingham, UK   Simon Duggal

Acknowledgements

I'd like to express my thanks to the following people: Eshan Duggal, Jayan Duggal and Ruth Edmondson, for their support and encouragement throughout. They've listened while I've read out sections and made valuable comments about how I can make the content easier to understand.

Thanks to Errol Reid, Nauwshaad Abdoelgafoer, Tatiana Ferrer and Ruchi Parikh for all of their help.

Thanks to Gabriela Kettle for providing vocals for the audio examples.

Thanks to all those who have contributed 'Tips from the Pros' to the book. I appreciate you taking time out of your busy schedules to share your knowledge and expertise.

They are, in no particular order:

Kevin Churko—Producer, Songwriter and Musician
Disturbed, Ozzy Osbourne, Shania Twain, Five Finger Death Punch, The Corrs, Britney Spears and more.

Axwell—Producer and Songwriter
Swedish House Mafia, Flo Rider, Brandon Flowers, Faithless, Usher and more.

Steve Osborne—Producer
U2, A-ha, New Order, Suede, Paul Oakenfold, Happy Mondays and more.

Peter Duggal—Producer and Composer
Wolfgang Flür, Peter Hook, Midge Ure, Claudia Brücken, Carl Cox, Juan Atkins, Maps and more.

Simone Torres—Vocal Producer, Engineer and Vocalist.
Normani, Chlöe Bailey, Billy Porter, Anitta, Camila Cabello, Cardi B, Monsta X, Sia, The Backstreet Boys, Dua Lipa, Jessie J and more.

Marcus Byrne—Producer and Musician
Take That, ELO, MIKA, Taio Cruz and more.

Mike Exeter—Producer, Engineer, Mixer and Composer
Engineer, Mixer and Composer - Black Sabbath, Judas Priest, Ronnie James Dio, Cradle Of Filth and more.

Hans-Martin Buff—Engineer and Producer
Prince, The Beatifics, Boney M, The New Power Generation and more.

Diamond Duggal—Producer, Songwriter and Musician
Shania Twain, Apache Indian, Erasure, The Beat, Maxi Priest, Swami and more.

Iwan VanHetten—Producer, Songwriter and Musician

Brooklyn Funk Essentials, Sister Sledge, The Pointer Sisters, Candy Duffer and more.

Alex Picciafuochi—Producer & Mastering Engineer
Robert Miles, Luca Agnelli, Claudio Coccoluto, Caneschi and more.

Richard Taylor—Producer, Songwriter and Musician
Emin, Ronan Keating, Bananarama, XFactor, David Foster, Nile Rodgers, Little Mix, 1D, Boyzone, Westlife, James Arthur, Mcfly and more.

Chris Taylor—Producer, Songwriter and Musician
Ruby Turner, Paul Potts, Robbie Williams, George Ezra, The Shires, Emili Sande and more.

TJ Rehmi —Producer, Composer and Musician
Nusrat Fateh Ali Khan, Natacha Atlas, Mumiy Troll, Trilok Gurtu, Cheb i Sabbah and more.

Meldra Guza—Managing Director at The SongLab
Senior Lecturer, Voice Over Artist (Mattel), Session musician, Songwriter.

Dr Paul J Rogers—Producer, Songwriter and University Lecturer
Composer, Producer, Sound designer and University lecturer.

Mark Gittins—FOH engineer, Broadcast Engineer and Studio Owner.
The Wytches, Youth Man, Robert Craig Oulton, Premier League Productions, BT sports, BBC and more.

Jonny Amos—Songwriter, Producer, Lecturer and Director at The SongLab.
Shayne Ward, Jpop Idols EXIT, Miss D, Jackie Paladino, Glow Beets, Native Instruments Sounds. MTV, Sky One and Film Four and more.

Martin 'Magic' Johnson—Session Drummer, Producer, Mixer:
B*witched, Guthrie Govan, Jo Harman, Sam Fox, Mike Farris, Praying Mantis and more

Jaclyn Sanchez—Engineer
Jon Batiste, H.E.R., Anderson Paak, Lauren Hill and Common.

I'd also like to express my thanks to the following companies for their kind permission to use their product images.

Waves Audio	www.waves.com
Audified	www.audified.com
Oeksound	www.oeksound.com
Focusrite	www.focusrite.com
FabFilter	www.fabfilter.com
Celemony	www.celemony.com
HEDD	www.hedd.audio
Laurent Colson	www.dev.laurentcolson.com
Soundtoys	www.soundtoys.com
Giraffe Audio	www.giraffeaudio.com
United Plugins	www.unitedplugins.com
Golden Age Project	www.goldenageproject.com
Neumann	www.neumann.com

Finally, I'd like to thank Dr Paul J Rogers for his support and contributions. His input has been invaluable.

Contents

Part I Record   1

1 An Introduction to How Sound Works 3
    Soundwaves... 3
    Amplitude 5
    Sound Dispersion 6
    Equal Loudness Contours..................................... 7
    Speaker to Room Relationship 7

2 Speakers... 11
    Types of Speakers.. 11
    Speaker Placement 17
    Speaker Listening Levels 24

3 Digital Audio Workstation 29
    Pro Tools DAW Controls and Functions......................... 30
    Mix Window 33
    Tools 34
    MIDI Edit Window 35
    Labelling Tracks 39

4 Digital... 41
    Sample Rate 41
    Bit Depth (Word Length) 45
    Nyquist Frequency, Aliasing and Oversampling................... 47
    Word Clock, Jitter and Frequency Drift 50
    DC Offset 52
    Hardware Buffer Size and Latency.............................. 53
    File Formats 57

5 Hardware... 59
    Audio Interface 59
    Audio Cables.. 60
    Equipment Connections 65
    Preamps (Pre-Amplifier)..................................... 68
    Controller Keyboards 69
    Headphones... 70

6	**Gain Staging**	75
	Analogue Gain Staging	75
	Digital Gain Staging	76

7	**Microphones**	81
	Types of Microphones	81
	Microphone, Instrument and Line Level	90
	Recording Vocals	93

8	**Phase**	99

9	**Room Acoustics**	105
	Room Acoustic Treatment	105
	DIY Broadband Bass Trap	113

10	**Recording Tips**	123
	General	123
	Drums	124
	Bass Guitar	126
	Electric Guitar	126
	Acoustic Guitar	127
	Vocal Tips	127

Part II   Mix   131

11	**Equalisers**	133
	Graphic Equalisers	134
	Parametric Equalisers	134
	Additive and Subtractive Eq	135
	Types of Equaliser Filters	135
	Q—Bandwidth	140
	Dynamic Eq	141
	Minimum Phase	141
	Linear Phase	142
	Baxandall Curve	142
	Frequency Range	143
	Equaliser Tips	144
	Modelled Equalisers	145
	Piano Display	146

12	**Dynamics**	149
	Compressors	149
	Limiters	163
	Expanders	165
	Noise Gates	166
	De-Essers	166
	Resonance and Spectral Shaping	170

13	**Effects**	173
	Reverberation (Reverb)	173
	Delay and Echo	177
	Modulation: Phasers, Flangers and Chorus	179
	Distortion and Saturation	180
	Inserting Effects	181
	Pitch Correction	182
14	**Subgroups**	185
	Subgroups and VCA	185
	Step-By-Step Guide to Routing	186
15	**Monitoring in Mono**	189
16	**Mid/Side Processing**	193
17	**Transients**	197
18	**Panning**	201
	Pan Law	204
19	**Plosives**	205
20	**Zero Crossing and Crossfades**	209
21	**Mixing Tips**	215
	Getting Ready to Mix	216
	Drums and Bass	218
	Vocals	220
	Guitars and Synths	220
	General	222

Part III Master   227

22	**What is Mastering?**	229
23	**Prepare Your Track for Mastering**	231
24	**Mastering Tools**	235
	Compression	235
	Equalisation	236
	Harmonic Exciter	236
	Reverb	236
	Stereo Enhancement	236
	Limiting and Clipping	237
25	**Dither**	239
26	**Metering: Peak, RMS and LUFS**	243
	Peak Program Meter (PPM)	244
	Root Mean Square (RMS)	244
	Loudness Units Full Scale (LUFS)	245

27 Mastering Your Song: Things to Consider 247
   Listen. 248
   Dynamics and Compression 249
   Corrective Eq and Tone Shaping. 250
   Harmonic Enhancement 250
   Limiting. 250
   Dither 251
   Mastering Chain 251
   Stem Mastering. 251

Glossary 253
Index 259

About the Author

Simon Duggal is an award-winning producer, composer and musician with over 30 years in the music industry. He has produced records for Shania Twain, Maxi Priest, Erasure, The Beat, Errol Reid (China Black), Apache Indian, Swami, Desmond Dekker, Nusrat Fateh Ali Khan, Janet Kaye, Luciano, Dillinger and many more. He has composed music for many television commercials for clients including Pepsi, Toshiba, Intel, Etihad and Etisalat and has songs featured in Hollywood, Bollywood and British movies.

Records produced and composed by Simon have been nominated for two Grammy Awards, three Brit Awards and a Mercury Music Prize and have achieved a combined 14 x Platinum sales. He was also nominated for a coveted Ivor Novello Award in the category of best contemporary song alongside Take That and M People.

Simon is also an MA Specialist Mentor in Music Production at The British and Irish Modern Music University, an ambassador at DMS, the UK's largest independent music school, and an ambassador at The Birmingham Music Awards.

List of Figures

Fig. 1.1	Soundwaves vibrating air molecules	4
Fig. 1.2	Soundwave vibrating four hundred and forty times per second	4
Fig. 1.3	Low-, mid- and high-frequency wavelengths	5
Fig. 1.4	Length of a 50 Hz wave	5
Fig. 1.5	Amplitude	6
Fig. 1.6	Sound radiation from a speaker	6
Fig. 1.7	Equal loudness contours	7
Fig. 1.8	A simplified example of how sound reflects off a room's boundaries	8
Fig. 2.1	HEDD Type 07 near/mid-field active studio monitors. Image courtesy of HEDD Audio	12
Fig. 2.2	Classic Yamaha NS-10M studio speaker	13
Fig. 2.3	Dual concentric speaker	14
Fig. 2.4	Conventional speaker	14
Fig. 2.5	A typical subwoofer	15
Fig 2.6	Connecting subwoofer and satellite speakers	16
Fig. 2.7	Closed and ported speaker cabinets	17
Fig. 2.8	Speaker positioning	18
Fig. 2.9	The sweet spot	19
Fig. 2.10	Speaker distance from side walls	20
Fig. 2.11	Listening position for improved stereo image	21
Fig. 2.12	Comb filtering	22
Fig. 2.13	Comb filtering caused by speakers placed on desk	23
Fig. 2.14	Comb filtering eliminated by placing speakers on stands behind desk	23
Fig. 2.15	A typical sound pressure level metre	25
Fig. 2.16	Mark your ideal listening level	26
Fig. 2.17	Subwoofer placement	27
Fig. 3.1	The different types of tracks in Pro Tools	30
Fig. 3.2	Typical DAW transport controls	32
Fig. 3.3	Pro Tools arrangement window grid settings	32
Fig. 3.4	Pro Tools mix window	34
Fig. 3.5	Pro Tools MIDI edit window showing unquantized notes	35
Fig. 3.6	Pro Tools MIDI edit window showing quantized notes	36

Fig. 3.7	Pro Tools groove quantise menu	37
Fig. 3.8	Pro Tools MIDI note velocity slider	38
Fig. 3.9	Adjusting MIDI note length	38
Fig. 4.1	Analogue to digital and digital to analogue signal path	42
Fig. 4.2	Audio signal sampled at 44.1 kHz—44,100 samples per second	43
Fig 4.3	Audio signal sampled at 88.2 kHz—88,200 samples per second	43
Fig. 4.4	Upsampling—zero filling	44
Fig. 4.5	Downsampling—decimation	45
Fig. 4.6a	Bit depth—24 bit	46
Fig. 4.6b	Bit depth—16 bit	46
Fig. 4.7	Audio file size per minute	47
Fig. 4.8	Audio signal sampled at multiple points	48
Fig. 4.9	Nyquist frequency at 44.1 kHz	48
Fig. 4.10	An anti-aliasing filter is essentially a squared low-pass filter	49
Fig. 4.11	Oversampling	50
Fig. 4.12	Jitter	50
Fig. 4.13	Frequency drift	51
Fig. 4.14	DC offset	52
Fig. 4.15	Reduced headroom resulting from DC offset	53
Fig. 4.16	Unevenly weighted waveform resulting from DC offset	53
Fig. 4.17	Hardware buffer size	54
Fig. 4.18	Input signal monitoring	55
Fig. 4.19	Automatic delay compensation	56
Fig. 5.1	Focusrite Scarlett 18i20 (front). (Image courtesy of Focusrite Audio Engineering Ltd)	60
Fig. 5.2	Focusrite Scarlett 18i20 (back). (Image courtesy of Focusrite Audio Engineering Ltd)	60
Fig. 5.3	Balanced TRS jack plug	60
Fig. 5.4	Normal and reversed polarity	61
Fig. 5.5	Balanced signal path	62
Fig. 5.6	Unbalanced signal path	62
Fig. 5.7	Balanced and unbalanced TRS jak plugs	63
Fig. 5.8	Male and female XLR connectors	63
Fig. 5.9	RCA (Phono) coaxial connector	64
Fig. 5.10	Optical (Toslink) connector	65
Fig. 5.11	AES/EBU cable	65
Fig. 5.12	Typical equipment connections	67
Fig. 5.13	Pre-amplifier (front)	68
Fig. 5.14	Pre-amplifier (back)	69
Fig. 5.15	A typical MIDI/USB controller keyboard	70
Fig. 5.16	Listening on speakers	72
Fig. 5.17	The stereo image is wider when listening on headphones	73
Fig. 5.18	Typical frequency response of headphones	73
Fig. 5.19	Calibrated frequency equals a flat response	74

List of Figures

Fig. 6.1	Analogue VU metres	76
Fig. 6.2	Digital signal headroom	77
Fig. 6.3	Ideal input signal level	78
Fig. 6.4	Individual channels summed to master bus	79
Fig. 7.1	Neumann KMS 104 Plus dynamic microphone. (Image courtesy of Neumann GmBH)	82
Fig. 7.2	Neumann U87 Ai condenser microphone. (Image courtesy of Neumann GmBH)	82
Fig. 7.3	Neumann KM 185 small condenser microphone. (Image courtesy of Neumann GmBH)	83
Fig. 7.4	Golden Age Project R1 Active Mk3 Ribbon Microphone. (Image courtesy of Golden Age Project)	84
Fig. 7.5	Cardioid pattern	85
Fig. 7.6	Hypercardioid pattern	86
Fig. 7.7	Bidirectional pattern	87
Fig. 7.8	Omnidirectional pattern	88
Fig. 7.9	Microphone proximity effect	89
Fig. 7.10	Microphone sensitivity to changes in level	90
Fig. 7.11	Microphone signal-to-noise ratio	91
Fig. 7.12	Line, consumer, instrument and microphone levels	91
Fig. 7.13.1	A typical passive DI Box	93
Fig. 7.13.2	A typical passive DI Box	93
Fig. 7.14	Cardioid pattern	94
Fig. 7.15	Neumann U87i with pop shield. Image courtesy of Neumann GmBH	95
Fig. 7.16	Typical microphone HPF	96
Fig. 7.17	Distance from microphone	97
Fig. 8.1	Peaks and dips in the frequency response	100
Fig. 8.2	Microphone 3:1 rule	100
Fig. 8.3	Signal entering second microphone delayed	101
Fig. 8.4	Constructive interference	102
Fig. 8.5	Destructive interference	102
Fig. 9.1	Room modes	106
Fig. 9.2	Speaker boundary interference response	106
Fig. 9.3	An example of how sound energy builds up in a room	108
Fig. 9.4	How speaker placement affects low-frequency response	109
Fig. 9.5	Broadband bass trap straddled across a corner	109
Fig. 9.6	Typical broadband absorber placement	111
Fig. 9.7	A typical calibration microphone	112
Fig. 9.8	The effect of SBIR on the frequency response	112
Fig. 9.9	A DIY broadband bass trap	113
Fig. 9.10	DIY broadband bass trap, Step 1	114
Fig. 9.11	DIY broadband bass trap, Step 2	115
Fig. 9.12	DIY broadband bass trap, Step 3	115
Fig. 9.13	DIY broadband bass trap, Step 4	116

Fig. 9.14	DIY broadband bass trap, Step 5	116
Fig. 9.15	DIY broadband bass trap, Step 5	117
Fig. 9.16	DIY broadband bass trap, Step 6	117
Fig. 9.17	DIY broadband bass trap, Step 6	118
Fig. 9.18	DIY broadband bass trap, Step 7	118
Fig. 9.19	DIY broadband bass trap, Step 7	119
Fig. 9.20	DIY broadband bass trap, Step 8	119
Fig. 9.21	DIY broadband bass trap, Step 8	120
Fig. 9.22	DIY broadband bass trap, Step 8	120
Fig. 9.23	DIY broadband bass trap, Step 8	121
Fig. 11.1	Graphic equaliser	134
Fig. 11.2	Parametric equaliser	134
Fig. 11.3	FabFilter Pro-Q2, low-pass filter. (Image courtesy of FabFilter)	135
Fig. 11.4	FabFilter Pro-Q2, high-pass filter. (Image courtesy of FabFilter)	136
Fig. 11.5	FabFilter Pro-Q2, notch filter. (Image courtesy of FabFilter)	137
Fig. 11.6	FabFilter Pro-Q2, bell filter. (Image courtesy of FabFilter)	137
Fig. 11.7	FabFilter Pro-Q2, band-pass filter. (Image courtesy of FabFilter)	138
Fig. 11.8	FabFilter Pro-Q2, high-shelf filter. (Image courtesy of FabFilter)	138
Fig. 11.9	FabFilter Pro-Q2, low-shelf filter. (Image courtesy of FabFilter)	139
Fig. 11.10	FabFilter Pro-Q2, tilt filter. (Image courtesy of FabFilter)	139
Fig. 11.11	Frequency bandwidth	140
Fig. 11.12	Filter type symbols	140
Fig. 11.13	Minimum phase Eq	141
Fig. 11.14	FabFilter Pro-Q2, Baxandall curve. (Image courtesy of FabFilter)	143
Fig. 11.15	Frequency range	143
Fig. 11.16	Audified RZ062 equaliser. (Image courtesy of Audified)	145
Fig. 11.17	Waves H-Eq. (Image courtesy of Waves Audio Ltd)	146
Fig. 12.1	Waves API 2500 compressor. (Image courtesy of Waves Audio Ltd)	150
Fig. 12.2	Compression ratio	151
Fig. 12.3	Compression knee	152
Fig. 12.4	Compressor circuit	154
Fig. 12.5	Compressor feedforward circuit	154
Fig. 12.6	Compressor feedback circuit	155
Fig. 12.7	An example of a compressed signal	156
Fig. 12.8	A mix before compression	157
Fig. 12.9	A mix after compression	157
Fig. 12.10	A mix after limiting	158
Fig. 12.11	Sidechain compression setup	159

List of Figures

Fig. 12.12	Sidechain Eq filter	160
Fig. 12.13	Parallel compression setup	161
Fig. 12.14	Waves LinMB multiband compressor. (Image courtesy of Waves Audio Ltd)	162
Fig. 12.15	Waves L2 ultramaximiser limiter. (Image courtesy of Waves Audio Ltd)	163
Fig. 12.16	Signal before and after limiting	164
Fig. 12.17	Expander	165
Fig. 12.18	Automating a reduction in level on sibilant parts of the signal	167
Fig. 12.19	Waves De-Esser. (Image courtesy of Waves Audio Ltd)	168
Fig. 12.20	Editing sibilant parts of the signal on a separate track	169
Fig. 12.21	Resonance	170
Fig. 12.22	OEK-sound Soothe—dynamic resonance suppressor. (Image courtesy of OEK-sound)	171
Fig. 13.1	Waves H reverb. (Image courtesy of Waves Audio Ltd)	174
Fig. 13.2	MusicMath by Laurent Colson	175
Fig. 13.3	Reverb tail decays before the next drum strike	176
Fig. 13.4	Delayed repeats fading out	177
Fig. 13.5	Waves H-delay. (Image courtesy of Waves Audio Ltd)	178
Fig. 13.6	Phaser, flanger and chorus effects	179
Fig. 13.7	Soundtoys PhaseMistress. (Image courtesy of Soundtoys)	180
Fig. 13.8	Celemony Melodyne plugin. (Image courtesy of Celemony)	182
Fig. 14.1	Channel outputs routed to auxiliary input	186
Fig. 15.1	Monitoring in mono	190
Fig. 16.1	Stereo processing	194
Fig. 16.2	Mid/side processing	194
Fig. 16.3	Waves centre mid/side processor. (Image courtesy of Waves Audio Ltd)	194
Fig. 17.1	Transients	198
Fig. 17.2	Sound envelope—attack, decay, sustain and release	198
Fig. 17.3	The controls on a typical transient shaper plugin	198
Fig. 18.1	Typical DAW pan controls	202
Fig. 18.2	Panning visualised as a clock	202
Fig. 18.3	An example of how instruments may be placed in the stereo field	203
Fig. 19.1	High-pass filter	206
Fig. 19.2	Automating reduction in level on plosives	206
Fig. 19.3	Neumann U87 microphone. (Image courtesy of Neumann GmBH)	207
Fig. 20.1	Zero crossing point	209
Fig. 20.2	Audio edited at zero crossing. No jump in amplitude	210
Fig. 20.3	Audio edited at non-zero crossing. Signal jumps in amplitude	210
Fig. 20.4	Crossfade applied to edited signal	211
Fig. 20.5	Audio section to be edited	211
Fig. 20.6	Audio section edited	212

Fig. 20.7	Crossfade applied to edited section	212
Fig. 21.1	Mixing desk and hardware effects	215
Fig. 21.2	Mixing desk faders	217
Fig. 22.1	Waves L3 multimaximiser mastering plugin. (Image courtesy of Waves Audio Ltd)	230
Fig. 23.1	Signal headroom and dynamic range	232
Fig. 23.2	Inter-sample peak	233
Fig. 24.1	Hard and soft clipping	237
Fig. 25.1	Analogue input and digital output	240
Fig. 25.2	Bit depth reduction and dither	240
Fig. 26.1	Signal peak and RMS value	244
Fig. 26.2	Peak program metres	244
Fig. 26.3	RMS meter	245
Fig. 26.4	Loudness units full scale	245
Fig. 27.1	Typical frequency response of a mastered track	249

Part I
Record

An Introduction to How Sound Works

1

▶ **Learning Outcomes**

By the end of this chapter, the reader will be able to:
- Define the properties of soundwaves and sound pressure levels.
- Explain units of measurement in relation to amplitude and wavelengths.
- Recall how sound behaves in critical listening environments.

Soundwaves

Sound is the result of the energy that is created when air molecules are vibrated. When a speaker cone moves forwards and backwards, a person speaks, or a guitar string vibrates, it causes air molecules to move in sympathy, which in turn causes our eardrums to vibrate. The vibrations in our eardrums are transmitted through the middle ear bones to the inner ear, where they are converted into electrical signals that are interpreted by our brains as the sounds we hear (Fig. 1.1).

Sound travels through the air in waves at approximately 344 metres per second. The speed can vary up or down slightly depending on air temperature. This behaviour is much like when a stone is dropped into water, causing waves to radiate outwards.

Frequency is determined by the number of wave cycles per second and is measured in Hertz (Hz) per second. For example, a guitar string vibrating at 440 Hz (the note A above middle C) is equal to 440 vibrations or cycles per second. Frequencies of 1000 Hz and above are referred to as kilohertz or KHz (Fig. 1.2).

Supplementary Information The online version contains supplementary material available at https://doi.org/10.1007/978-3-031-40067-4_1. The videos can be accessed individually by clicking the DOI link in the accompanying figure caption or by scanning this link with the SN More Media App.

© The Author(s), under exclusive license to Springer Nature Switzerland AG 2024
S. Duggal, *Record, Mix and Master*,
https://doi.org/10.1007/978-3-031-40067-4_1

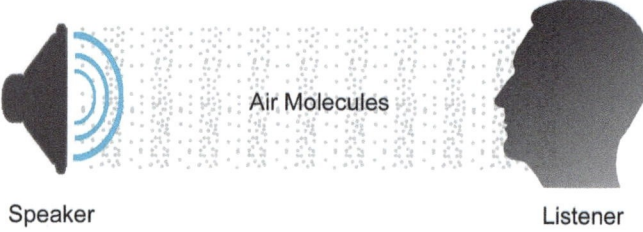

Fig. 1.1 Soundwaves vibrating air molecules

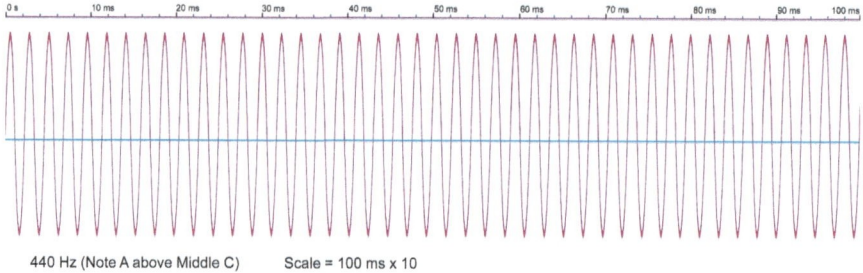

Fig. 1.2 Soundwave vibrating four hundred and forty times per second

The lower the frequency and therefore the lower the note in pitch, the longer the wave is. In Fig. 1.3, you can see the difference in wavelength between low, mid and high frequencies over the same time span.

The length of a single wave at any given frequency can be calculated by dividing the speed of sound by the frequency. For example, the length of a 50 Hz wave would be (Fig. 1.4):

$$344 \left(speed\ of\ sound\ in\ metrers\ \text{per}\ second \right) \div 50 \left(\text{Hz}\ or\ cycles\ \text{per}\ second \right) = 6.88\ metrers$$

By contrast, the length of a 5000 Hz (5 kHz) wave would be 344 ÷ 5000 = 0.0688 metres (6.88 centimetres).

Amplitude

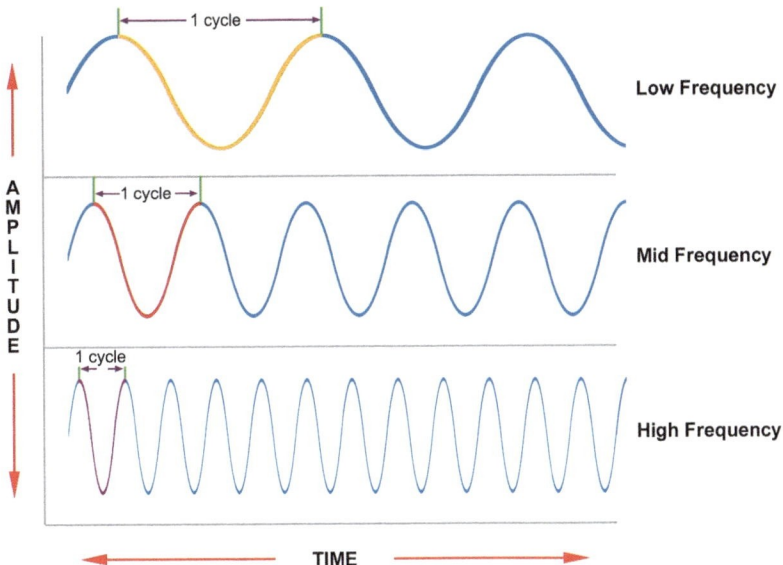

Fig. 1.3 Low-, mid- and high-frequency wavelengths

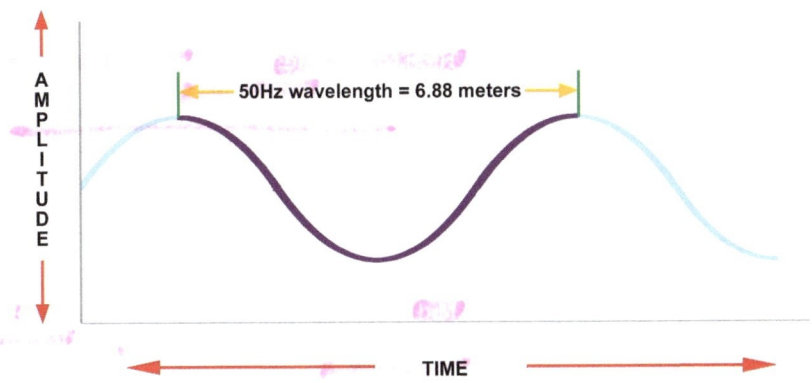

Fig. 1.4 Length of a 50 Hz wave

Amplitude

Amplitude is the maximum extent of a vibration or oscillation of sound measured from the position of equilibrium—the point from which the signal level either rises or falls. Amplitude determines how loud or quiet the sound is and is measured in Decibels (dB), a unit used to measure the intensity of a sound. The decibel scale is logarithmic. When the sound pressure is doubled, it corresponds to an increase of 3 dB in level (Fig. 1.5).

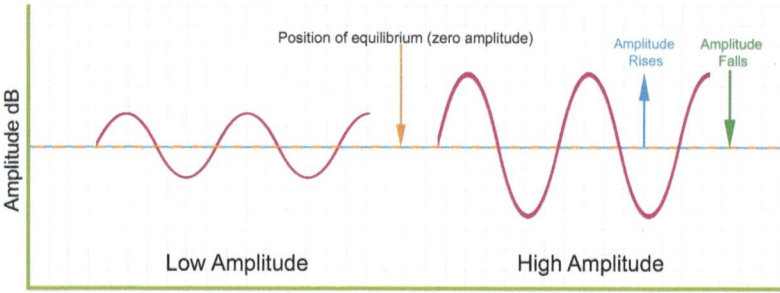

Fig. 1.5 Amplitude

Sound Dispersion

Low-frequency sounds played through a speaker are omnidirectional. That means the sound radiates outwards from the speaker in all directions, including behind the speaker cabinet. Mid frequencies are more directional, and the highest frequencies travel directly towards the ear from the speaker (Fig. 1.6).

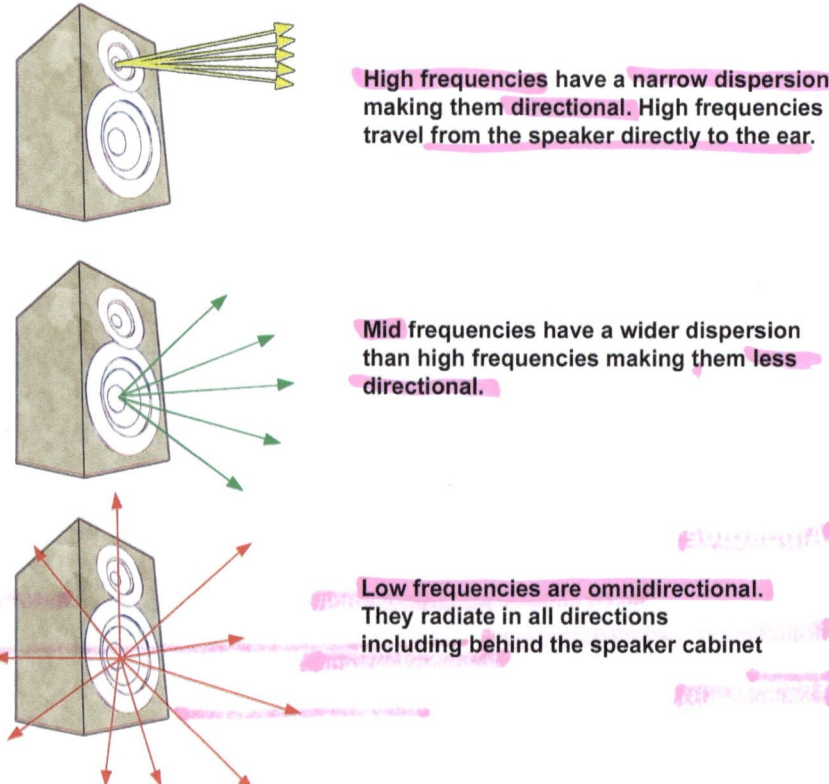

Fig. 1.6 Sound radiation from a speaker

Equal Loudness Contours

In 1933, two physicists, Harvey Fletcher and Wilden A. Munson, conducted research into how humans hear sound at different volume levels. They measured sound pressure levels (dB SPL) over the frequency spectrum of human hearing −20 Hz to 22 kHz using the Phon unit of measurement. They determined that, in the simplest of terms, the quieter we listen to audio material, the less bass and treble we hear. There have since been many studies into Equal Loudness Contours; however, the Fletcher–Munson curve is probably the best known (Fig. 1.7).

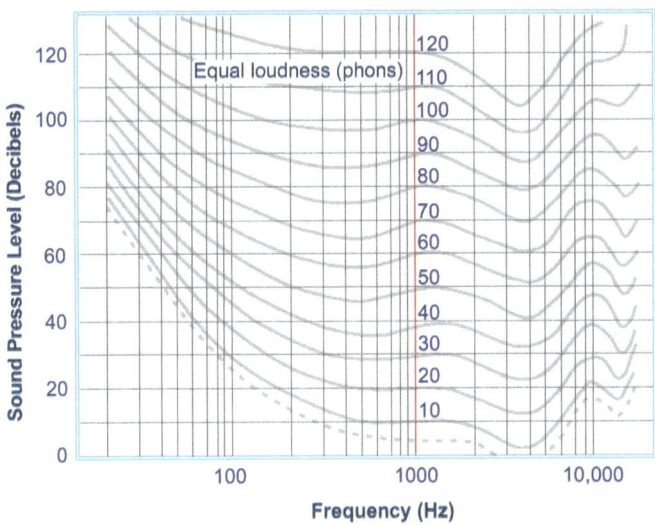

Fig. 1.7 Equal loudness contours

Many Hi-Fi amplifiers have a loudness switch. When listening quietly to a Hi-Fi system, engaging the loudness switch compensates for the Equal Loudness Contours by boosting the bass and treble frequencies.

It is important to be aware of this when recording and mixing music. If you mix your track whilst monitoring too loud, you will hear more bass and treble frequencies. When the mixed track is played back on other systems, it will sound dull and lack weight. If monitored too quietly, the opposite can happen. Your mixes may end up sounding bass-heavy and overly bright (See Chap. 2: Speakers—Speaker Listening Levels).

Speaker to Room Relationship

When we hear sound, what we are actually hearing is a combination of direct sound from the source—for example, a person speaking or music playing through a speaker and reflected sound bouncing off surfaces such as walls, ceilings, tables, windows or any other object that is nearby. There are multiple reflections at every frequency.

Whilst in most everyday listening situations this is not a problem, in studios and critical listening environments, this can have a big impact on the audio decisions you make. Our brains cannot distinguish between reflected sound arriving at our ears less than approximately 20 milliseconds after the direct sound from the speakers, so we perceive it to be one sound. These reflections interfere with the direct sound causing dips and peaks in the frequency response, which fool us into thinking that a particular frequency is too quiet or too loud when in actual fact it is not (Fig. 1.8).

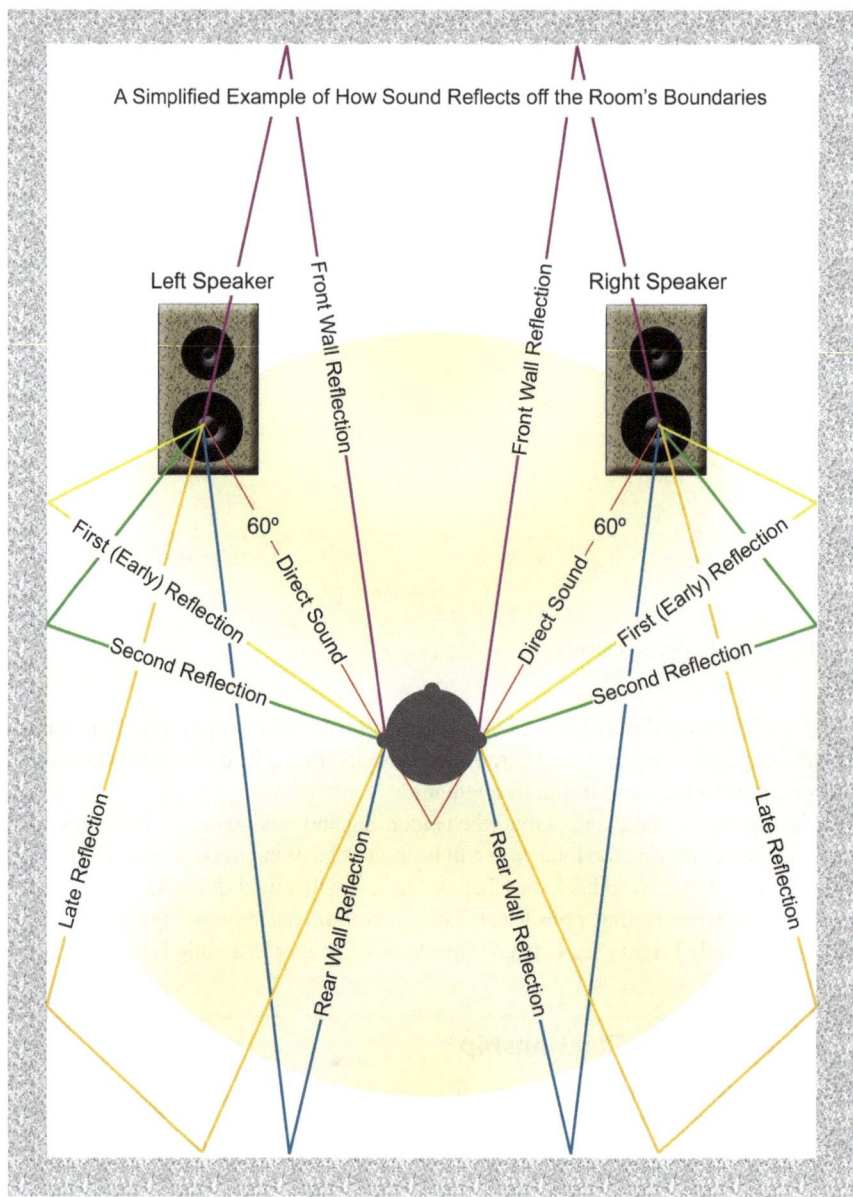

Fig. 1.8 A simplified example of how sound reflects off a room's boundaries

When a reflection is in phase (See Chap. 8: Phase) with the source sound, constructive interference reinforces the signal. This causes a boost in amplitude at the given frequency. When the reflection is out of phase, it causes a cancellation at the given frequency, thereby causing a reduction in amplitude. By acoustically treating the room, we can absorb, diffuse or scatter reflections so that we can hear more of the speaker and less of the room (See Chap. 9: Room Acoustics).

Understanding how sound behaves in critical listening environments will help you create an ideal studio space and listening position where you can trust what is coming out of your speakers. This means you will be able to make the right decisions about your audio and ensure that it translates well to a variety of playback systems.

▶ **Chapter 1 Tasks:** The following tasks will audibly demonstrate sound dispersion, speaker to room relationships and the interaction of soundwaves to the local environment. The provided audio tracks will reveal how high frequency soundwaves are directional, low frequencies are omnidirectional, and the ways in which our ears receive sound sources from both the speakers and room reflections.

- **Download the stereo Audio example 2.2a and import it into your DAW.**
- Loop the audio for continuous playback.
- Play the audio track through your speakers at a comfortable volume and allow the sound to travel around the room.
- Listen carefully to the sound from in front of your speakers, then slowly start moving and tilting your head from side to side. Note the differences in the way you perceive the sound.
- Stand up slowly and quietly and begin moving around the room. Position your head in a range of places, heights and angles and note the changes in what you hear, despite the audio being played remaining constant.
- Consider how you perceive changing levels in amplitude, clarity of sound, stereo imaging, oscillations of frequency and the directional certainty of where the sound is coming from.
- **Download the stereo Audio example 2.2b and import it into your DAW.**
- Loop the audio for continuous playback.
- Play the audio track through your speakers at a comfortable volume and allow the sound to travel around the room.
- Move slowly around the room and place your head at a range of heights and positions. Make a note of changes in amplitude in your perception of the audio.
- Try standing in the corners of your room and listen for changes in intensity of the low frequencies.
- Consider how the low-frequency sound is behaving, depending on your listening position, and how this could affect recording and mixing. Note how more omnidirectional the low frequencies are compared to the directional high frequencies.

Speakers 2

Types of Speakers

▶ **Learning Outcomes**

By the end of this chapter, the reader will be able to:
- Define the differences between a range of speaker types.
- Create an appropriate listening environment utilizing correct speaker placement.
- Calibrate suitable speaker listening levels.

Studio speakers, also referred to as monitors (not to be confused with your computer screen), are designed specifically for recording studios, film studios, home and project studios and other critical listening environments where accurately reproduced sound is crucial. They are designed to give an honest representation of what is going on in your audio material.

Studio speakers are designed to have a narrow field of dispersion (see Chap. 1: An Introduction to How Sound Works—Sound Dispersion), which helps to reduce the amount of sound reaching the room's boundaries and reflecting back at the listening position.

There's some debate over whether or not Hi-Fi speakers can be used for critical listening purposes. One point of contention is that Hi-Fi speakers do not usually have such a narrow field of dispersion, thereby increasing the likelihood of early reflections from nearby sidewalls (see Chap. 4: Room Acoustic Treatment), and they are designed to artificially enhance the sound with adjusted bass and treble to

---

Supplementary Information The online version contains supplementary material available at https://doi.org/10.1007/978-3-031-40067-4_2. The videos can be accessed individually by clicking the DOI link in the accompanying figure caption or by scanning this link with the SN More Media App.

make them sound more exciting. This of course depends on the particular speakers in question as well as the quality of the amplifier used.

For the purpose of understanding different types of speakers for your studio, the following pages will focus only on studio monitors and not on Hi-Fi speakers.

Active Studio Speakers

Active speakers have amplifiers built into the cabinets and often have a separate amplifier for the woofer (bass speaker) and tweeter (treble speaker). Active speakers use an active crossover, the circuitry that prevents low frequencies being fed to, and causing damage to the tweeter. Active crossovers can automatically adjust to changing frequency levels.

An advantage with active speakers over passive speakers (see below) is that the amplifiers are designed specifically to match the woofer and tweeter, and the physical design of the cabinet. Active studio speakers connect directly to the output of your audio interface via balanced XLR or jack cables (see Chap. 5: Hardware—Audio Cables).

Some active speakers have EQ shelving filter controls built in (see Chap. 11: Equalisers). These allow for adjustments to be made to the bass and treble responses to better suit your listening environment and preferences. It is important to use these controls sparingly whilst referencing commercial music that you are familiar with, or after using room EQ measurement software (see Chap. 4: Room Acoustic Treatment—Room Measurement) to get an accurate picture of the frequency response of your speakers/room. Typical shelving filter ranges for nearfield monitors might be low-Frequency shelving 0 Hz–300 Hz @ +/− 6 dB and high-frequency shelving 4.5 kHz–22 kHz @ +/−3 dB (Fig. 2.1).

Fig. 2.1 HEDD Type 07 near/mid-field active studio monitors. Image courtesy of HEDD Audio

Types of Speakers

Passive Studio Speakers

Passive speakers do not have amplifiers built into the cabinets and as such are generally cheaper than active ones. However, a separate amplifier will also need to be purchased. That is not to say that passive speakers are inferior to active ones but a lot will depend on the quality of the amplifier used.

Passive speakers use a passive crossover, which is the circuitry that prevents low frequencies from being fed to the tweeter. Passive crossovers force high frequencies through a capacitor and low frequencies through an inductor.

The most commonly used passive speaker is the classic Yamaha NS-10M which can be found in many professional recording studios around the world (Fig. 2.2).

Passive speakers connect to the speaker outputs of the amplifier via standard speaker cable. The outputs of the audio interface connect to the line inputs on the amplifier.

Fig. 2.2 Classic Yamaha NS-10M studio speaker

Two Way Speakers

Two-way speakers have two drivers in each cabinet: a single driver for bass and midrange frequencies usually between 4 and 8 inches in diameter and a single driver feeding the tweeter for high frequencies. The tweeter is usually placed above the woofer.

Three Way Speakers

Three-way speakers have three speakers in each cabinet. A woofer for bass frequencies, a midrange driver for midrange frequencies and a tweeter for high frequencies. The midrange driver is usually placed above the woofer with the tweeter placed above that. Three-way speakers have a three-way crossover which feeds the correct frequencies to the correct driver.

A typical three-way crossover design may look something like this:

Driver	Frequency Range	Sensitivity
Tweeter	2 kHz–25 kHz	89 dB SPL
Mid	200 Hz–3 kHz	88 dB SPL
Woofer	40 Hz–300 Hz	88 dB SPL

Dual Concentric Speakers (Coaxial Speakers)

Dual concentric speakers have a single woofer with the tweeter placed in the centre of it. Conventional speakers transmit sound from as many points as there are drivers. This can cause phase and timing inaccuracies—different frequencies reach the listeners' ears at different times.

With dual concentric speakers, the sound emanates from a single source point which greatly reduces or even eliminates the possibility of distortion caused by phase and timing inaccuracies.

This is not to say that conventional speakers are inferior. In higher quality studio speakers, the crossover is fitted with a baffle step filter—a component which time aligns the signals from both (or more) drivers. This reduces or removes phase and timing inaccuracies ensuring all frequencies leave the speaker at precisely the same time and arrive at the ear at the same time (Figs. 2.3 and 2.4).

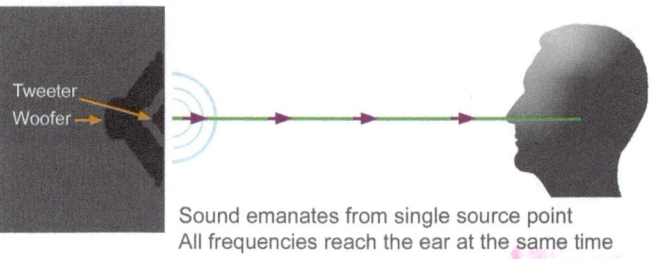

Fig. 2.3 Dual concentric speaker

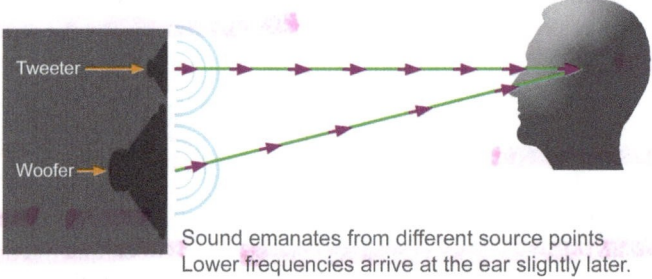

Fig. 2.4 Conventional speaker

Subwoofer

Subwoofers are single speakers designed to extend the low-frequency response of your monitoring system by outputting frequencies below the cut-off point of your satellite speakers. They most commonly have active circuitry (Fig. 2.5).

In a home or project studio, a single subwoofer is connected to the satellite speakers. The left and right outputs of the audio interface are connected to the inputs of the subwoofer. The left and right outputs of the subwoofer would then be connected to the inputs of the left and right satellite speakers (Fig. 2.6).

Some subwoofers have a fixed upper frequency limit, usually around 85 Hz, whilst others have a selectable upper frequency limit, usually up to around 150 Hz (see Chap. 2: Speakers—Speaker Listening Levels—Setting up a Subwoofer).

Fig. 2.5 A typical subwoofer

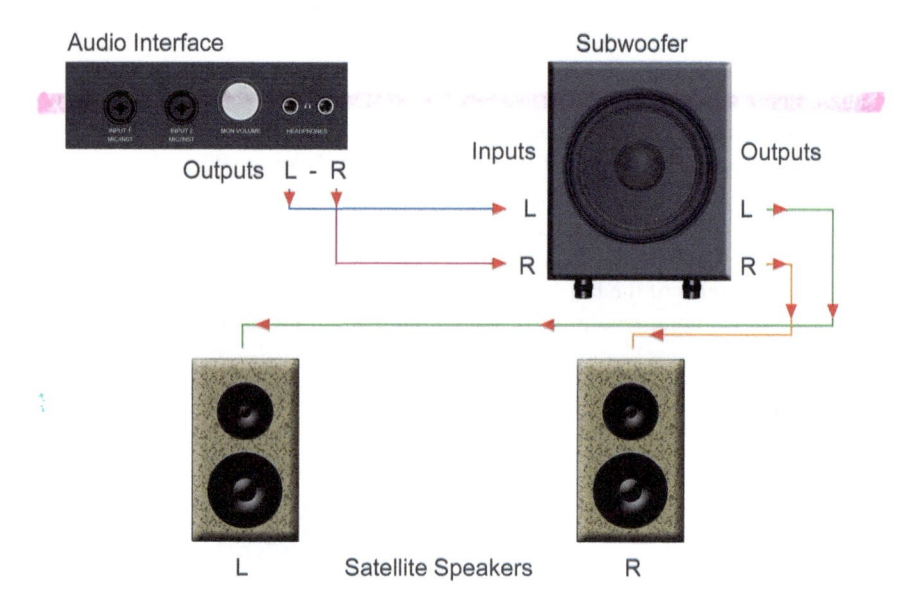

Fig 2.6 Connecting subwoofer and satellite speakers

Ported (Vented) vs Closed (Sealed) Speaker Cabinets

Some speaker cabinets have a port (or two) on them. This is a hole in the cabinet that is designed to artificially extend the bass frequency response to below what the speaker would otherwise be able to deliver. Ports can be on the front or rear of the cabinet.

When you blow over the top of a bottle, it makes a sound at the resonant frequency of the bottle. The frequency depends on the size and shape of the bottle and the size of the hole. For example, if you add liquid to the bottle and blow, it will make a higher-pitched sound than when it is empty. This is how the ports on a speaker cabinet work, the difference being that the vibration of air molecules required to cause the cabinet to resonate is generated by the back and forth movement of the speaker cone.

Ports can be beneficial where an extended low-frequency response is required from a small speaker, though cheaper poorly designed ported cabinets may not be as sonically accurate as closed cabinets, particularly in the low-frequency range. Also, port noise can occur at the resonant frequency which can sometimes sound a bit raspy when the speaker is driven hard. Ringing on low frequencies may also be induced; this is when low frequencies continue to sound momentarily after the signal has stopped.

If extended bass from a small speaker is what you need, then a ported speaker may be a good option. Higher quality speaker manufacturers such as HEDD Audio spend large sums of money on the research and development of their speakers to ensure they deliver precise low-frequency extension and to prevent port noise and ringing. So, when budgeting for equipment for your studio, be sure to get the best possible speakers you can afford (Fig. 2.7).

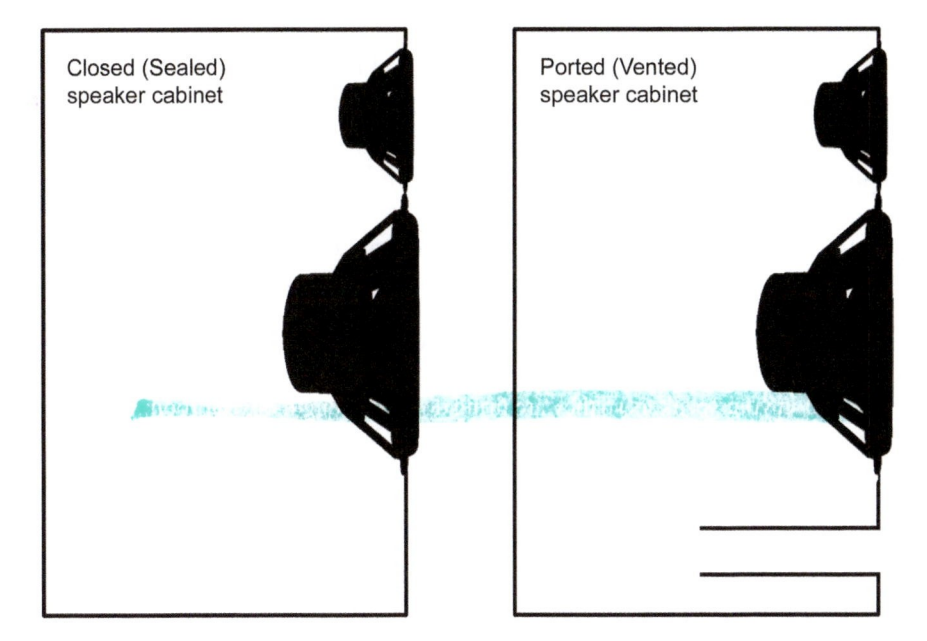

Fig. 2.7 Closed and ported speaker cabinets

Choosing Monitors

Choosing the right speakers for your room depends on many factors, including room size, how close to the speakers you will sit and what kind of music you make. If you make music with heavy bass content such as EDM, House or Reggae, you will need speakers with a frequency response that lets you hear more detail in the low bass range. If you make mostly bass shy music such as Rock or Folk, the low-frequency response will be less important.

Wherever possible, it is best to test speakers in the room that they will ultimately be used in before you buy. Some music shops will let you have a demo pair to trial for a few days.

Once you've bought the right speakers, you'll need to position them correctly in your room.

Speaker Placement

When playing music in your studio, what you hear is a combination of direct sound from the speakers and reflected sound from the room's surfaces—walls, ceiling, floor and furniture. This is known as speaker boundary interference response (SBIR). In order to make accurate recording and mixing decisions, you need to hear the sound coming from the speaker with as little interference from SBIR as possible.

The balance between direct and reflected sound depends on the size and shape of your room, materials in the room such as carpets, curtains and windows and the positioning of your speakers in relation to the boundaries of the room.

Getting this balance right is crucial to getting accurate information from your speakers. If the balance is wrong, making critical recording and mixing decisions will be very difficult.

Speaker Positioning

Correct speaker placement can play a big part in minimising interfering reflections from the room's boundaries and is an important step in creating an accurate listening position. This will be the position where you sit whilst monitoring the recording and mixing of instruments and voices. This position is known as the sweet spot.

Here are some key points to help you set up your speakers properly:

Position your speakers so they are firing down the length of your room. This way, sound energy has more time to dissipate before any reflections bounce back at you from the rear wall. Strong low-frequency modes will lose energy when they travel further away from the sweet spot. The returning reflection will be weaker and therefore cause less interference with the direct sound.

A good starting point for finding the ideal location for your speakers is to follow the 38% trick. Measure the full length of your room and position your chair at approximately 38% (room length × 0.38) from the front wall—the wall behind your speakers. This will be the sweet spot (Fig. 2.8).

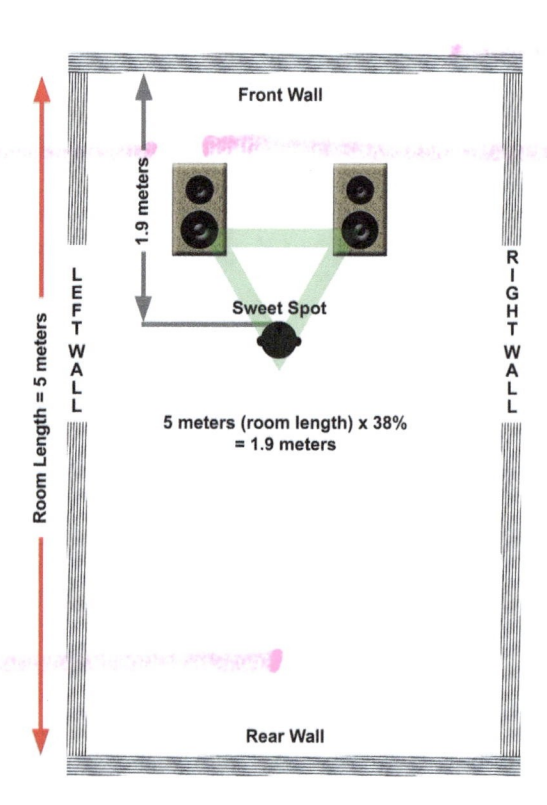

Fig. 2.8 Speaker positioning

Speaker Placement

Make sure the distance from the sweet spot to the centre of the woofer on Speaker 'A' (left speaker) is equal to the distance from the centre of the woofer on Speaker 'A' (left speaker) to the centre of the woofer on Speaker 'B' (right speaker), thereby forming an equilateral triangle.

Turn the speakers in so they are angled towards you. You should not be able to see the sides of the speaker cabinets when sitting at the sweet spot and looking directly at either one (Fig. 2.9).

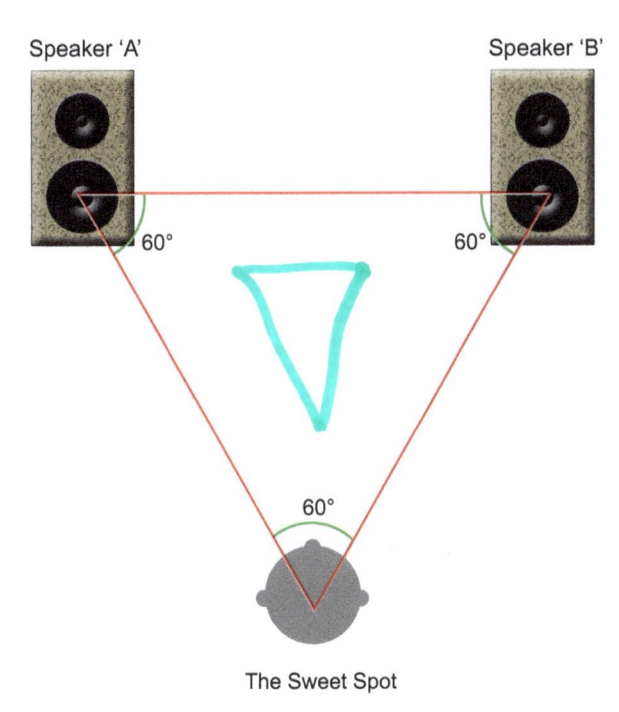

Fig. 2.9 The sweet spot

Make sure your speakers are positioned at an equal distance from both of the side walls, and the front wall—the wall behind the speakers (Fig. 2.10).

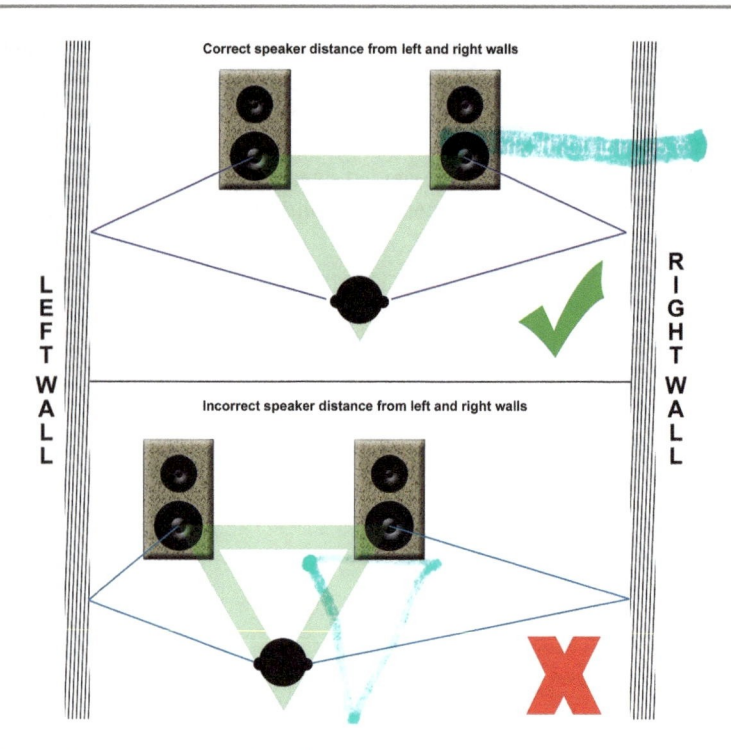

Fig. 2.10 Speaker distance from side walls

▶ *Tip: The distance from the speakers to the side walls should be different to the distance from the speakers to the front wall in order to avoid overlapping reflections of the same frequencies.*

Speaker height should be adjusted so that the tweeter in each cabinet is slightly above ear level when sitting. If it is necessary to have your speakers higher or lower than this, they can be angled up or down so that the tweeter is aimed towards your ear. The angle should be no more than 15°. Any more than this will cause the high-frequency response to change noticeably as you move your head backwards or forward.

Sit in the sweet spot and listen to a variety of commercial music that you know well, preferably something that has lots of varied bass notes. Each bass note or tone should sound roughly the same volume.

Try playing all notes in the two lowest audible octaves on a bass synth or virtual instrument and listen for any variations in the volume of each note. Each note should sound roughly the same level. You can also use pure sine wave tones starting at 40 Hz and increasing incrementally in 10 Hz steps up to 150 Hz, with each lasting for a few seconds. These can be generated from within most DAWs or you can download **2.3 Audio File 40 Hz to 150 Hz Pure Sine Wave.wav** file from the Audio examples folder accompanying this book.

► *Tip: Record your bass synth notes or sine wave tones to your timeline and play it back on a loop to help you focus on what you are listening for.*

Even in professional studios, it is not uncommon for the levels to vary by a few dB up or down, but if you find big differences in level between notes after careful speaker placement, there will be some room acoustics issues to address (see Chap. 9: Room Acoustics).

The stereo image should not sound artificially wide or narrow, and the centre mono image should sound tight and focused. You may find that you need to shuffle your speakers back, forward, left, right or up and down a few centimetres until they sound just right. You may also need to reduce or increase the size of the sweet spot. You can do this easily by moving them forward or backwards along the axis line of the equilateral triangle (Fig. 2.11).

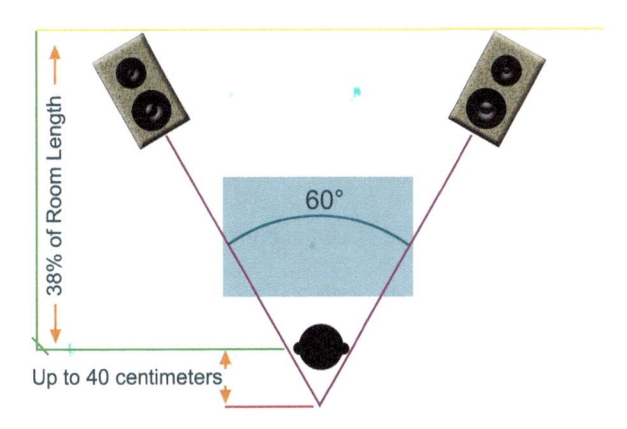

Fig. 2.11 Listening position for improved stereo image

► *Tip: In some instances, it may be necessary to place your speakers upside down or on their sides. Check your speaker manufacturer's user guide to see if they have been designed to allow this.*

► *Tip: Try sitting just inside the sweet spot so that the third point of the equilateral triangle is up to 40 cm behind your head. This position can give you an improved stereo image.*

Comb Filtering

Comb filtering occurs when frequencies reflecting off the room's surfaces combine with the direct sound from your speakers. The reflected frequencies arrive at the ear within milliseconds of the sound from the speakers. This can result in either

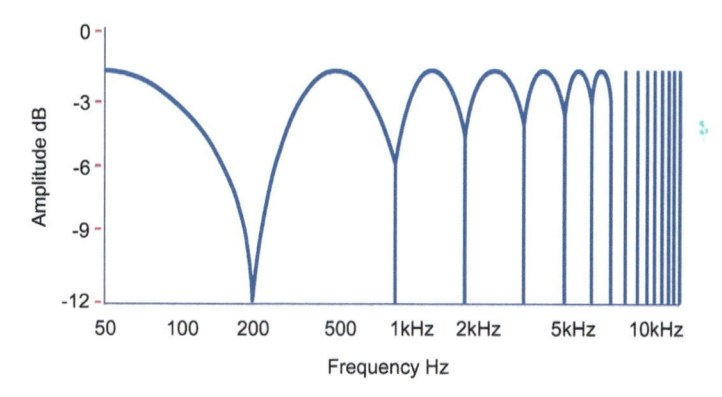

Fig. 2.12 Comb filtering

constructive or destructive interference in the form of peaks or dips in the frequency response at multiples of the lowest resonant frequency. Furthermore, the frequency response changes noticeably as you move your head. Even small movements of a centimetre or so can have a big effect on the frequency response.

In Fig. 2.12, you can see that an analysis of comb filtering resembles the teeth of a comb.

Ideally your speakers should be placed at either:

(a) a distance from the wall behind them that causes the ¼ wavelength cancellation to be below their lowest cut-off frequency (see Chap. 9: Room Acoustics).
(b) close enough to the wall so that the cancellation is moved to a much higher frequency. At higher frequencies, the speaker will have greatly reduced omni-directional energy (see Chap. 1: An Introduction to How Sound Works—Sound Dispersion) which will be easier to absorb with acoustic panels (see Chap. 9: Room Acoustics).

Reflections from the room's boundaries can be dealt with using broadband absorption, diffusion or a combination of both placed strategically around the room (see Chap. 9: Room Acoustics). However, sound can also reflect off your desk. This can be particularly problematic when your speakers are sitting on the desk because the angle of incidence of the reflected sound reaches your ears very soon after the direct sound from the speakers. It is not usually practical to position acoustic treatment there, so ideally your speakers should be mounted on sturdy stands behind the desk. This changes the angle of incidence, thereby directing the reflections away from your ears (Figs. 2.13 and 2.14).

Speaker Placement

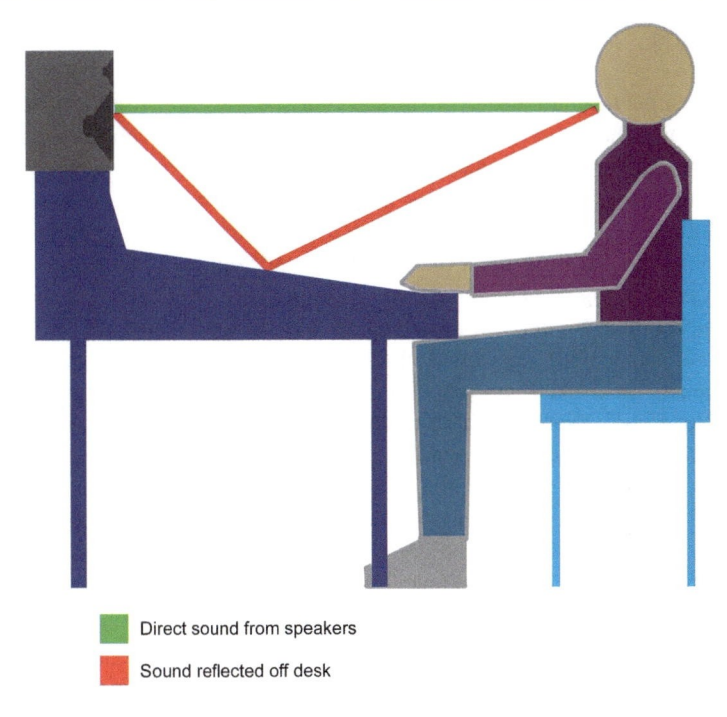

Fig. 2.13 Comb filtering caused by speakers placed on desk

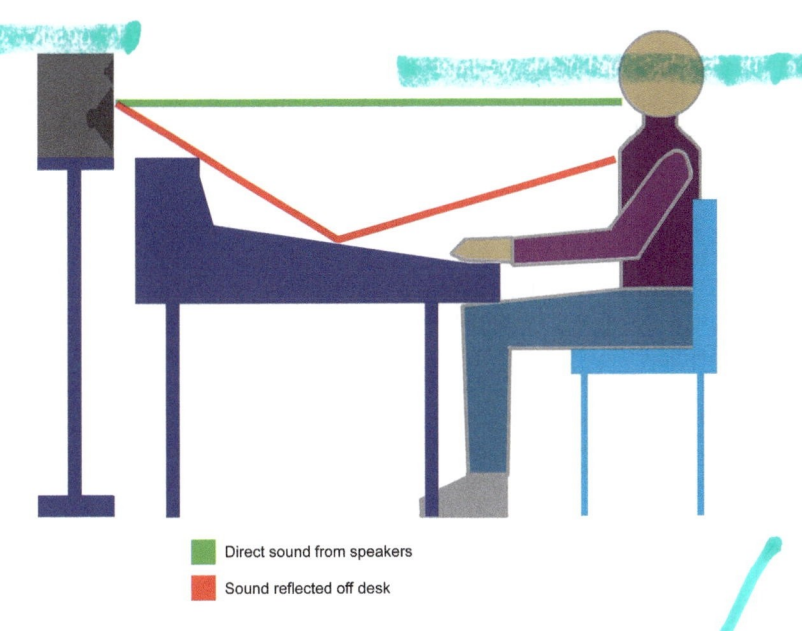

Fig. 2.14 Comb filtering eliminated by placing speakers on stands behind desk

Decoupling

Sound transmits through whatever surface your speakers are sitting on. Lower frequencies travel through your desk, stands or floor, and can reach your ears within milliseconds of the direct sound from the speakers. This also results in comb filtering causing peaks and dips in the low-frequency response.

A solution is to decouple your speakers from whatever surface they are sitting on. Decoupling reduces or can even prevent sound from being transmitted through the surface, resulting in a clearer and more defined low-frequency response.

Decoupling can be done in a number of ways: using heavy stands filled with sand; using stands with spikes that minimise contact with the floor; or by placing your speakers on dense foam pads, rubber feet, sorbothane or a number of other absorbent materials. Some methods of decoupling perform much better than others. The method you choose will depend on the type of speakers you use, their size and weight and the surface they are sitting on. There are a variety of decouplers available commercially and a number of DIY solutions can be found online.

Once your speakers are set up correctly, you can start to look at the type and positioning of acoustic treatment (see Chap. 9: Room Acoustics).

Speaker Listening Levels

We hear frequencies differently depending on what level we are listening at. For example, as discovered by Fletcher and Munson in 1933 (see Chap. 1: An Introduction to How Sound Works—Equal Loudness Contours), the quieter we listen, the less bass and treble we hear.

Setting an optimal listening level will ensure that you consistently hear all frequencies accurately. It will also ensure that you always have plenty of digital headroom—which will make you add more dynamic range to your mixes. For example, if you calibrate your listening level to K14 as described later on in this chapter, you will have 14 dB of headroom before hitting the maximum digital ceiling of 0 dBFS (zero decibels full scale).

The K-System, created by world-renowned mastering engineer Bob Katz, is a metering and monitoring system through which consistent listening levels can be set.

Calibrating the K-System is relatively straightforward. To set it up, you will need a sound pressure level (SPL) meter. You can use a free SPL meter app on your phone or tablet though you will need to ensure it is calibrated for accuracy (Fig. 2.15).

You will also need a −20 dBFS RMS pink noise audio file to play through your speakers. A −20 dBFS RMS pink noise file is used as it closely matches the level of normal conversational dialogue. You can download 2.4 Audio File Pink_min_20_dBFS_RMS 441.wav file from the Audio examples folder accompanying this book.

Speaker Listening Levels

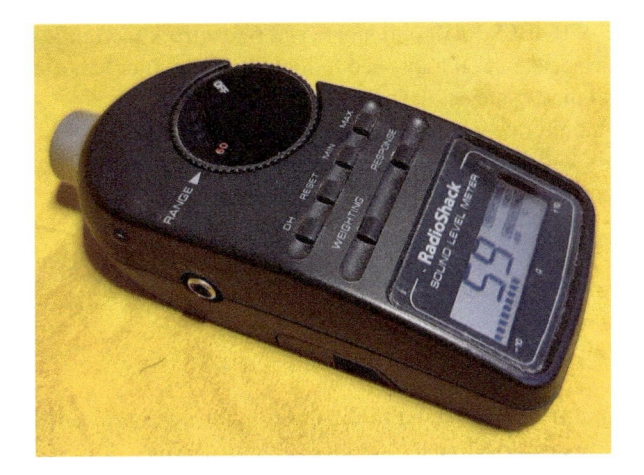

Fig. 2.15 A typical sound pressure level metre

How to Calibrate Your Listening Levels

There are three K metering calibration settings:

K20—Monitoring Levels for Film Music Production. This gives you 20 dB of headroom before hitting 0 dBFS.

K14—Monitoring Levels for Commercial Music Production. This gives you 14 dB of headroom before hitting 0 dBFS.

K12—Monitoring Levels for Broadcast. This gives you 12 dB of headroom before hitting 0 dBFS.

K20—Monitoring Levels for Film Music Production

1. Set the SPL meter on a stand in the position where your head would be when sitting at the mix position.
2. Set the SPL meter to C weighting and a slow response time.
3. Import the −20 dBFS RMS pink noise audio to a track in your DAW and play it through one speaker. You may need to loop the audio file. Make sure your DAW channel and master are set to 0 dB.
4. Turn your monitor controller volume level up or down until the SPL meter reads 83 dB. This will be 0 dB on your monitor controller. Mark the level on your monitor controller so that you know where 0 dB is.
5. Follow the same process for your other speaker/s.
6. Your monitors are now calibrated to K20 which is an ideal listening level when producing music for film.

K14—Monitoring Levels for Commercial Music Production

1. Set the SPL meter on a stand in the position where your head would be when sitting at the mix position.
2. Set the SPL meter to C weighting and a slow response time.

3. Import the −20 dBFS RMS pink noise audio to a track in your DAW and play it through one speaker. You may need to loop the audio file. Make sure your DAW channel and master are set to 0 dB.
4. Turn your monitor controller volume level up or down until the SPL meter reads 79 dB. This will be 0 dB on your monitor controller. Mark the level on your monitor controller so that you know where 0 dB is.
5. Follow the same process for your other speaker/s.
6. Your monitors are now calibrated to K14 which is an ideal listening level when producing commercial music. K14 is 6 dB quieter than K20.

K12—Monitoring Levels for Broadcast

7. Set the SPL meter on a stand in the position where your head would be when sitting at the mix position.
8. Set the SPL meter to C weighting and slow response time.
9. Import the −20 dBFS RMS pink noise audio to a track in your DAW and play it through one speaker. You may need to loop the audio file. Make sure your DAW channel and master are set to 0 dB.
10. Turn your monitor controller volume level up or down until the SPL meter reads 77 dB. This will be 0 dB on your monitor controller. Mark the level on your monitor controller so that you know where 0 dB is.
11. Follow the same process for your other speaker/s.
12. Your monitors are now calibrated to K12 which is an ideal listening level when producing music for broadcast. K12 is 8 dB quieter than K20.

You can mark your monitor level control for all three settings or choose the one that best suits your regular work (Fig. 2.16).

Fig. 2.16 Mark your ideal listening level

Setting Up a Subwoofer

If you are using a subwoofer, a good trick for setting it up is to place it on your chair in the sweet spot and play some sine wave tones through it in mono, with your satellite speakers switched off. Download 2.3 Audio File 40 Hz to 150 Hz Pure Sine Wave.wav which is ideal for this purpose.

Put the audio file on a track in your DAW and play it on a loop at normal listening levels. Now spend some time crawling around on the floor behind your speakers and under your desk whilst listening to the tones. You will notice that some sound louder than others. Find the spot where there is the least difference in level between the tones, and that is where you should place your sub. You can use your SPL meter to measure the level at each spot for accuracy if needed, or you can do this by ear (Fig. 2.17).

Once you have positioned the sub, you will need to carefully adjust its level in relation to the satellite speakers. The purpose of a subwoofer in a studio is to extend the frequency response of your monitoring system so that you can hear the lowest octave at the correct level relative to the rest of the frequency range.

> ▶ *Tip: It's tempting to have your subwoofer set too loud as more bass equals more vibe. But your studio isn't a nightclub and excessive bass will only serve to mask other frequencies, making it very difficult to get a mix that translates well to other systems outside of your studio.*

Remember to high pass (see Chap. 11: Equalisers—Types of Equaliser Filters) your satellite speakers as you don't want the same low frequencies playing through them as your sub. The recommended crossover frequency from satellite speakers to the subwoofer is 85 Hz. This can be adjusted up or down depending on the type of speakers you are using and the available controls on your subwoofer.

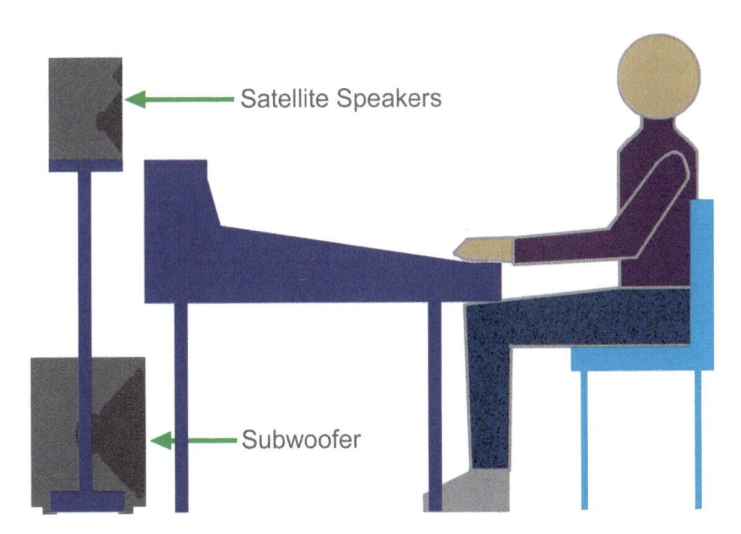

Fig. 2.17 Subwoofer placement

It may take a bit of time to get the level of your subwoofer absolutely right in relation to your satellite speakers, but these steps will help you to get pretty close.

1. Disconnect your subwoofer (or set its level to zero if it has a level control).
2. Play pink noise through your satellite speakers. You will find a −20 dBFS RMS pink noise file in the downloadable resources folder.
3. Switch off one of your satellite speakers.
4. Position your SPL meter at the sweet spot, preferably on a stand where your head would be and pointed towards the centre spot between your speakers. If you don't have an SPL meter, you can use an app on your mobile device.
5. Set the SPL meter to C-weighted and slow response.
6. Play the pink noise and adjust the speaker level until the SPL meter reads 85 dB. You may also need to adjust the monitor control level on your audio interface too. Repeat this step for the other speaker.
7. Switch off your satellite speakers and reconnect your subwoofer.
8. Play the pink noise through the subwoofer and adjust its level until the SPL meter reads 79 dB.
9. You can now switch on the satellite speakers and listen to music through your system. You may need to tweak the subwoofer level up or down a dB to fine tune it.

In essence, you can see that the subwoofer is set approximately −6 dB lower than the output of a single satellite speaker.

▶ **Chapter 2 Tasks:** The following tasks will demonstrate the perception and importance of speaker placement and listening levels.

- Play a stereo track through your speakers with clear left and right localization (e.g. a track with guitar in the left speaker and vocals in the right speaker).
- Move your speakers to a range of positions such as in the room corners, the middle of the room or close to the walls.
- How does it change the way you perceive the sound? Where do you consider the best position?
- Try listening again at low volume and then at high volume. Does this affect your perception of the stereo image or frequency ranges?
- Listen to a stereo track through your speakers and use MixChecker (trial version is available at www.audified.com) to hear how different speakers sound.
- Note your observations.

Digital Audio Workstation   3

▶ **Learning Outcomes**

By the end of this chapter, the reader will be able to:
- Explain the working environments within a digital audio workstation (DAW).
- Construct a clear workflow within a DAW.
- Recall functional tools available within audio and MIDI editing.

A digital audio workstation (DAW) is a software designed to enable multitrack audio and MIDI recording, editing and mixing on your computer.

There are several DAWs available and although they may operate slightly differently, they all have the same core functions and features. Whichever DAW you use, the recording, editing and mixing processes will be pretty much the same.

Here are some examples of popular DAWs:

DAW	Manufacturer
Pro Tools	Avid
Live	Ableton
Logic	Apple
Reason	Propellerhead
Reaper	Cockos
Studio One	Presonus
Sonar Platinum	Cakewalk
Cubase Pro	Steinberg
GarageBand	Apple
FL Studio	Image Line
Mixbus	Harrison
Digital Performer	MOTU

Pro Tools DAW Controls and Functions

Arrange Window

Tracks

Tracks in the arrange window are for recording audio, MIDI and virtual instruments. One instrument or voice is recorded onto the timeline of one track which can be either mono or stereo depending on the source sound. Tracks can be created as needed, or a template can be created if you intend to use the same setup as a starting point for each session.

The timeline scrolls from left to right, starting on the first beat of Bar 1 and can be as long as is required for your song, limited only by the amount of free hard disc space. The timeline has a grid which can be set to display divisions in bars and beats, minutes and seconds or samples and frames per second. A playhead scrolls from left to right displaying the current song position.

There are six different types of tracks in most DAWs (Fig. 3.1):

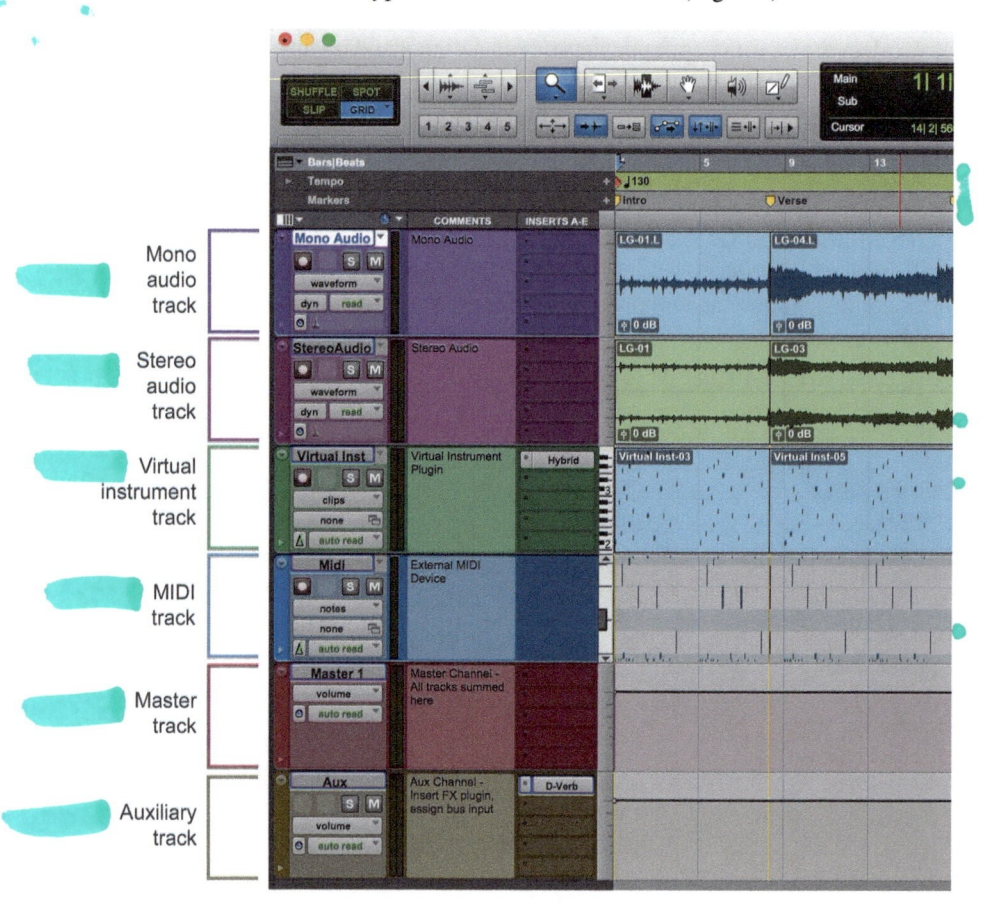

Fig. 3.1 The different types of tracks in Pro Tools

Pro Tools DAW Controls and Functions

1. **Mono audio track**—for recording a single mono audio source such as a single microphone or guitar.
2. **Stereo audio track**—for recording a stereo audio source such as two overhead drum microphones or the stereo output of an external sound module.
3. **Instrument track**—for recording MIDI data relating to an inserted virtual instrument plugin.
4. **MIDI track**—for recording the MIDI data of an external hardware sound module, synthesizer or sampler.
5. **Master channel track**—for recording master fader and effect automation data.
6. **Auxiliary track**—for recording auxiliary effect automation data.

Transport

The transport section is where you will find the buttons that control the operation of the DAW. These buttons are:

Synchronise: For synchronising two devices to keep them playing in time with each other. This may be another DAW on another computer or a DAW and an analogue tape machine for example.

Stop: Stops playback or recording. Depending on how you set this in the preferences, it can either stop playback and leave the playhead where it has been stopped or stop playback and return the playhead to where you started playing from. In most DAWs, double clicking stop will return the playhead to the first beat of the first bar on the timeline.

Play: Plays the content of your session starting at the location of the playhead. Play can be set to cycle your selection or play continuously until stop is pressed.

Record: In some DAWs, the record button prepares the session to record on any track that is record armed. Engage the record button and recording will start once play is pressed. In other DAWs, pressing record will start recording immediately on any track that is record armed, without having to press play. Recording can be set to cycle your selection and can be destructive or non-destructive. Destructive recording permanently erases any previous recording on the same track from the hard drive. Non-destructive replaces the previous recording but keeps the file in the session's audio pool. Loop recording is a great way of capturing the perfect take.

Skip Backward: Skips the session back to the start or to a point that you have previously defined.

Rewind: Press and hold the rewind button to skip backwards through the session whilst hearing playback.

Fast Forward: Press and hold the fast forward button to skip forwards through the track whilst hearing playback

Skip Forward: Skips the session to the end of the track or to a point that you have previously defined (Fig. 3.2).

Fig. 3.2 Typical DAW transport controls

Counter
The counter displays the current arrangement position in bars and beats, minutes and seconds and the time signature.

Grid
Most DAWs give you the option to adjust the grid display. You can select whether the grid in the edit window shows divisions in bars, 1/2 note, 1/4 note, 1/8 note, 1/16 note, 1/32 note or 1/64 note. You can also select whether any of these notes are dotted or triplet, as well as setting the grid to display minutes/seconds, time code, feet/frames, samples and clips/markers (Fig. 3.3).

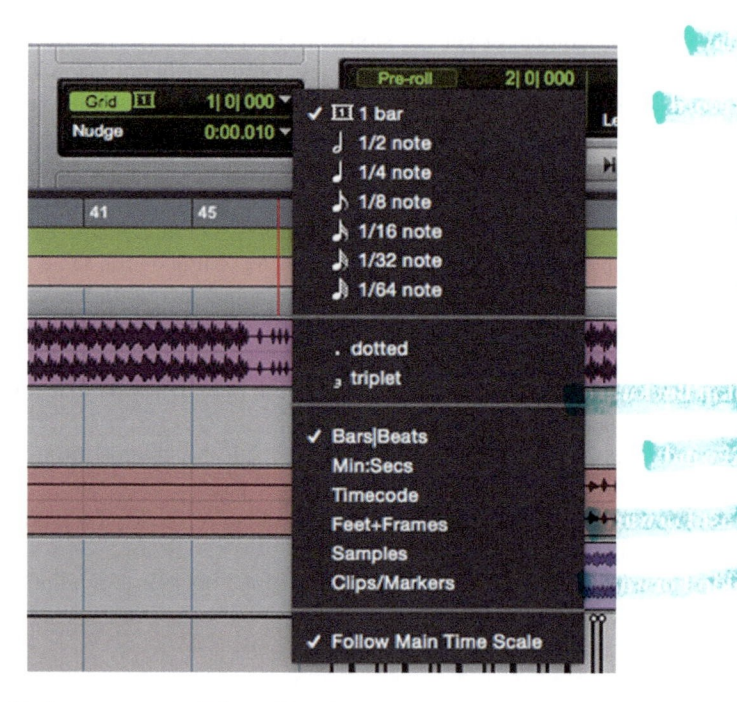

Fig. 3.3 Pro Tools arrangement window grid settings

Place the playhead on the grid in the arrange window where you want to begin recording. You can set a count-in in the metronome window. This can be set to as many bars as you need. Recording and playback will start from where you place the playhead.

▶ ***Tips from the pros:*** *For editing in the finest detail—set snap to samples. Steve Osborne—Producer—U2, A-ha, New Order, Suede, Paul Oakenfold, Happy Mondays and more.*

Mix Window

Mixer

Each track in the arrange window has a corresponding mix channel in the mix window. All mix channels are summed to the master channel inside your DAW, so that your finished mix can be bounced (exported) as a single stereo or mono WAV or AIFF file. Some DAWs also give the option for exporting as an MP3.

The mix channel for each track has the following controls:

1. **Fader**—for changing the level of the track.
2. **Mute**—for silencing the signal.
3. **Solo**—for soloing the signal, effectively muting all other channels.
4. **Record**—for arming the track ready for recording.
5. **Pan**—for changing the panoramic position of the signal in the stereo field.
6. **Group assignment**—multiple mix channels can be grouped so that an action performed on one channel will affect all channels in the group.
7. **Automation assignment**—for setting the channel ready to read, write or modify automation data.
8. **Output assignment**—usually set to your main outputs but also used to assign channels to an auxiliary channel.
9. **Input assignment**—for setting which input channel of your audio interface is assigned to the channel.
10. **Send**—for setting the bus assignment to an auxiliary track.
11. **Insert**—for inserting plugins and virtual instruments.

Some of the mix channel controls such as record, mute and solo can also be found on each track in the arrange window.

Additionally, many DAWs have a track freeze function. This allows the user to render the track content as well as any plugin inserts, in place. This is a very handy feature for reducing CPU usage when many plugins are used throughout the session. The track freeze function is undoable, so that at any stage, the user can unfreeze, make adjustments to the material or plugin settings, and then refreeze. Each time a track is frozen, a new audio file is created in the session's audio folder (Fig. 3.4).

Fig. 3.4 Pro Tools mix window

Tools

Each DAW has a selection of tools with which you can edit and manipulate audio and MIDI regions, notes and events. Most DAWs have some or all of the following tools:

MIDI Edit Window

1. **Pointer**—used for selecting and moving things
2. **Pencil**—for creating regions and drawing automation data
3. **Eraser**—for erasing regions, notes, events and automation data
4. **Scissors**—for splitting regions or notes
5. **Glue**—for joining regions or notes
6. **Solo**—for soloing regions
7. **Mute**—for muting regions
8. **Zoom**—for zooming in on audio and MIDI regions
9. **Fade**—for creating fades and crossfades on audio regions

MIDI Edit Window

When MIDI has been recorded, on either a MIDI track or a virtual instrument track, its data can be edited in several ways.

Quantise: Single or multiple notes can be selected and quantised to the grid. Quantise moves the note so that its start point lines up with a precise point on the grid. Quantise is a useful feature for tightening things up though it can make parts sound rigid and unnatural if overused (Figs. 3.5 and 3.6).

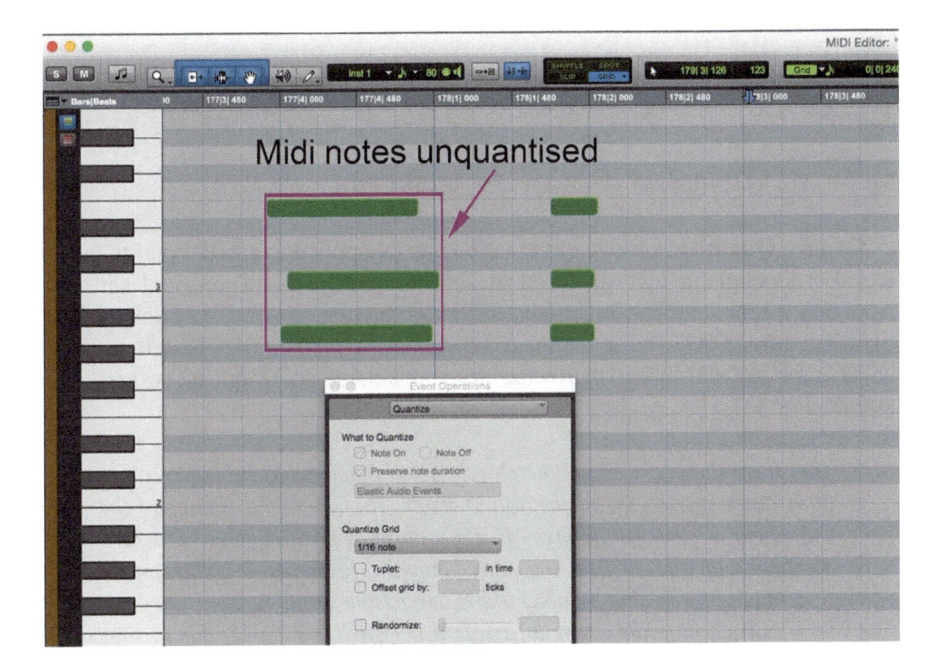

Fig. 3.5 Pro Tools MIDI edit window showing unquantized notes

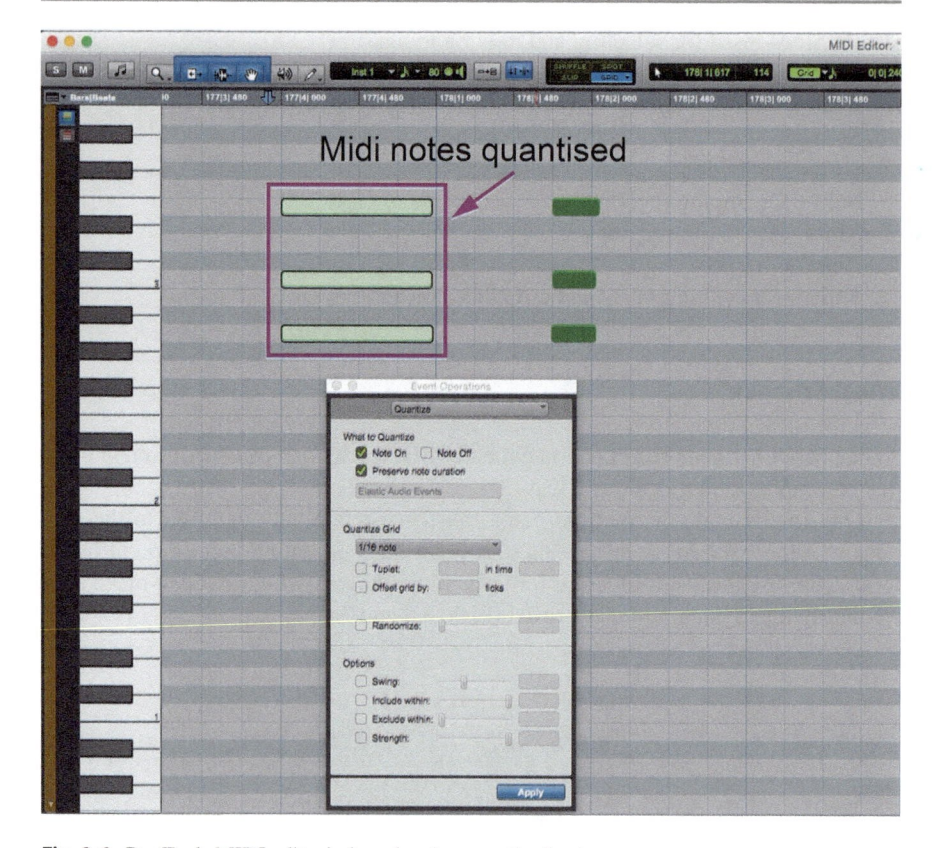

Fig. 3.6 Pro Tools MIDI edit window showing quantized notes

Groove Quantise: Groove quantisation can be applied to a MIDI part to give it feel. For example, a part quantised to 16th notes may sound too rigid and stiff. Applying a groove quantise can give it a more natural feel whilst maintaining its tightness. Most DAWs have several groove quantisation templates built in, some of which replicate the feel of hardware drum machines and sequencers, and other DAWs (Fig. 3.7).

▶ *Tips from the pros: To get the classic drum machine sound (such as the 808) don't just focus on the sound itself. The jitter and timing of the sequencer in those old boxes is even more important. Get hold of a sampled loop directly from the source machine (even better if you can get a sample of a rim shot or other short percussive sound doing 16ths) and then extract the groove template from it in your DAW. Apply this to your drums to really get the feel of the original machine.* **Peter Duggal—Producer/Composer**—Wolfgang Flür (Kraftwerk), Peter Hook, Midge Ure, Claudia Brücken, Carl Cox, Juan Atkins, Maps and more.

MIDI Edit Window

Fig. 3.7 Pro Tools groove quantise menu

▶ *Tip: For best results, quantise to the grid before applying groove quantise.*

Velocity: The velocity of single or multiple notes can be altered by dragging the slider up or down. Velocity simulates the behaviour of piano keys, whereby there are differences in tone and dynamics depending on how hard or soft the note is struck (Fig. 3.8).

Note Length: The length of single or multiple notes can be extended or reduced, usually by dragging left or right from anchor points at the start or end of the note. For example, perhaps that piano chord you played felt great but didn't sustain for as long as you wanted, or a sample you triggered didn't play to the end (Fig. 3.9).

In addition to the control you have over the timing, velocity and length of MIDI notes, most DAWs offer several other functions including the ability to split notes at a desired point and alter control data such as modulation, pitch bend, portamento time, expression, pan, volume, effect control and custom controller data.

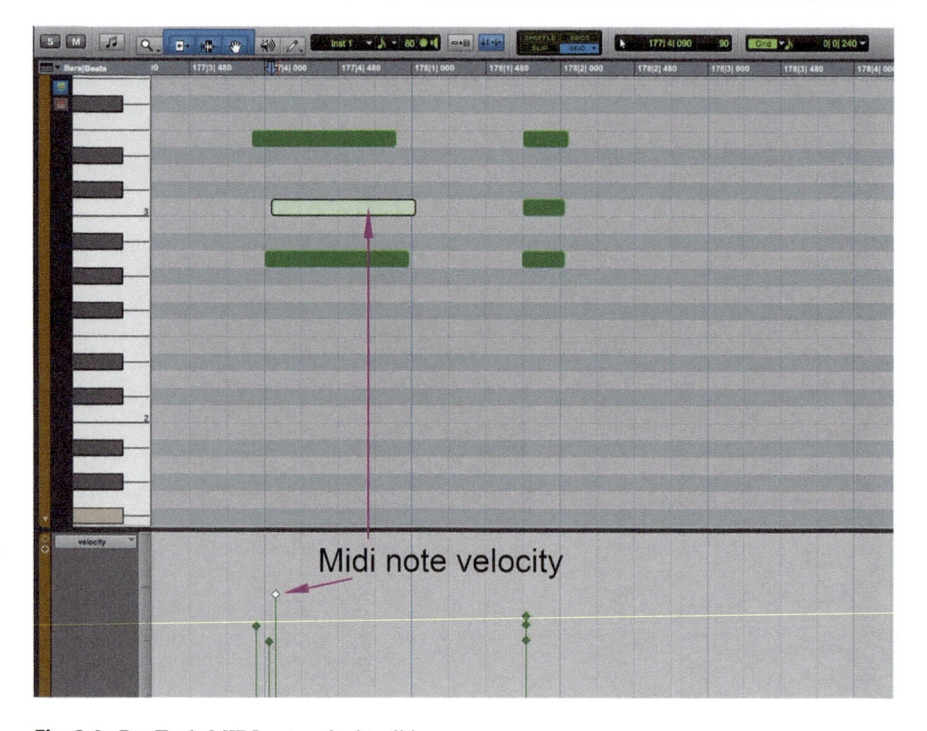

Fig. 3.8 Pro Tools MIDI note velocity slider

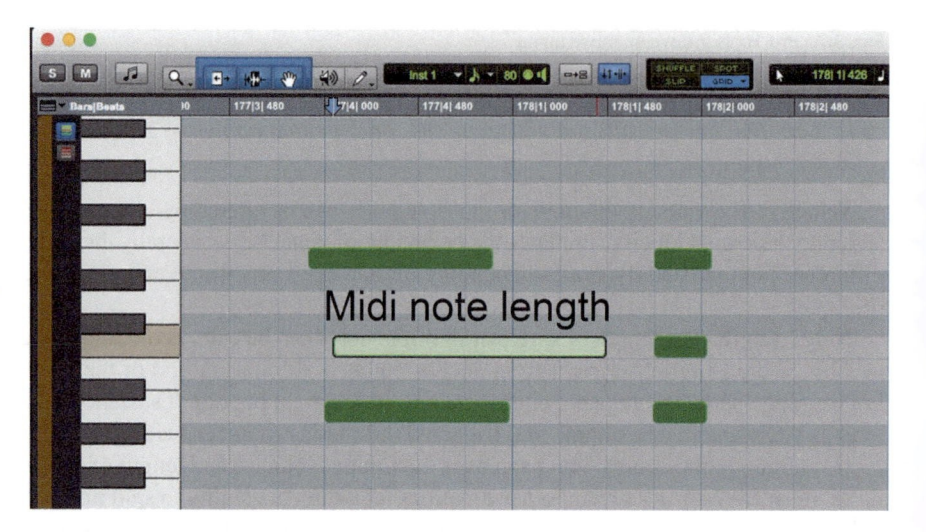

Fig. 3.9 Adjusting MIDI note length

In many DAWs, double clicking a MIDI or virtual instrument part opens the MIDI editor window.

▶   *Tips from the pros*: Don't be afraid to commit to sounds. Make decisions in the early stages of the recording process as to 'how' things should actually sound. This will help you and the Artist to create a general feel and artistic direction for the project early on. In addition, it demonstrates that you have a vision as a producer. **Iwan VanHetten—Producer, Songwriter and Mix Engineer**—Brooklyn Funk Essentials, Sister Sledge, The Pointer Sisters, Candy Duffer and more.

Labelling Tracks

It's important to label your tracks correctly so that you can see what's on them at a glance and so there's no confusion if and when you share a session with someone else.

You can make up your own naming convention though there are some standard abbreviations that professionals use. Keeping the names short helps to avoid clutter on the screen too. Below you'll see the abbreviations I use:

Drums

Drum Bus-	Drm Bus
Drum Bus Parallel Comp-	Drm Para
Bass drum-	Kick
Snare Drum-	SN
Snare Drum Top Mic-	SN T
Snare Drum Bottom Mic-	SN B
Hi Hats-	HH (or Hats)
Tom Tom-	Tom (followed by number of Tom—Tom 1, Tom 2 etc)
Crash Cymbal-	Crash
Ride Cymbal-	Ride
Percussion-	Perc

Instruments

Bass guitar-	Bass
Synth bass-	S Bass
Synthesizer-	Abbreviate name of patch
Piano-	Pno

Organ-	Org
Electric guitar-	GTR E (If needed add the style too—GTR E Strum)
Acoustic guitar-	GTR A (If needed add the style too—GTR A Strum)
Lead vocal-	L Vox
Backing vocals-	BV (followed by number—BV1, BV2 etc)

▶ *Tips from the pros*: Sometimes certain sections sound great in reverse. Try cutting into a quantised clip of a vocal or instrument track and reverse it into a new song segment. It can add a really interesting texture and neatly depart from one section of a song into another. ***Jonny Amos—Songwriter, Producer, Lecturer and Director at The SongLab.*** Shayne Ward, Jpop Idols EXIT, Miss D, Jackie Paladino, Glow Beets, Native Instruments Sounds. MTV, Sky One and Film Four.

▶ **Chapter 3 Tasks:** The following tasks will enable you to begin building a library of DAW templates to ensure a quick start to recording sessions.

- Create a DAW session and use the Save As Template function to build a personalised template for a basic audio recording session.
- Create three Mono Audio tracks in your template.
- Create a stereo auxiliary track with input from BUS 1–2 in your template and name it 'Reverb'.
- Create a stereo master output track (note some DAW create these automatically).
- Add a Reverb plug-in to the INSERTS of the auxiliary track and check the Reverb's mix of wet/dry is set to fully wet (or mix on full).
- Add Aux SENDS in each of the mono audio tracks and set the outputs to BUS 1–2.
- Add an EQ to the INSERTS to the first slot in each of the mono audio tracks.
- Use the colour palette function to give each track a different colour.
- Save this as your template for a quick-start audio recording session.
- Create similar templates using virtual instrument and/or MIDI tracks for quick-start MIDI-based sessions.

Digital

4

▶ **Learning Outcomes**

By the end of this chapter, the reader will be able to:
- Define the importance of different sample rates and bit depths.
- Create analogue and digital workflows to optimise sampling quality.
- Recall a range of audio file formats.
- Listen to and recognise glitches in audio recordings caused by sampling inconsistencies.

Sample Rate

When an analogue audio signal is recorded into a digital audio workstation (DAW), it has to be converted into digital bits—a binary sequence of zeros and ones. This is done by the A/D converter in the audio interface. The incoming analogue signal is sampled at precise and regular intervals, tens of thousands of times per second. This is known as the sample rate.

The analogue signal, such as a microphone capturing a voice, a guitar or bass going into your DAW through a preamp or DI Box, or any other analogue signal, will pass through an analogue to digital converter (A/D). The sound leaving your computer will be converted back to analogue in order for you to be able to hear it through your speakers. The diagram below shows the path a signal takes from entering to exiting your digital audio workstation (Fig. 4.1).

Supplementary Information The online version contains supplementary material available at https://doi.org/10.1007/978-3-031-40067-4_4. The videos can be accessed individually by clicking the DOI link in the accompanying figure caption or by scanning this link with the SN More Media App.

© The Author(s), under exclusive license to Springer Nature Switzerland AG 2024
S. Duggal, *Record, Mix and Master*,
https://doi.org/10.1007/978-3-031-40067-4_4

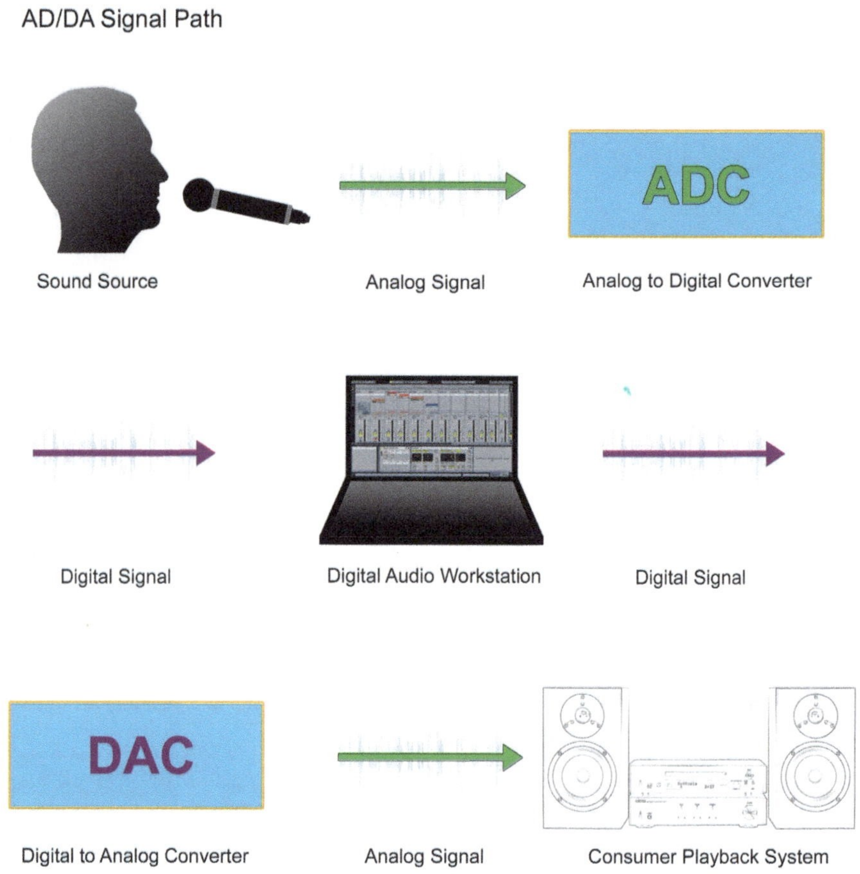

AD/DA Signal Path

Fig. 4.1 Analogue to digital and digital to analogue signal path

The number of samples recorded per second of an incoming analogue audio signal is measured in Hz (Hertz) and kHz (kilohertz). For example, when an analogue signal is recorded at a sample rate of 44,100 Hz (44.1 kHz), every second of audio is sampled 44,100 times.

The standard sample used for CD, MP3, FLAC, AAC and other consumer playback formats is 44.1 kHz, and it is approximately double the highest frequency of human hearing. Higher sample rates are available, for example, 48,000 Hz (48 kHz), which is used more commonly when audio is synced to film. These sample rates and above give us high-quality recording and playback (Figs. 4.2 and 4.3).

A higher sample rate means the analogue audio signal will be captured at more points of the wave, giving a better digital representation of the analogue sound. The maximum achievable sample rate will be determined by the capabilities of your audio interface (see Chap. 5: Hardware—Audio Interface).

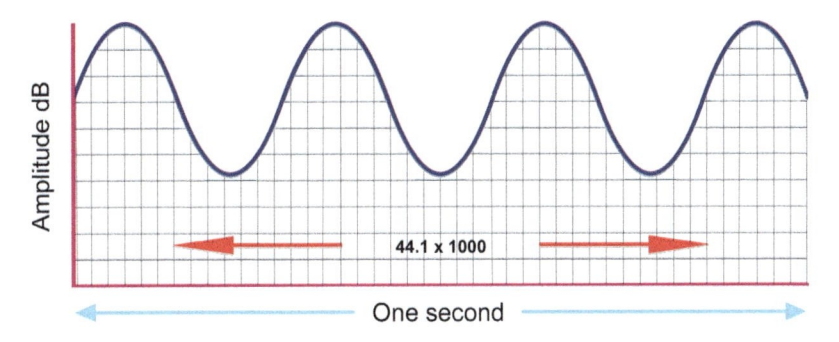

Fig. 4.2 Audio signal sampled at 44.1 kHz—44,100 samples per second

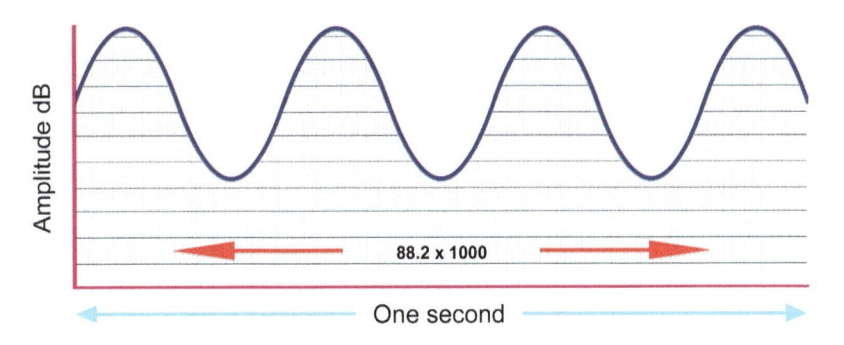

Fig 4.3 Audio signal sampled at 88.2 kHz—88,200 samples per second

Due to the extra load on your audio interface, the highest sample rates may reduce its processing capacity, resulting in a reduction of the available input and output channels. For example, an audio interface with 8 inputs and outputs running at 44.1 kHz may only have 4 inputs and 4 outputs available when running at 96 kHz.

The most commonly available sample rates that you can choose from are given below:

Sample rate	Number of times the audio signal is sampled per second
44.1 kHz	44,100
48 kHz	48,000
88.2 kHz	88,200
96 kHz	96,000
176.4 kHz	176,400
192 kHz	192,000

Upsampling

Upsampling is the process of increasing the sampling rate of an audio file. For example, when an audio file has been recorded at 44.1 kHz but you want to use it in a session you are working on that is at 96 kHz. In this instance, the audio material would be upsampled at the higher sample rate and saved as a new file, which would then be imported into your 96 kHz session.

When increasing the sampling rate of the given audio file, interpolation is used. Interpolation adds samples to the signal. Interpolation estimates the value of the signal between each sample and fills the gaps with zeros. When upsampling by a factor of 2, or doubling the sampling rate, for example, from 44.1 kHz to 88.2 kHz, one zero is inserted between each original sample. If upsampling by a factor of 4, for example, from 44.1 kHz to 176.4 kHz, 3 zeros would be inserted between each original sample and so on. This is known as zero filling (Fig. 4.4).

Some plugins have an option to oversample the signal. This is the process of increasing the sample rate within the plugin for processing, and then outputting the signal back at the session's original sample rate (see Chap. 4: Digital—Nyquist Frequency, Aliasing and Oversampling—Oversampling).

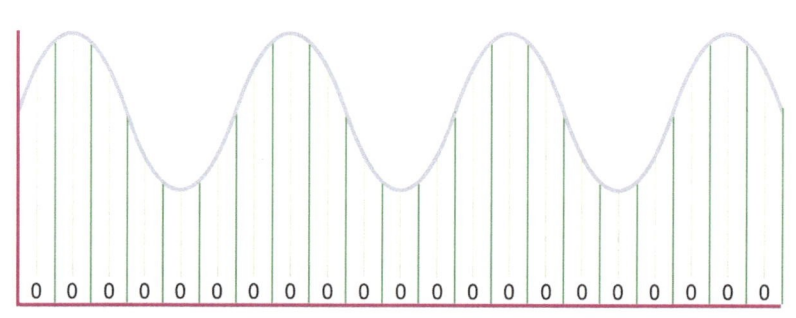

Zero Filling - Upsampling By a Factor of 2

■ = Original sampling instances
0 = Interpolation - One zero added between each sample

Fig. 4.4 Upsampling—zero filling

Downsampling

When decreasing the sample rate of an audio file, decimation is used. Decimation removes samples from the signal. An anti-aliasing filter has to be used to remove frequencies higher than the Nyquist frequency to prevent aliasing. Therefore, the signal has to be filtered before Decimation (see Chap. 4: Digital—Nyquist Frequency, Aliasing and Oversampling) (Fig. 4.5).

Recording at any sample rate other than 44.1 kHz will mean that the finished mix will have to be downsampled to 44.1 kHz in order to make it compatible with

Downsampling

■ = Original sampling instances
■ = Decimation - sampling instances removed

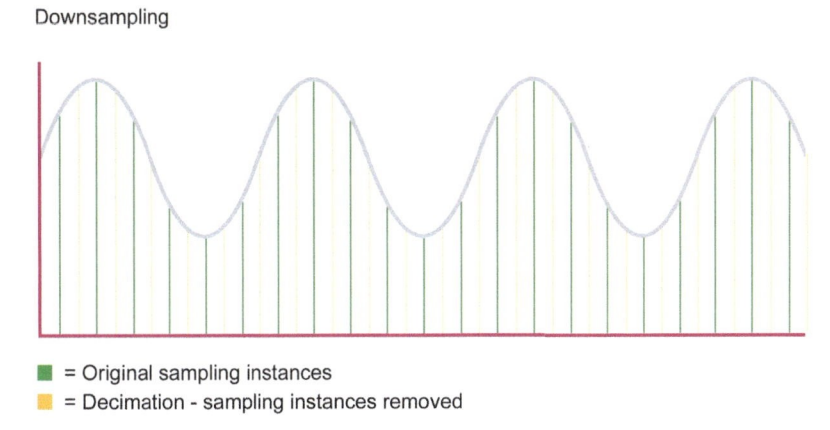

Fig. 4.5 Downsampling—decimation

consumer playback devices. It is quite common for professionals to record at higher sample rates and then downsample at the final stage.

There are no rules to which sample rate you work with, though recording at the highest rate your computer and audio interface can handle, and then downsampling to 44.1 kHz at the final stage will mean that maximum quality is maintained throughout the recording, mixing and mastering stages.

Listen carefully to each of the audio examples below. Can you hear a difference between the signal recorded at 44.1 kHz and 96 kHz?.

Bit Depth (Word Length)

In one second of audio recorded at 44.1 kHz, there are 44,100 samples. Each one of those samples has a depth which is measured in bits. Bit depth, also called word length, is the number of bits of information in a single sample of digital audio and determines the maximum dynamic range of the signal.

Bit depths used for recording digital audio are 16, 24 and 32 bits. The higher the bit depth, the more accurately the dynamic range of the sound is able to be captured.

Each sample recorded at 16 bits contains any one of 65,636 unique values. When recorded at 24 bits, there are 16,777,216 unique values. The difference between 16 bits and 24 bits is clearly huge.

The examples below show 24 bits and 16 bits of data for each of the 44,100 samples in one second of audio recorded and played back at 44.1 kHz (Figs. 4.6a and 4.6b).

Bit depth determines the dynamic range of the audio signal. 24-bit digital audio has a maximum dynamic range of approximately 144 dB, whereas 16 bit has a maximum of 96 dB. Modern high-quality analogue to digital converters can achieve a maximum dynamic range of approximately 120 dB at 24 bit.

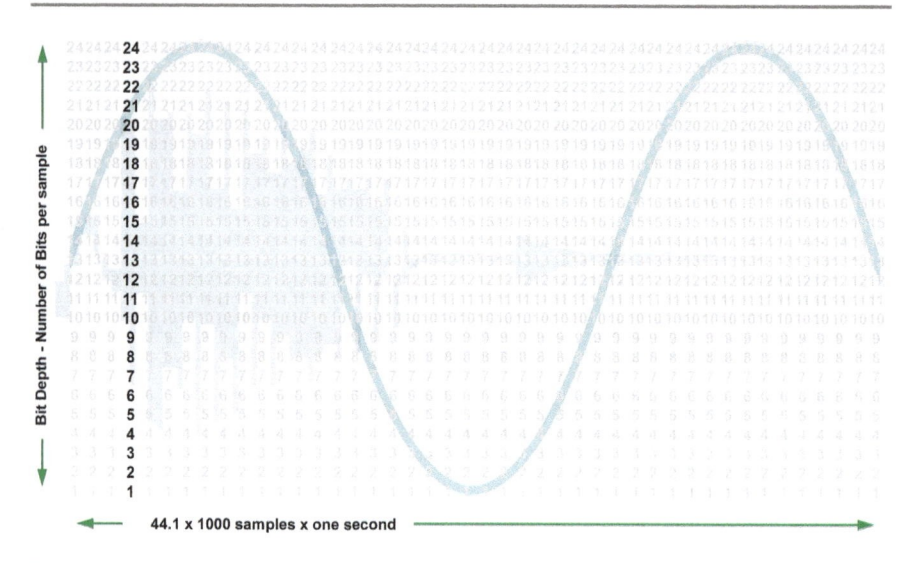

Fig. 4.6a Bit depth—24 bit

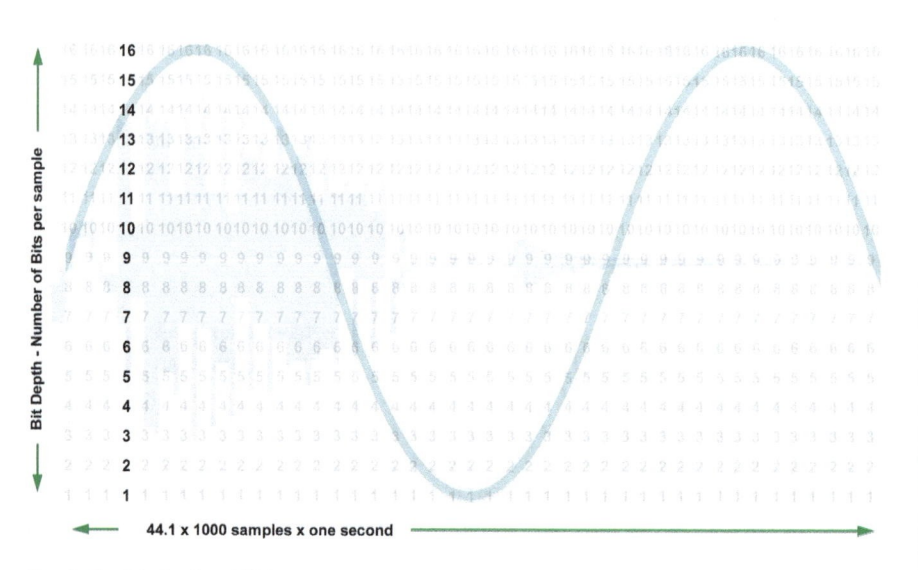

Fig. 4.6b Bit depth—16 bit

32-bit fixed-point binary has a dynamic range of somewhere around 192 dB, that is, 6 dB per bit. The dynamic range of 32-bit floating point is nearly 1700 dB. That is a massive increase compared to the dynamic range at 32-bit fixed point and at 24 bit. Whilst 32-bit floating point will remove the chance of any clipping during audio rendering and prevent mathematical quantisation errors during signal processing, the big increase in file size will result in the need for huge computer processing power in order to be able to playback large sessions at higher sample rates.

Fig. 4.7 Audio file size per minute

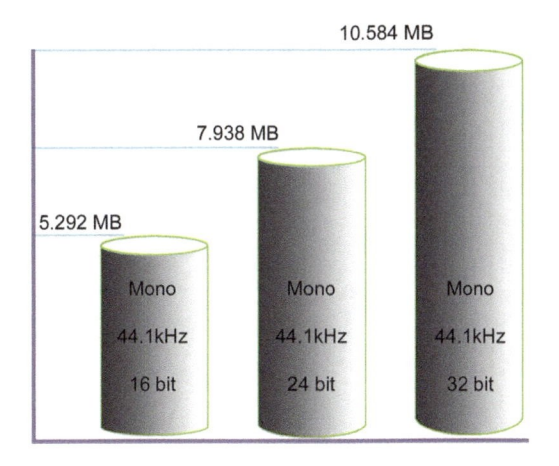

32-bit files are twice as big as 16-bit files and one and a half times as big as 24-bit files. Coupled with the fact that audio interface A/D and D/A converters are either 16 bit or 24 bit, it would seem that despite 32-bit floating point offering greater dynamic range, the benefit is outweighed by the limitations of the computer, the maximum bit depth of your audio interface and the big increase in file size (Fig. 4.7).

Listen carefully to each of the audio examples below. Can you hear a difference between the signal recorded at 16 bits and 24 bits?

Nyquist Frequency, Aliasing and Oversampling

In order to use an analogue signal in a digital audio workstation, it has to be sampled at multiple points of the cycle. Much like taking a photograph, the digital signal is a snapshot of the analogue signal. It does not represent an entire frequency range. For example, a photograph may look great, but when you zoom in, you can see that it starts to become pixelated. Also, the higher the frequency there are, the less sample points per cycle. By using high sample rates, we can get a good representation of the analogue signal. The most common sample rate used is 44.1 kHz or 44,100 samples of the analogue signal per second (see Chap. 4: Digital—Sample Rate) (Fig. 4.8).

The highest frequency that can be recorded at any sample rate is known as the Nyquist Frequency and is half of whatever the sample rate is.

So, if the sample rate is 48 kHz, the highest frequency that can be recorded is 24 kHz. If the sample rate is 44.1 kHz, the highest frequency that can be recorded is 22.050 kHz.

Any frequencies above the Nyquist Frequency would be moved by the digital to analogue converter to a frequency band below the Nyquist Frequency, thereby changing the frequency response of the signal. This is called Aliasing (Fig. 4.9).

Aliasing causes distortion and can make frequencies indistinguishable from each other. Our ears are sensitive to aliased frequencies as they are not harmonically related to the source.

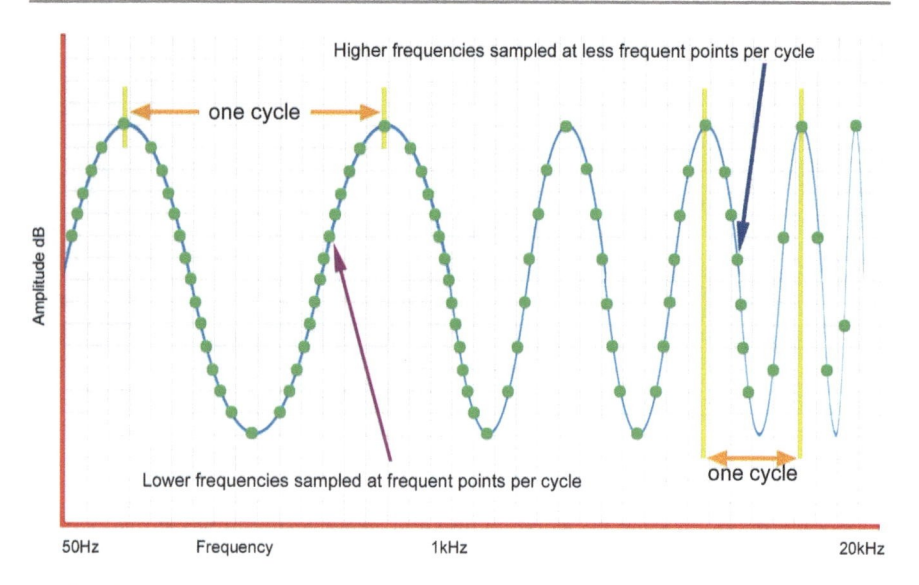

Fig. 4.8 Audio signal sampled at multiple points

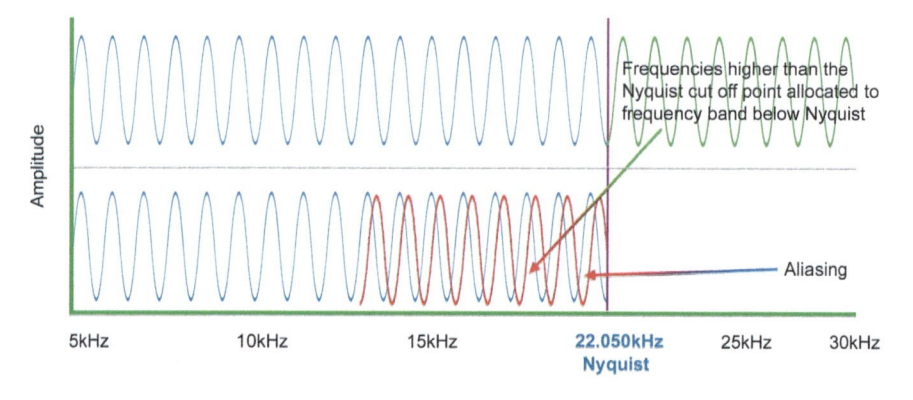

Fig. 4.9 Nyquist frequency at 44.1 kHz

Digital to analogue and analogue to digital converters in your audio interface have a component called an anti-aliasing filter which prevents frequencies above the Nyquist frequency from being converted, thereby preventing aliasing. The anti-aliasing filter is essentially a squared low-pass filter, cutting off everything above Nyquist (Fig. 4.10).

▶ *Tip: Be mindful that cheaper audio interfaces may not have such great AD/DA converters so aliasing may still occur. Purchase the best quality audio interface you can afford. There are plenty of reviews online and all good manufacturers provide detailed specifications.*

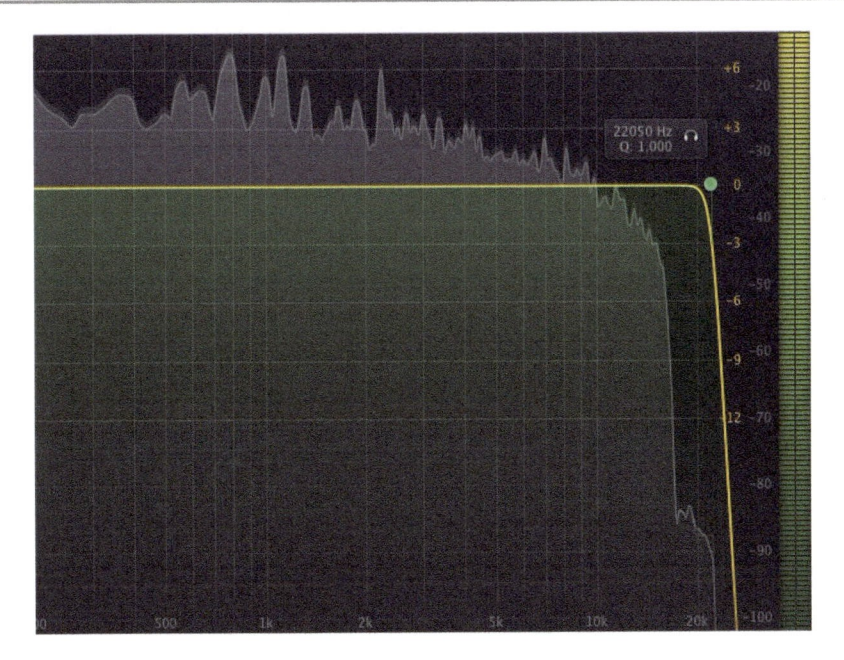

Fig. 4.10 An anti-aliasing filter is essentially a squared low-pass filter

Oversampling

Some plugins give you the option to oversample the input signal. When oversampling is engaged, the plugin resamples the audio at a higher sample rate than the session sample rate. If your DAW is set to 44.1 kHz for example and 4 × oversampling is selected, the plugin will sample the audio at 176.4 kHz. Oversampling allows the plugin to process the signal at a much higher resolution before outputting it back at the session's sample rate (Fig. 4.11).

The sound entering the plugin is first upsampled in order to maintain the original signal quality. Processing inside the plugin takes place at the oversampled rate to ensure the best possible sound from the plugin, and the output is then downsampled back to the session sample rate. If any of the processing is non-linear, unwanted frequencies above Nyquist may be added. These frequencies would be filtered out by an anti-aliasing filter before downsampling to the session sample rate.

So, if the audio material will ultimately end up at the same sample rate that it started at, what's the point of oversampling? Briefly speaking, oversampling prevents aliasing distortion from non-linear signals, particularly when modulation or distortion effects are used.

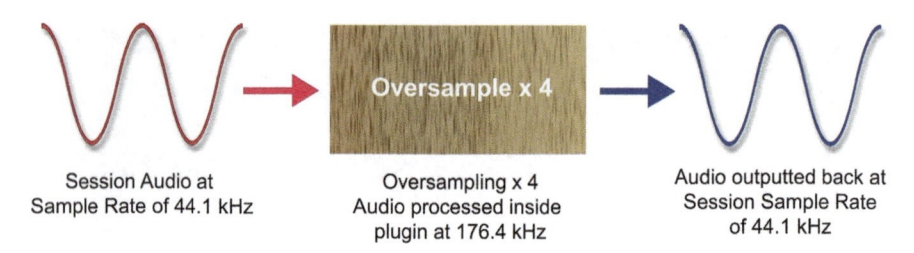

Fig. 4.11 Oversampling

Word Clock, Jitter and Frequency Drift

Word Clock and Jitter

One of the most important parts of an A/D and D/A convertor is the word clock. When an analogue signal is converted to digital, it has to be sampled at regular and precise intervals. A word clock is essentially a digital timekeeper that determines exactly when each sample (see Chap. 4: Digital—Sample Rate) should be recorded and played back. If there is any variation in the timing of the word clock, samples would be recorded and played back at the wrong time resulting in a distorted waveform. This is known as jitter. Jitter can also introduce pops and clicks at the output stage (Fig. 4.12).

Accurate word clock timing is critical to achieving the best possible sound quality. Any piece of equipment that converts A/D and D/A will have a word clock.

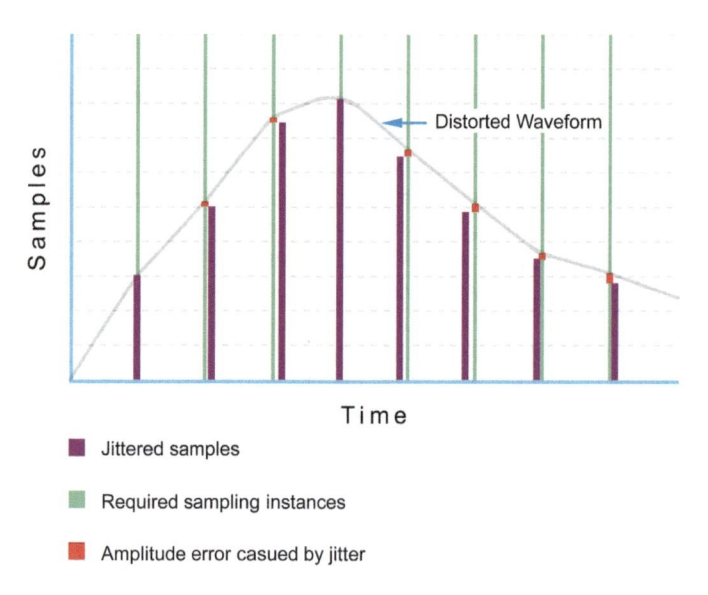

Fig. 4.12 Jitter

However, not all word clocks are equal. Just as some wrist watches keep more accurate time than others, some word clocks keep more accurate time than others.

If multiple A/D and D/A devices need to be synchronized, an external word clock should be used to keep recording and playback of all devices jitter-free. Using an external clock on a single audio interface can actually introduce jitter and is not generally necessary.

If you are using multiple digital devices, it is best to use a clock distribution box rather than daisy chaining devices together. Daisy chaining adds jitter progressively on each device. A clock distribution box will send the same signal through multiple outputs, ensuring each device receives identical timing information.

Frequency Drift

Frequency drift is when the signal is sampled at regular intervals of the required sampling instances but it is not in time with the clock. Whilst this is undesirable, it is not as much of a problem as jitter as it does not have a noticeable audible impact on the recording. However, it does affect the timing of the signal which could be problematic if, for example, you were synchronising the audio to film or video or you were sending stems to another studio (Fig. 4.13).

When choosing an audio interface, consider the quality of the word clock in addition to your input and output requirements.

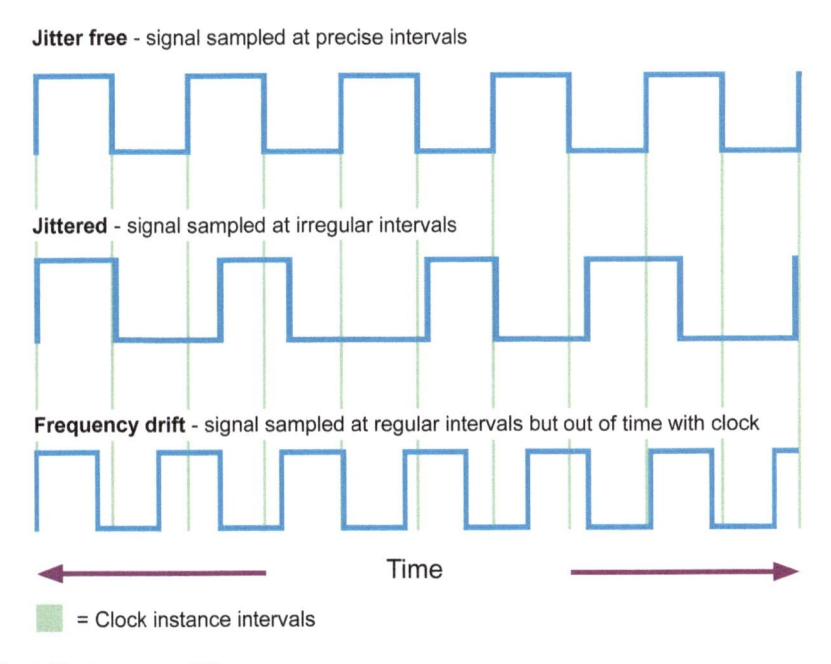

Fig. 4.13 Frequency drift

DC Offset

On occasion, your recorded audio wave may appear to be offset on the timeline of your DAW. The signal becomes offset from the centre zero point, the point of zero amplitude from where the signal either rises or falls in level. This is known as DC offset. It can be introduced into the recording when using poor-quality analogue-to-digital converters and/or some modulation effects such as chorus, flangers and phasers (Fig. 4.14).

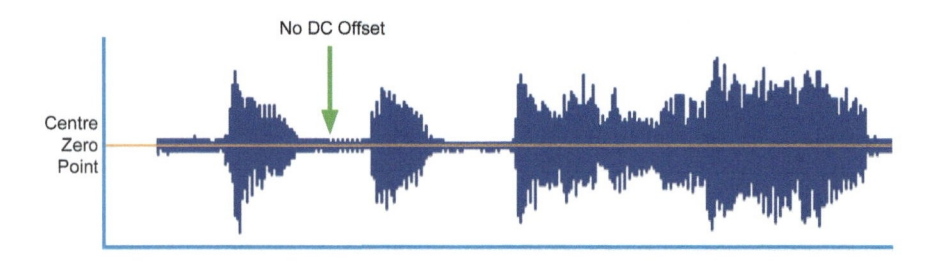

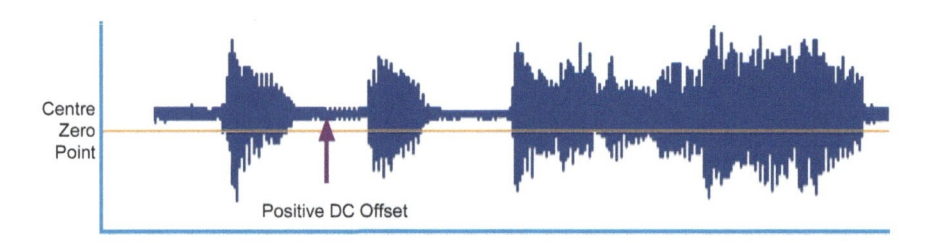

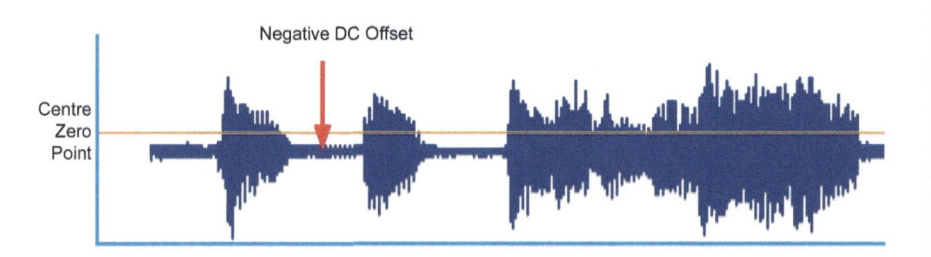

Fig. 4.14 DC offset

The result of DC offset is a reduction in the amount of headroom available between the peak of the signal and the loudest possible level. DC offset can occur on individual audio tracks or even a whole mix (Fig. 4.15).

DC offset can introduce low-level distortion which becomes apparent when the audio material is converted to lossy formats such as MP3, or when frequency-changing effects such as phasers, are applied. It can also cause audible clicks and pops when sections of audio are cut and pasted together.

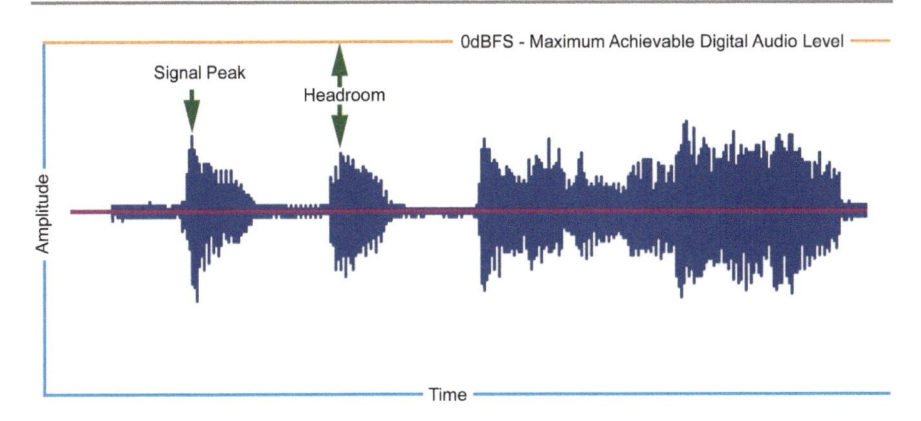

Fig. 4.15 Reduced headroom resulting from DC offset

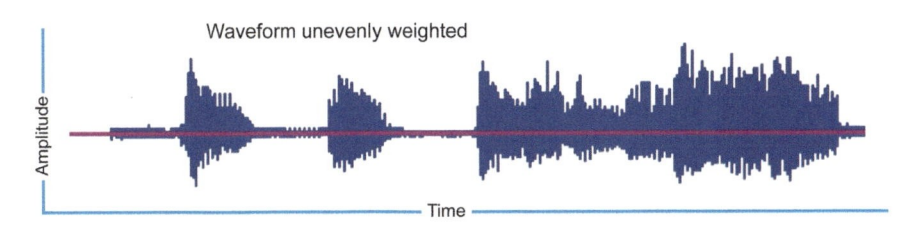

Fig. 4.16 Unevenly weighted waveform resulting from DC offset

Sometimes, rather than the wave being displayed as offset from the centre zero-point, dc offset can cause the wave to be displayed as unevenly weighted on either the top or the bottom (Fig. 4.16).

There can be varying degrees of DC offset, so it might take a keen ear and eye to spot it. Most DAWs and some plugins have a 'remove DC offset' function which corrects the problem easily by realigning the wave so that it sits correctly at the centre zero point.

▶ *Tip: Not all DC Offset removal tools respond to audio in the same way, so you may have to try a couple to see which one works best.*

Hardware Buffer Size and Latency

The hardware (H/W) buffer setting in your DAW determines the size of the cache that the computer uses to temporarily store audio input and output data. The buffer can be set to store 32, 64, 128, 256, 512 or 1024 samples of audio. Some DAWs can store more.

The bigger the buffer size, the longer it takes for the computer to process the audio data. This is because the computer has to process a greater number of temporarily stored samples. The result is an audible delay between audio entering and leaving the computer. A benefit of larger buffer sizes is that you'll be able to run bigger sessions with more tracks and plugins, though this will come at the cost of some latency.

Latency is the time delay between a live audio signal entering the DAW and leaving it. This delay, usually measured in milliseconds or samples, can have a noticeable impact on the timing of your recording.

For example, having recorded some virtual instrument parts into your DAW, a programmed drum beat, a bass line and some keyboard parts, you now need to record a live guitar part. You've armed your audio track ready for recording and jammed along with your track only to find that there is a delay between you striking the guitar strings and hearing it playing back in time with your virtual instrument parts. All of your virtual instrument parts are playing together in time; however, the delay you are hearing when you strike a guitar string is making it impossible to play with feeling.

One solution is lowering the buffer setting in your DAW's playback engine. This can reduce the latency but depending on how powerful your computer is, it may come at the cost of possible sporadic glitches or stutters during recording and playback (Fig. 4.17).

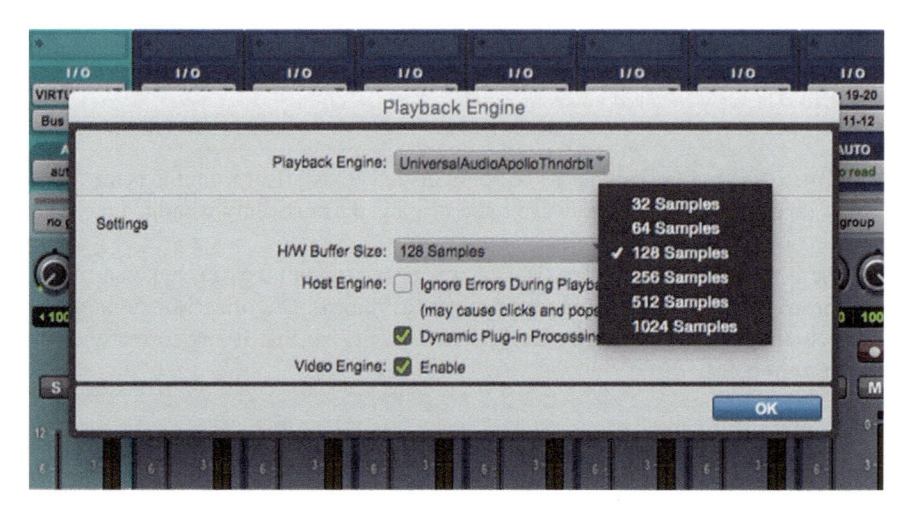

Fig. 4.17 Hardware buffer size

Another solution is to free up computer power temporarily by deactivating tracks that you can do without whilst playing your guitar part. You could try recording your guitar whilst listening to just the drums, bass and lead vocal and deactivate all keyboard and backing vocal tracks. By freeing up computer processing power, you may be able to set the buffer size low enough so that latency is not an issue.

The preferred solution is to monitor the live input of the guitar through your audio interface mixer software instead of through the record-armed track in your

Hardware Buffer Size and Latency

DAW. The mixer for your audio interface routes the live guitar input to the record channel of your DAW and simultaneously directly to the speakers with near-zero latency, so you can easily play in time with the previously recorded parts. Be sure to keep the record-armed track in your DAW muted so you don't hear the delayed signal as well as the monitored signal. One downside of this is that you won't be able to monitor through any plugins you have inserted on your record channel but the upside of near zero latency may well be worth the trade-off (Fig. 4.18).

The buffer size and sample rate setting both have an impact on latency. Higher sample rates offer less audible delay but at the cost of higher CPU usage.

To calculate exactly how much latency is induced, divide the buffer size by the sample rate. For example, a buffer setting of 256 samples at 44.1 kHz would be:

$$256\, samples \div 44100 = 0.0058 = 5.8\,ms$$

Whereas, 256 samples at 96 kHz would be: $256 \div 96000 = 0.0026 = 2.6$ ms. 64 samples at 44.1 kHz would be:

$$64 \div 44100 = 0.0014 = 1.4\,ms$$

Buffer size	Sample rate	Calculation	Result	Result in ms
256 samples	44.1 kHz	256 ÷ 44100	0.0058	5.8 milliseconds
256 samples	96 kHz	256 ÷ 96000	0.0026	2.6 milliseconds
64 samples	44.1 kHz	64 ÷ 44100	0.0014	1.4 milliseconds

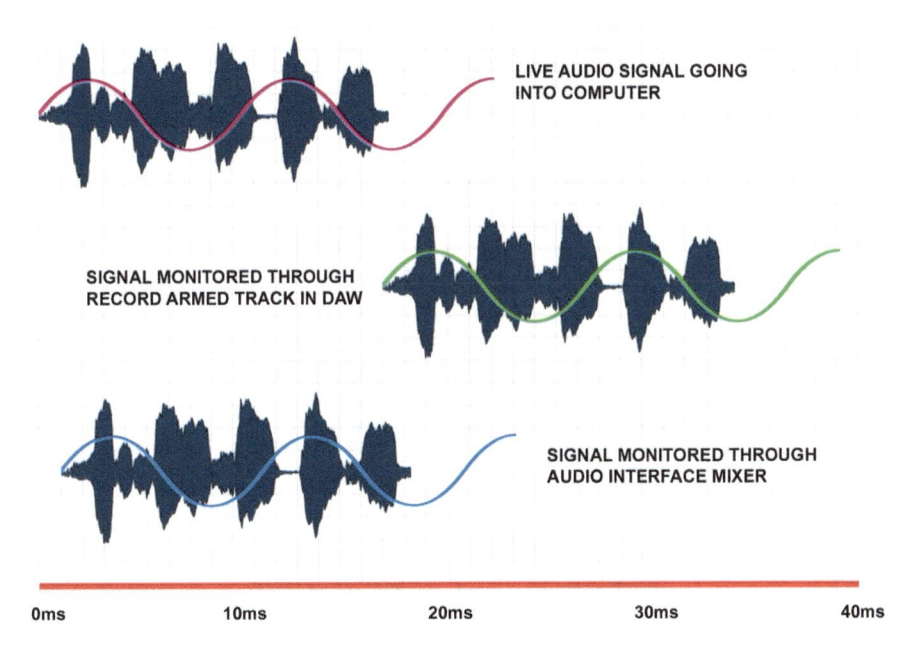

Fig. 4.18 Input signal monitoring

Latency can also be caused by inserting certain plugins on a track which cause the recorded audio or midi to be delayed in relation to other tracks in the session. This is due to the time it takes for certain plugins to process the audio material. The more intensive the calculation the plugin has to perform, the longer the delay will be. With multiple plugins inserted on lots of tracks, this can become a bit of a mess resulting in tracks playing back out of time with each other. It would be a huge task to calculate how much latency has affected each track, and then to move each one on the timeline so that it is in time again. Fortunately, most recording software compensates for this with automatic delay compensation (ADC). ADC calculates the delay induced by each plugin and compensates for any shift in time. This keeps all of the tracks in the session in time with each other and with the DAW's metronome (Fig. 4.19).

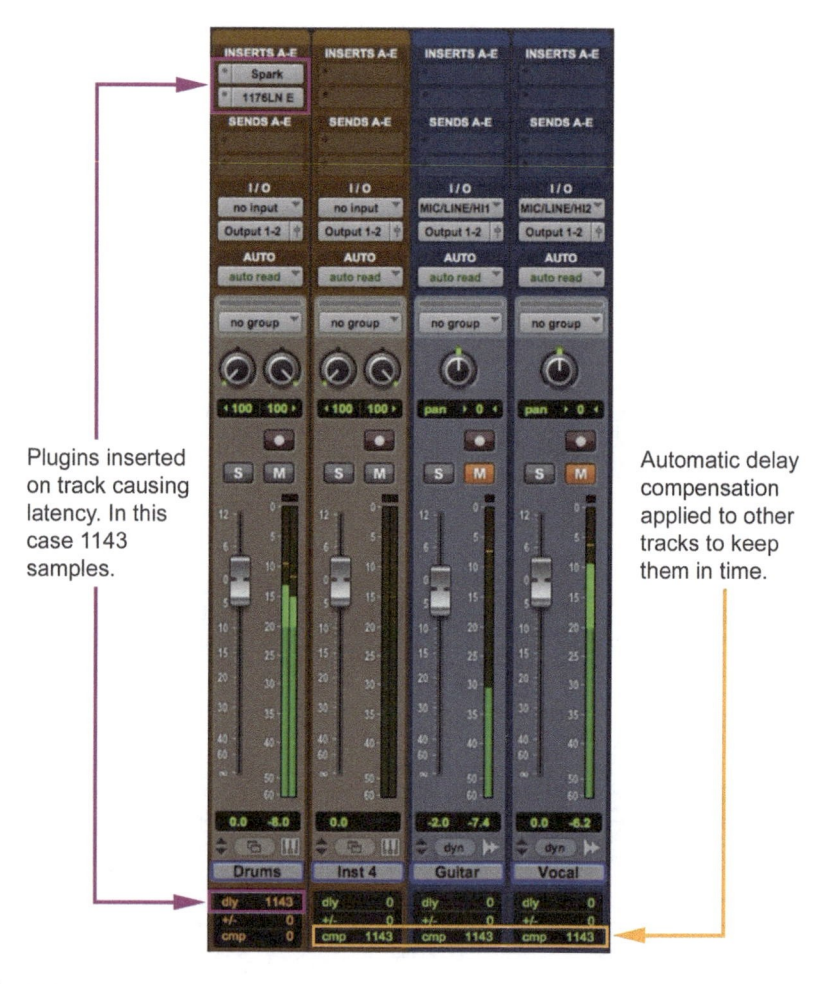

Fig. 4.19 Automatic delay compensation

File Formats

Pulse code modulation (PCM) is the most common audio file format. It is used in CD and DVD. PCM is the most accurate digital representation of an analogue audio signal. When an analogue audio signal is recorded into a digital audio workstation, it has to be converted into digital bits (see Chap. 4: Digital—Bit Depth). The incoming analogue signal is sampled at regular intervals. This is known as the sample rate (see Chap. 4: Digital—Sample Rate).

The most common file types that use the PCM format are WAV (wave) and AIFF (audio interchangeable file format). Both are uncompressed formats with no difference in sound quality between the two. Generally speaking, WAV files are compatible with more devices/software programs. Broadcast wave format (BWF) is a type of WAV file that was created for film and TV and carries additional information such as timestamps and metadata, as well as the audio material.

WAV and AIFF are uncompressed lossless formats, whereas AAC, MP3, MP4 and others are compressed lossy formats. Lossy formats get rid of part of the data to make the file size smaller. Lossy formats can have greatly reduced file sizes compared to lossless formats, though the trade-off is a reduction in audio quality. Lossy formats are most commonly found on streaming and file-sharing sites.

Listen and compare the audio signal in WAV and MP3 formats.

▶ **Chapter 4 Tasks:** The following tasks will sharpen your listening skills in identifying a variety of file types and associated issues.

- Listen to the provided Audio Examples 3, 4, 5 and 6.
- How would you describe in words how the different sample rates and bit depths sound? Can you hear a difference between 44.1 kHz and 96 kHz?
- Listen to Audio example 4.5 and identify where the buffer size glitches appear.
- Try doing a listening test of Audio examples 4.6 and 4.7 without knowing which one you are listening to—can you tell which one is .wav and which one is .mp3? Describe the differences.

Hardware 5

▶ **Learning Outcomes**

By the end of this chapter, the reader will be able to:
- Show a working knowledge of a range of audio and MIDI hardware.
- Categorize a range of audio cables and explain how they work.
- Define the strengths and weaknesses of working with headphones.

Audio Interface

An audio interface is a hardware device that connects to your computer to give you much better sound quality and connection capabilities than the computer's own sound card. An audio interface will allow you to connect professional microphones and instruments to your computer, and output high-quality sound to your studio speakers and headphones.

The most important job your audio interface does is converting incoming analogue signals to digital, and outgoing digital signals back to analogue. Some audio interfaces do this job more accurately than others (see Chap. 4: Digital—Word Clock, Jitter and Frequency Drift) (Fig. 5.1).

Audio interfaces connect to your computer via FireWire, USB or Thunderbolt cables. Driver software supplied with your particular interface will need to be installed on your computer so that the devices can communicate with each other.

Supplementary Information The online version contains supplementary material available at https://doi.org/10.1007/978-3-031-40067-4_5. The videos can be accessed individually by clicking the DOI link in the accompanying figure caption or by scanning this link with the SN More Media App.

© The Author(s), under exclusive license to Springer Nature Switzerland AG 2024
S. Duggal, *Record, Mix and Master*,
https://doi.org/10.1007/978-3-031-40067-4_5

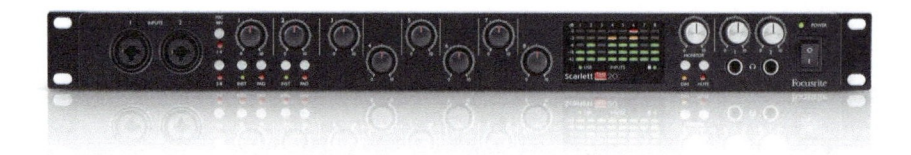

Fig. 5.1 Focusrite Scarlett 18i20 (front). (Image courtesy of Focusrite Audio Engineering Ltd)

Fig. 5.2 Focusrite Scarlett 18i20 (back). (Image courtesy of Focusrite Audio Engineering Ltd)

Audio interfaces provide a number of balanced analogue line inputs and outputs as well as headphone sockets, MIDI in and out and digital in and out—either SPDIF or ADAT optical—and have preamps built in. Many high-end interfaces can automatically detect whether the input signal is at microphone, instrument or line level (see Chap. 7: Microphones—Microphone, Instrument and Line Level) (Fig. 5.2).

The front face of the interface will usually have a master volume control, instrument/Hi-Z inputs, input gain controls and level metres, and one or two ¼" TRS jack headphone sockets.

Audio Cables

Balanced

There are three wires in a balanced cable, and three conductors in the connector plug. There are two signal wires—a positive and a negative. They are surrounded by a ground wire which helps protect the signal from noise and interference (Fig. 5.3).

Fig. 5.3 Balanced TRS jack plug

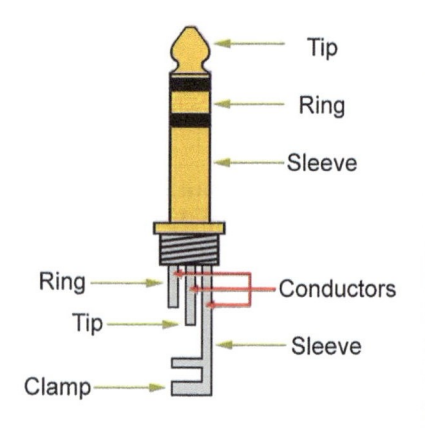

The positive (Tip) and negative (Ring) wires carry identical signals but with the polarity reversed. This means that the signal in one of the wires is inverted (see Chap. 8: Phase). Reversal of polarity affects all frequencies in the signal equally, unlike phase reversal which affects only some frequencies (Fig. 5.4).

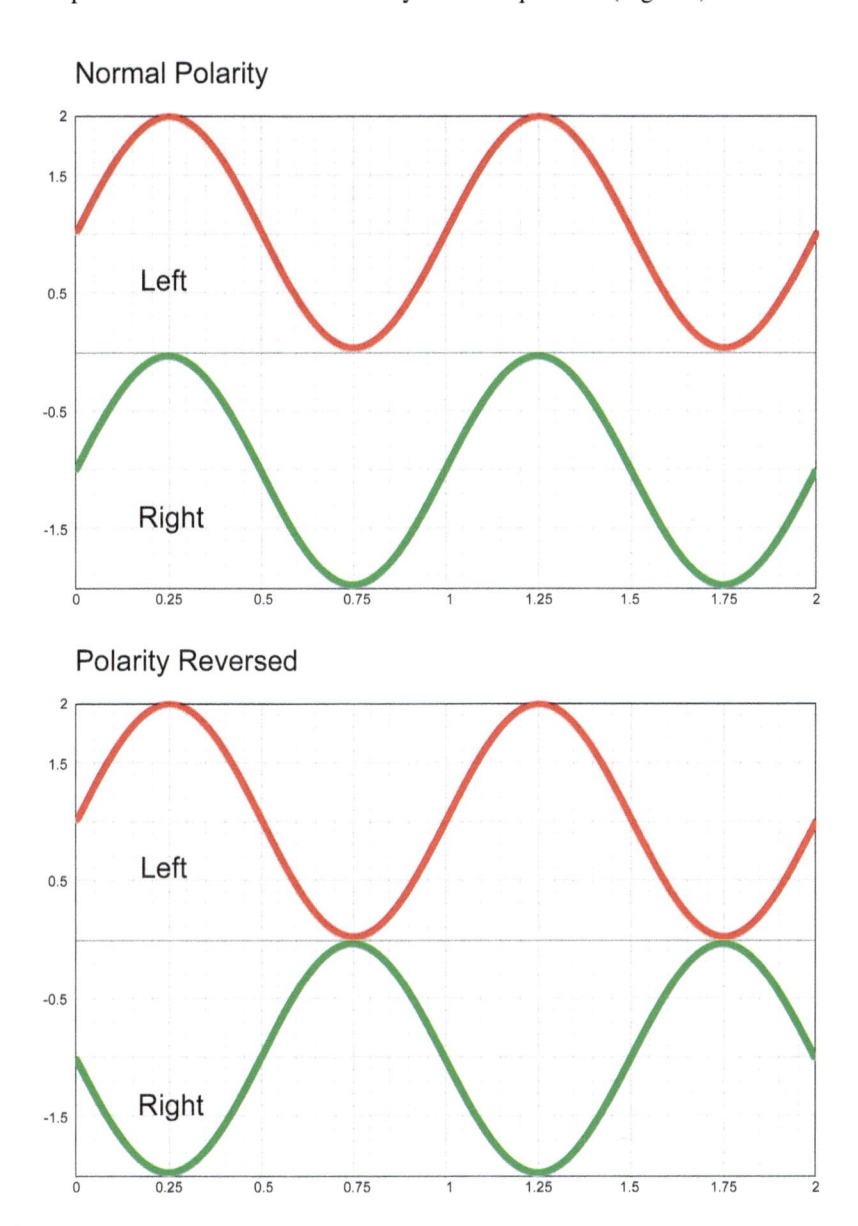

Fig. 5.4 Normal and reversed polarity

This reversal in polarity causes the signal to cancel itself out, which results in silence. When the signal reaches the preamp, audio interface, mixer or other equipment, the polarity is reversed again and the signal is restored. Any noise present in the signal is also carried by both the positive and negative wires. When the signal reaches the equipment and its polarity is restored, the polarity of the noise gets reversed and cancelled out, resulting in a clean signal with any noise silenced (Fig. 5.5).

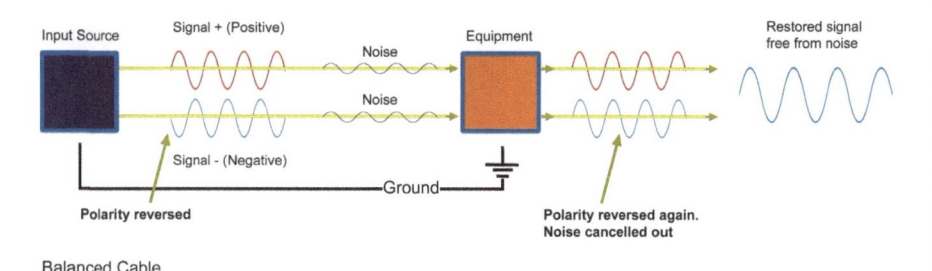

Fig. 5.5 Balanced signal path

Balanced cables are suitable for use in applications such as connecting active studio speakers to the outputs of an audio interface or connecting a microphone to an audio interface or preamp. They are also the best option when very long lengths are required. Balanced connector plugs can be either TRS jack, XLR or a combination of both.

Unbalanced

Unbalanced cables have two wires and two conductors in the connector plug. There is one signal wire and one ground wire. Unbalanced cables are most commonly used for connecting instruments such as guitars and keyboards to amplifiers and audio interface line inputs. Unbalanced cables can be prone to noise and interference, especially in long lengths. RCA (Phono) cables used in consumer hi-fi equipment are also unbalanced (Fig. 5.6).

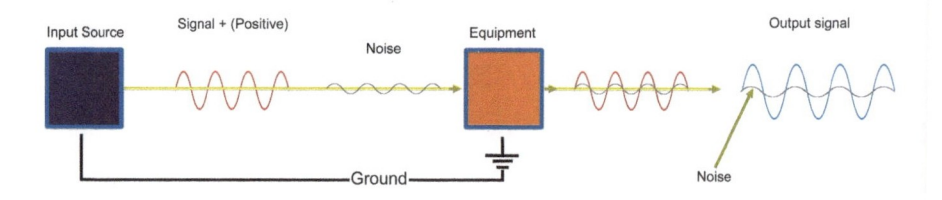

Fig. 5.6 Unbalanced signal path

You can tell the difference between balanced and unbalanced cables that have TRS jack plugs easily. The connector plug on a balanced cable has a tip, ring and sleeve and an unbalanced cable has just a tip and sleeve (Fig. 5.7).

Fig. 5.7 Balanced and unbalanced TRS jak plugs

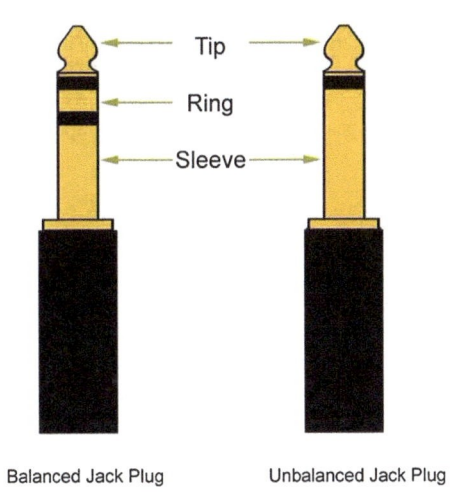

Balanced Jack Plug   Unbalanced Jack Plug

XLR

Generally speaking, cables with XLR connectors are pretty much always balanced. XLR cables have a three-pin male connector plug at one end and a three-pin female connector plug at the other. XLR cables can carry phantom power, usually +48v, as well as the balanced audio signal (Fig. 5.8).

Fig. 5.8 Male and female XLR connectors

Male XLR Connector   Female XLR Connector

The table below shows you what types of leads are balanced and unbalanced.

Type of cable	Connector type	Balanced	Unbalanced
Instrument/guitar	TS Jack to TS Jack		✓
Microphone	XLR to XLR	✓	
Audio interface into active speaker	TRS to TRS	✓	
	TRS to XLR	✓	
	XLR to XLR	✓	
Passive speaker to amplifier	Speaker wire		✓

Digital Audio Cables

Coaxial (Coax)

Coaxial cables have an RCA (Phono) connector at each end. They have a signal cable running through the centre, which is shielded by copper wire surrounding it. Although these cables are designed to carry a digital signal, they can pick up radio frequency and electromagnetic interference. Coaxial cables are not suitable for long distances as they are also prone to losing signal strength (Fig. 5.9)

Fig. 5.9 RCA (Phono) coaxial connector

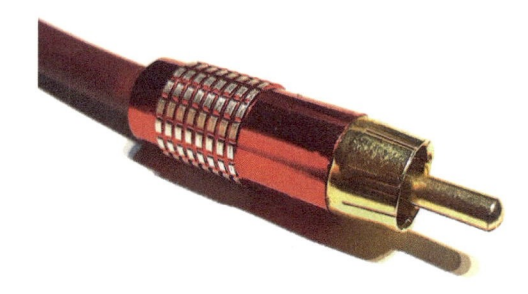

Optical (Toslink)

Optical cables have a glass or plastic fibre optic core which transfers the signal through a beam of red light. The source signal is converted from electrical to optical and then back again when it reaches the equipment. Optical cables do not pick up interference and are suitable for long distances. Usually, optical cables have a square plug with a small bump on it at each end. Optical cables are more delicate than coaxial cables, so care should be taken not to bend or twist them (Fig. 5.10).

Fig. 5.10 Optical (Toslink) connector

AES/EBU

AES/EBU (Audio Engineering Society/European Broadcasting Union) cables look like regular balanced XLR cables with a male XLR on one end and a female XLR on the other. These cables transfer digital PCM signals between devices. AES/EBU cables are fine to use for connecting analogue equipment, but analogue XLR cables cannot be used for connecting digital equipment due to the difference in impedance in the cable (Fig. 5.11).

Fig. 5.11 AES/EBU cable

Equipment Connections

A simple home or project studio setup comprises of:
1. A computer to run your DAW software. Whether you use Pro Tools, Ableton Live, Logic or any other DAW, you'll need a computer that's powerful enough to handle audio, plugin and virtual instrument processing. As a minimum, a MAC or PC desktop or laptop with an Intel i5 or i7 processor, at least 8 GB of RAM (ideally 16 GB), a 512 GB internal hard drive on which to install your DAW, plugins and sample libraries, and 4 USB ports. It's advisable to have an external hard drive for recording your audio projects and saving your sessions. In addition, you should have an additional external hard drive for backing up your projects.

2. A USB audio interface with as many inputs and outputs as you need. How many will depend on whether you record one microphone or instrument at a time, or more. It's also useful to have more than one headphone socket. If you are planning on recording at sample rates higher than 44.1 kHz, check the maximum sample rate available on your interface (see Chap. 5: Hardware—Audio Interface).
3. A USB controller keyboard so that you can input midi note data, pitch bend, aftertouch and modulation data (see Chap. 5: Hardware—Controller Keyboards).
4. A pair of studio speakers. Active speakers have amplifiers built in, so you don't need an external amp (see Chap. 2: Speakers—Types of Speakers).
5. Balanced cables to connect your audio interface to your speakers. USB cables to connect your audio interface and controller keyboard to your computer. If you are using an external sound module, you'll need MIDI (5 pin DIN) cables to connect it to the MIDI input and output on your audio interface. You'll also need unbalanced TRS to TRS cables to connect the audio outputs of your sound module to the line inputs of your audio interface.

NB: These recommendations are correct at the time of writing this book. Given the exponential growth of computing technology, these recommendations are subject to change.

Now that you have your equipment, you'll need to connect it together.

Install your DAW software (see Chap. 3: Digital Audio Workstation) and drivers for your audio interface, controller keyboard or any other device that requires a driver. See the manufacturer's guidelines for the installation process, as this may differ depending on what you are using. Once this is done, you can connect your equipment.

The diagram below shows how to connect a simple setup. Make sure all devices are switched off before connecting any cables (Fig. 5.12).

1. Connect the USB out of the audio interface to a USB input on your computer.
2. Connect the USB out of your controller keyboard to a USB input on your computer.
3. Connect the monitor outputs—sometimes labelled as outputs 1 and 2, on the audio interface to the inputs on your active speakers.
4. Connect the MIDI in and out on your sound module to the MIDI in and out on your audio interface.
5. Connect the audio outputs of your sound module to the line inputs on your audio interface.
6. Connect a microphone to the mic input on your audio interface.
7. Connect a guitar to the instrument input on the front of your audio interface. Note: The inputs on the front of most audio interfaces are microphone and instrument level, and on the back, they are line level (see Chap. 7: Microphones—Microphone, Instrument and Line level).

Equipment Connections   67

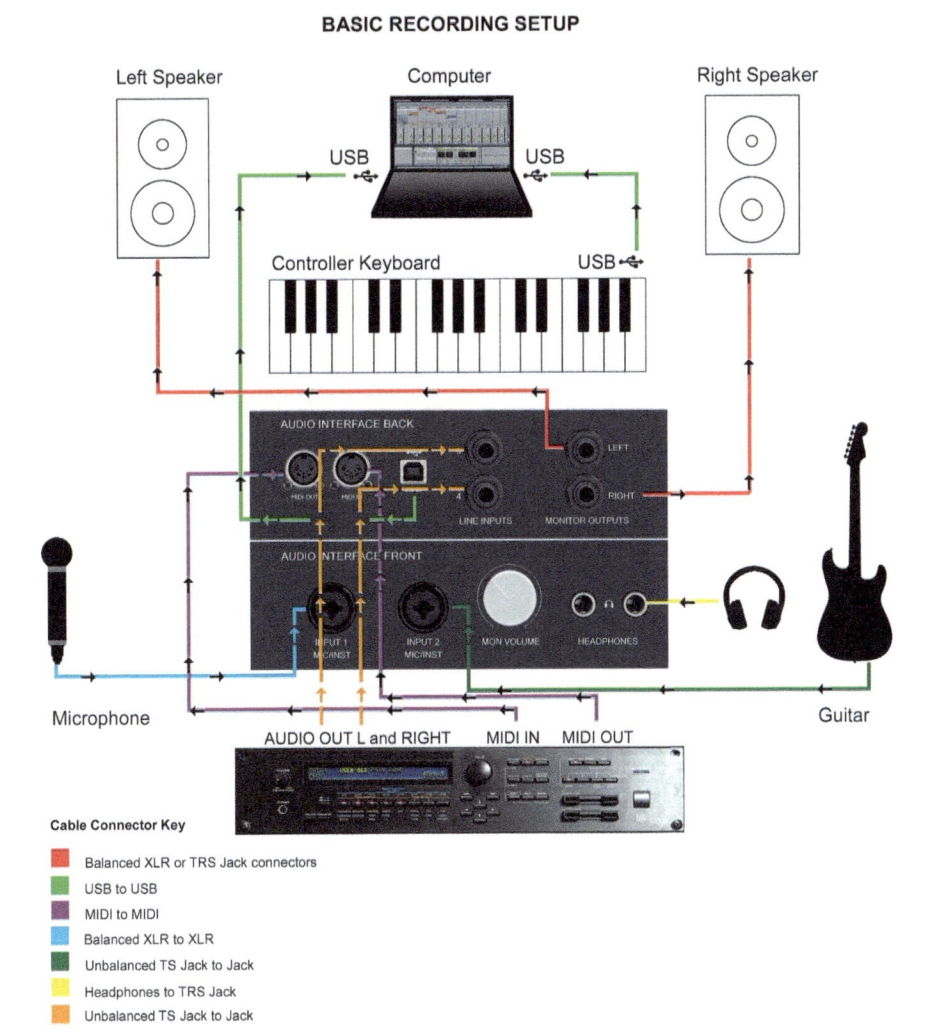

BASIC RECORDING SETUP

Fig. 5.12 Typical equipment connections

In order to protect your equipment from electrical spikes or sudden loud noises that may cause damage to your speakers, it's important to switch devices on and off in the following order.

Switching on:
1. Turn on your audio interface.
2. Boot up your computer.
3. Turn on your speakers.

Switching off:
1. Turn off your speakers.
2. Shut down your computer.
3. Turn off your audio interface.

NB: Make sure any external hard drives are ejected before unplugging their USB cables. Unplugging hard drives without ejecting them first can cause damage which may result in data loss.

Preamps (Pre-Amplifier)

Preamps are used to increase the gain—the input level—of a microphone or instrument, to change the tone of the sound and to change the input signal from unbalanced to balanced (see Chap. 5: Hardware—Audio Cables). Some preamps are designed to change the tone whilst others are designed to be totally transparent.

Preamps can be stand-alone units as well as being built into audio interfaces, guitar pedals and amplifiers. They can be solid-state or tube designs. The latter uses vacuum-sealed tubes that get physically warm and impart that warmth onto the signal (Fig. 5.13).

Fig. 5.13 Pre-amplifier (front)

The two main controls on the front of most preamps are gain and output. The gain knob controls the amount by which the signal level is increased, and the output volume control knob allows you to increase or decrease the overall level after the preamp stage.

Some preamps have tone controls, which can be used to alter the tone of the sound. Other preamps are more transparent, allowing the gain of the signal to be changed without altering the tonal quality in any way.

48v feeds phantom power to a microphone at 48 volts. Be careful not to activate the phantom power switch if anything other than a microphone requiring power is plugged in. Doing so will damage any equipment that is connected.

The direct injection (DI) input allows you to directly connect instrument-level sources. Keyboards and guitars output somewhere between mic and line level. To take the signal of an instrument to line level, an active DI Box is required. The DI input on the preamp negates the need for a separate DI Box (see Chap. 7: Microphones—Microphone, Instrument and Line Level).

The Z in low Z signifies impedance. Impedance affects the efficiency of how the signal is transferred to the input of the preamp. Low impedance means the current is stronger, therefore giving a better signal-to-noise ratio. High impedance signals are more prone to interference and noise, and should be connected to Hi-Z inputs.

The rear of a typical preamp has microphone and line inputs, a choice of TRS or XLR outputs and power supply input (Fig. 5.14).

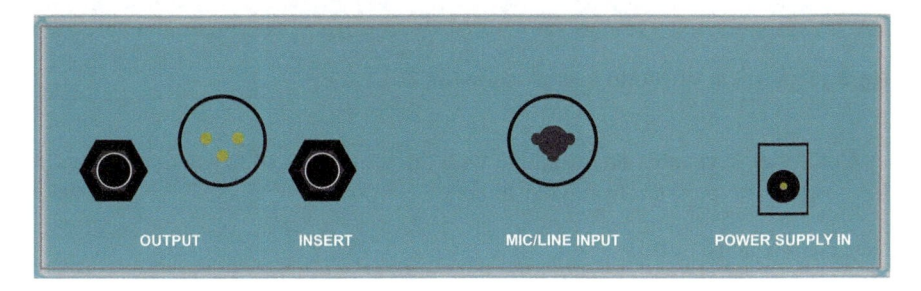

Fig. 5.14 Pre-amplifier (back)

▶ *Tip: Gain staging your preamp correctly can make the difference between a great sound and an ok sound (see Chap. 6: Gain Staging). If the input signal is too strong, try using the pad button to bring the level down. Most preamps have a sweet spot where the best input level is achieved. Try starting with the input gain at around 65% to 75% and adjust the output level accordingly.*

▶ *Tip: Some preamps sound better with some microphones. Experiment with different microphone and preamp combinations.*

Controller Keyboards

USB and MIDI controller keyboards do not have any on-board sounds. Instead they are used to control virtual instrument plugins inside your digital audio workstation. Some controller keyboards have built-in drum pads for use with virtual drum machines and samplers, as well as assignable control knobs and faders for controlling many other features of your software and plugins. Some current models are also compatible with the software on your tablets and smartphones (Fig. 5.15).

They come in a variety of sizes from portable 25-note versions with mini keys to 88-note versions with full-size piano keys. It's also possible to get even smaller (one octave) versions. Most have pitch bend and modulation wheels.

Fig. 5.15 A typical MIDI/USB controller keyboard

Controller keyboards are available with different types of key action—how the key responds to pressure from your fingers:

Key action	Response type
Synth action	This is the most common key type. These controllers have plastic spring-loaded keys that feel lightweight and have a quick response.
Semi weighted	These controllers have individual weights for each non-plastic key. The response is heavier than synth action and a touch slower.
Fully weighted	Fully weighted controller keyboards have weighted non-plastic keys too. These are designed to mimic the feel and response of a real piano.

Headphones

Headphones are necessary in studios because:

- They reveal fine detail that would otherwise be inaudible on your speakers. They are useful for checking audio tracks for noise, clicks and hums.
- When using a microphone for recording in the same room that you mix in, you will need to switch your speakers off so that the sound is not picked up by the microphone.
- If your vocalist or musician is in another room, they will need to hear the music and themselves.
- Headphones are great for checking the low frequencies in your mix, especially when your room is less than adequately acoustically treated.
- Room resonances and comb filtering that can affect the mix decisions you make are no longer an issue.

There are different types of headphones available:

For recording use in a studio environment, closed-back headphones are the most suitable as the sound does not spill out of them and get picked up by the microphone. Open-back headphones can be used for reference and mixing purposes.

The classic Beyer Dynamic DT100 Headphones have long been a popular choice for many professional studios though headphone technology has moved on somewhat in recent years. It's a good idea to get the best quality headphones your budget will allow, as they will, no doubt, be used for monitoring, referencing and perhaps mixing.

▶ *Tip: Some singers like to have one side of the headphones off their ears. This helps them to hear themselves properly and improves their pitching. Watch out for headphone spills getting picked up by the microphone.*

Headphone Impedance

Most consumer headphones, ones designed to be used with MP3 players, mobile phones, etc. are low impedance, usually less than 32 ohms as they don't need much power in order to deliver high volume. Headphones with impedances greater than 32 ohms up to as high as 600 ohms, are generally used for connecting to DJ mixers, audio interfaces and other professional audio equipment.

Cue Mix

A cue mix is another name for a headphone mix. This is a mix sent to the singer's headphones that is different from the actual mix you're hearing on your monitors.

Sometimes the cue mix may be simple, such as the mix you're working on fed to the headphones, together with the singer's live vocal so they can hear themselves with the music. Sometimes the singer might want to hear some reverb on their voice—this helps them to pitch correctly—but you may want to hear their voice dry on the monitors so you can more easily hear unwanted noises such as accidental knocks of the microphone stand, plosives or the singer rustling the lyric sheet.

Other times the cue mix may be more complex with the whole band being able to hear themselves just the way they want in their individual headphones, whilst you hear the actual mix on the studio monitors. For example, the bass player might want to hear more kick drum whilst the guitarist may want to hear more drums and bass and less keyboard.

The number of cue mixes you can have will be determined by the capabilities of your DAW, your audio interface and its mixer software. The setup of cue mixes will also vary depending on which interface you are using. Refer to the user guide for your audio interface for specific details on how to set up cue mixes for your requirements.

Mixing on Headphones

It is possible to get a good mix on headphones that translates well to other systems, as room acoustics issues such as resonances and comb filtering are taken out of the equation. It is, however, important to cross check the decisions you make on headphones through speakers.

There are differences in the way sound is perceived when listening on headphones versus speakers. When we listen to speakers, we hear the left speaker with our left ear and also some of it with our right ear, and vice versa. This gives us a sense of space, depth and direction and makes it easy for us to pinpoint elements in the stereo field. With headphones, we only hear the left speaker with the left ear and the right speaker with the right ear. This unnatural acoustic environment makes it difficult to place elements of a mix in the stereo field (Fig. 5.16).

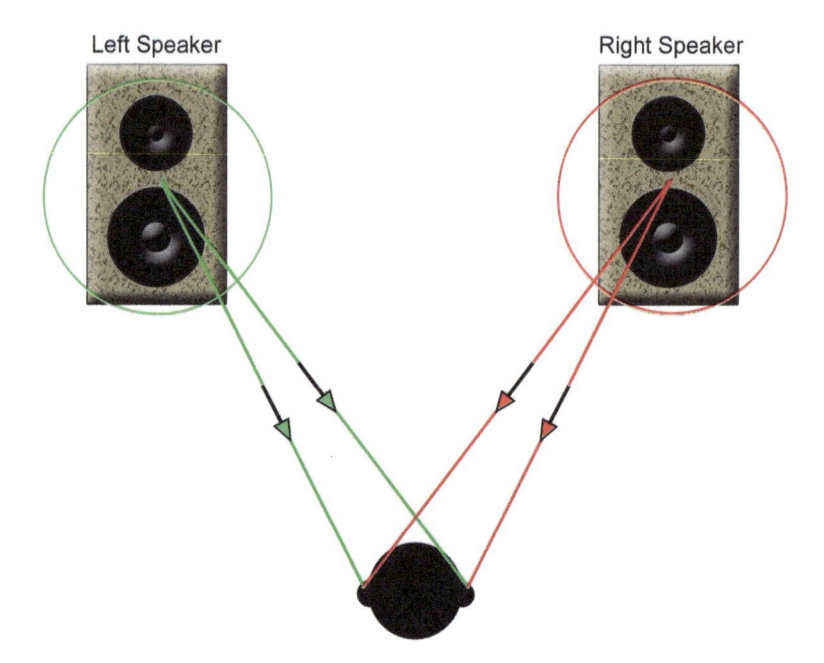

Fig. 5.16 Listening on speakers

We also hear a much wider 180° stereo image through headphones compared to 60° when sitting in front of a typical nearfield studio monitoring setup (Fig. 5.17).

With headphones, SBIR is not an issue (see Chap. 9: Room Acoustics). However, low and high frequencies are boosted on many headphones in order to make them sound impressive. When mixing audio, you need to hear a reasonably flat frequency response so that you can add the right amount of Eq, compression and effects. Using speaker and headphone calibration software such as SonarWorks Reference 4, you can achieve a pretty flat frequency response in your headphones (Figs. 5.18 and 5.19)

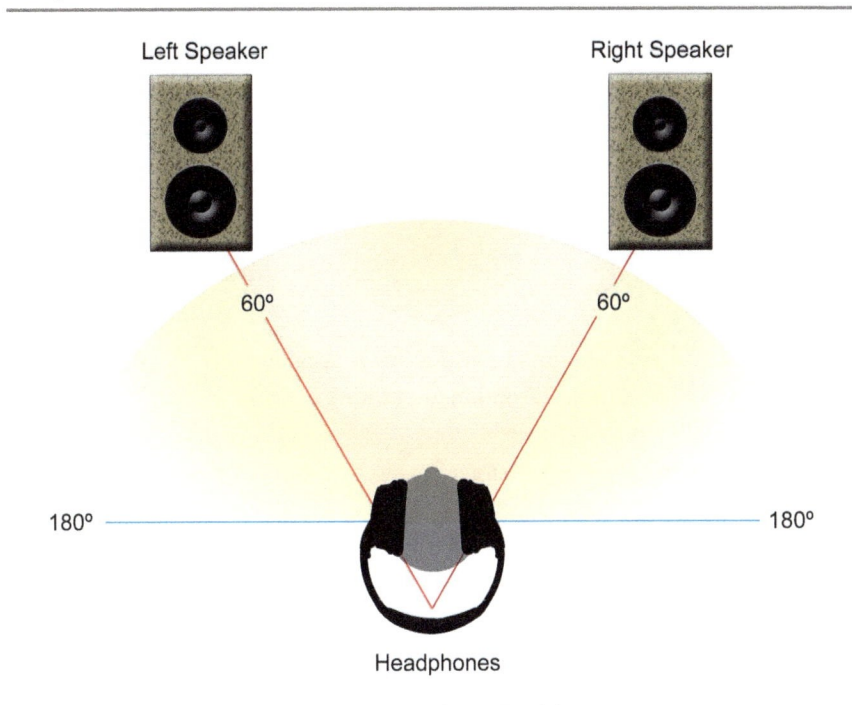

Fig. 5.17 The stereo image is wider when listening on headphones

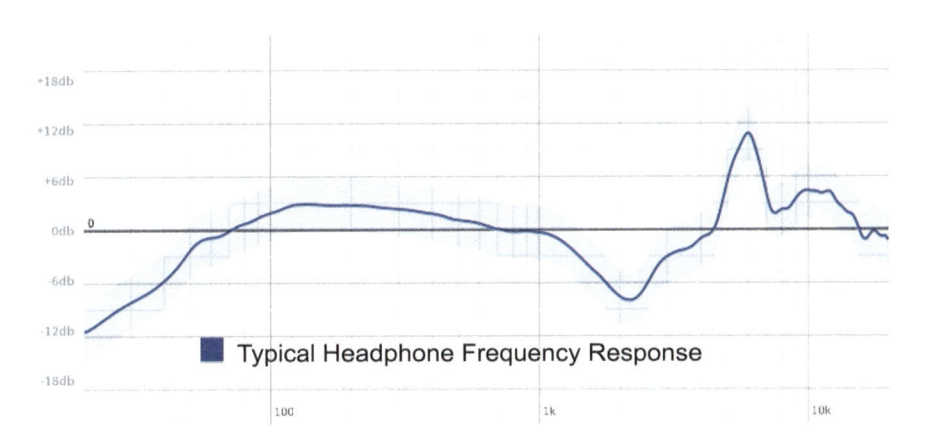

Fig. 5.18 Typical frequency response of headphones

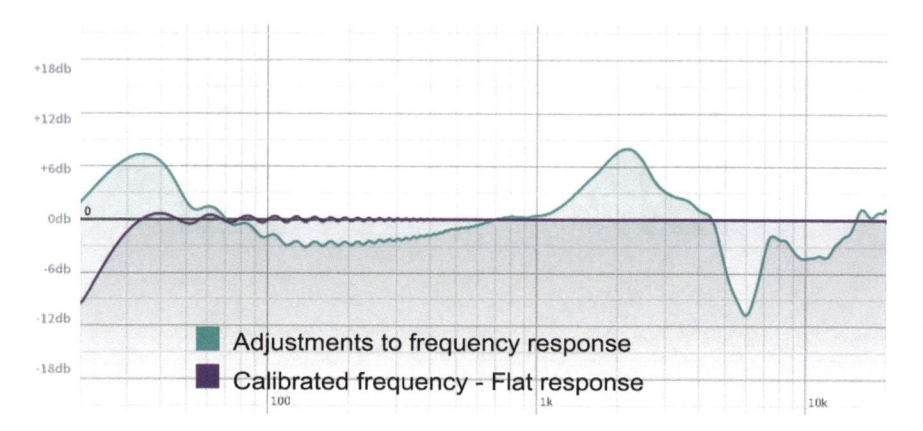

Fig. 5.19 Calibrated frequency equals a flat response

With a relatively flat frequency response, an understanding of the difference in the behaviour of the stereo field between headphones and speakers, and with constant checking on speakers, it is possible to get a professional quality mix on headphones that translates well to other systems.

▶ **Chapter 5 Tasks:** The following tasks will improve your listening skills in relation to hearing how preamps can influence a recording and get you started with a functioning recording setup.

- Listen to the provided Audio Examples 9, 10 and 11. Can you describe the differences you hear between the range of preamps?
- Follow the Basic Recording Setup in this chapter to connect your equipment and check if the signal flow is working for each component.

Gain Staging 6

▶ **Learning Outcomes**

By the end of this chapter, the reader will be able to:
- Explain the importance of signal-to-noise ratios.
- Illustrate suitable headroom for dynamic ranges within signal processing.
- Apply a working knowledge of how to maintain suitable levels across analogue and digital audio chains.

Analogue Gain Staging

Every piece of analogue hardware—e.g. a preamp, an amplifier, a compressor or an equaliser—has an ideal operating level at which its best sound is achieved, and at which it has a good signal-to-noise ratio. Gain staging refers to setting ideal input and output levels for each piece of equipment in an analogue recording chain. For example, an analogue chain could be a microphone going into a preamp, followed by a compressor and then into the line inputs of an audio interface. The preamp input gain would be set to achieve the desired sound, which may be clean, driven, distorted or anything in between. Its output level would then be set so the compressor receives the right amount of gain for its input. The output gain of the compressor would then be set so that the input of the audio interface receives the correct amount of gain.

Analogue equipment is not linear. Different levels will make it react differently, thereby changing the sound. For some equipment, finding the optimal setting may involve driving the input gain hard and reducing the output gain, or vice versa in order to find the sweet spot for that particular device. When an optimum gain is set for a device, the correct level can then be sent to the next device in the chain (Fig. 6.1).

Analog Input

Analog Output

Fig. 6.1 Analogue VU metres

Digital Gain Staging

In digital recording, DAWs do not have ideal operating levels. Correct gain staging is still important though so that the signal entering and leaving the DAW does not exceed 0 dBFS (zero decibels full scale)—the maximum achievable level in digital audio recording. Any signal exceeding this level will result in clipping, which causes an unpleasant, distorted sound.

▶ *Tip: A digital metre reading an average level of −18 dBFS is the same as an analogue VU metre reading an average of 0 dB. Be aware though that whilst most plugins operate at −18 dBFS, some, such as some of the UAD plugins, operate at −14 dBFS and −12 dBFS. Always check the plugin manufacturer's guide.*

When recording through an audio interface into a DAW, the signal still has to go through an analogue stage. The analogue input signal, be it a guitar or a microphone, has to be converted to digital and the output signal from your DAW converted back to analogue, so that you can hear it through your speakers. It's important to get the gain staging right at the input stage to ensure a good signal-to-noise ratio and maintain digital headroom.

Momentary inter-sample peaks, which may not be picked up by the metres in your DAW or plugins, can sometimes exceed 0 dBFS. This can cause unwanted distortion or clipping. Compressors are not usually fast enough to catch these peaks, so in order to avoid them, you must ensure there is enough digital headroom. Aiming for a maximum peak level of around −6 dBFS should allow sufficient headroom.

When the signal is too loud and exceeds 0 dBFS, the sound becomes clipped and distorted. When it is too quiet, the difference between the signal and the noise floor is reduced, making a less than ideal balance between noise and signal. When the signal is just right, noise is kept to a minimum, and the headroom of −6 dBFS ensures the signal will not clip (Figs. 6.2 and 6.3).

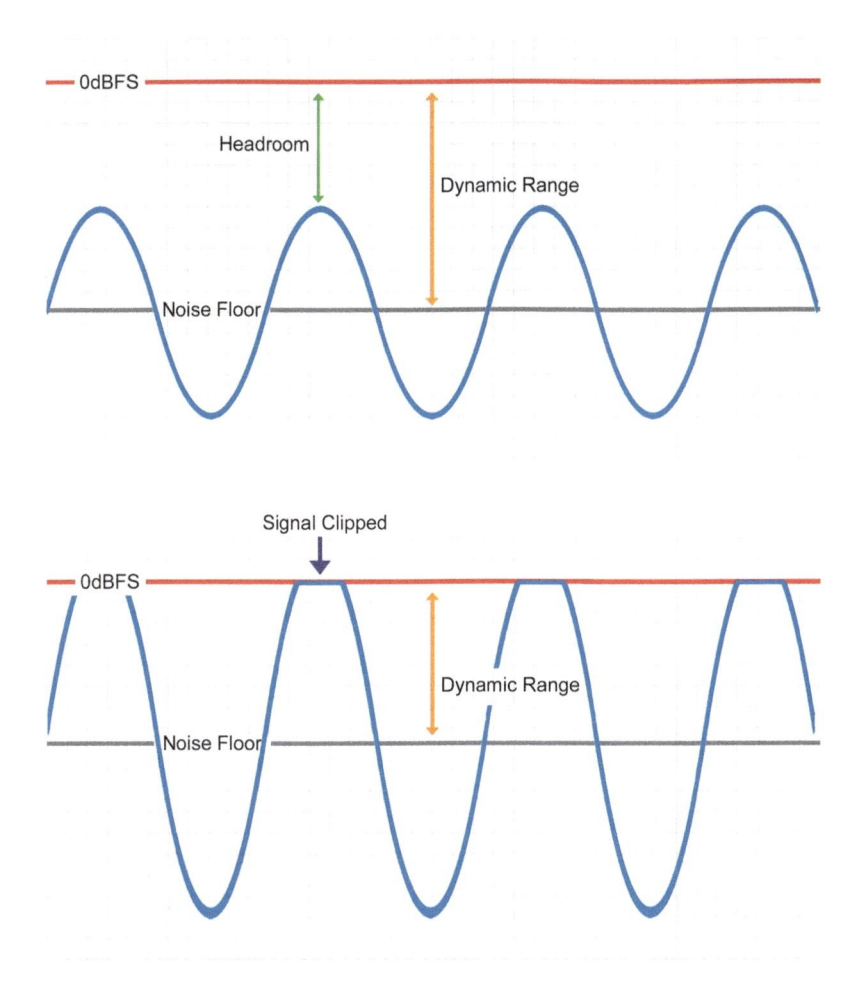

Fig. 6.2 Digital signal headroom

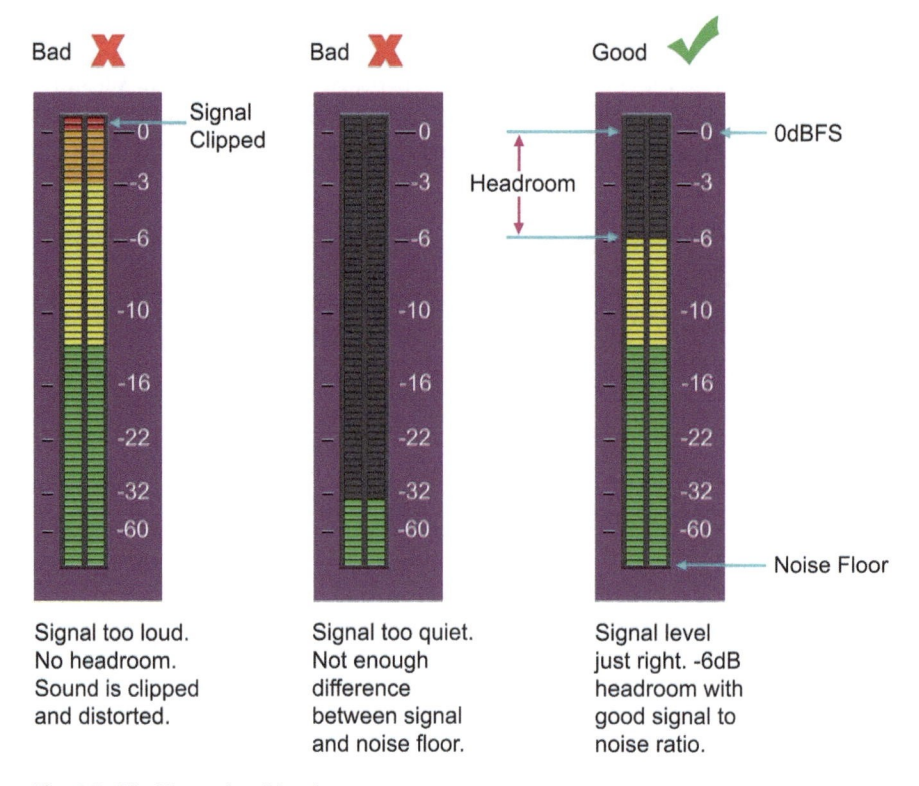

Fig. 6.3 Ideal input signal level

Bad ✗ — Signal Clipped. Signal too loud. No headroom. Sound is clipped and distorted.

Bad ✗ — Signal too quiet. Not enough difference between signal and noise floor.

Good ✓ — 0dBFS, Headroom, Noise Floor. Signal level just right. -6dB headroom with good signal to noise ratio.

The outputs of all individual channels are summed to the master channel in your DAW. Their combined level can overload the master channel, so it's important to leave plenty of headroom when starting a mix. Set the master fader to unity gain, 0 dB, and ensure that the loudest peak of your song leaves around 6 dB of headroom. That's enough to make sure inter-sample peaks won't clip the master channel. It will also ensure there's enough headroom at the mastering stage. If any plugins are inserted on the master channel, be sure to check their input and output levels too (Fig. 6.4).

Some plugins are precisely modelled on analogue equipment. This means that their behaviour is non-linear like that of their analogue counterparts and will change depending on how hard you drive them. The more you drive them, the more they will compress, saturate or distort. If you have a lot of plugins all being driven with high input and output gains, the resulting sound can be brittle and harsh. Check the input and output gain of each plugin in the chain to ensure the next plugin in the chain receives the correct input gain.

Digital Gain Staging

Individual channels summed to Master Bus

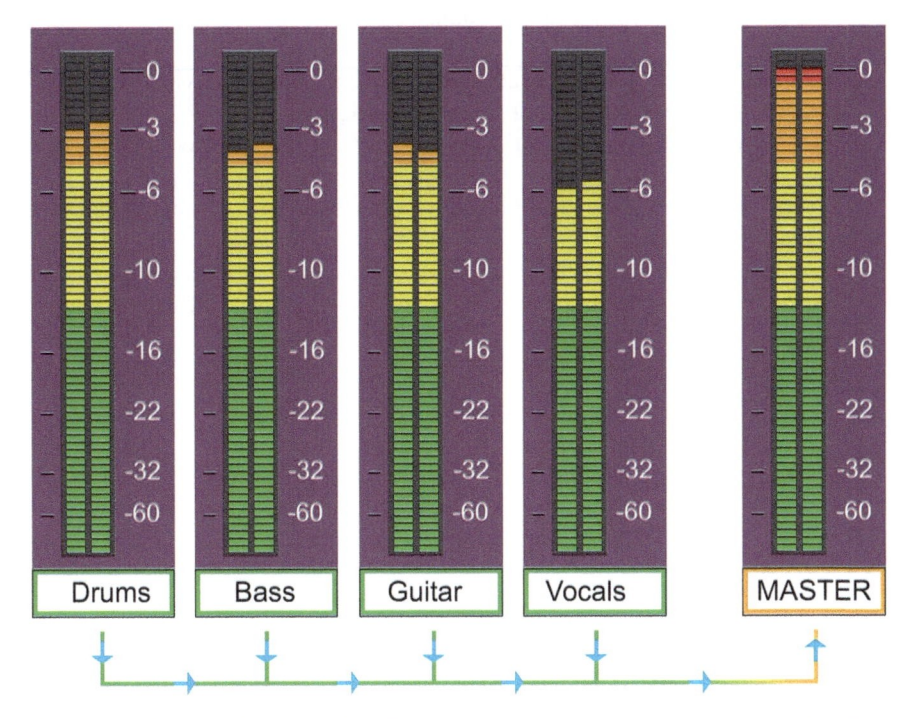

Combined output levels of individual channels overload the master bus

Fig. 6.4 Individual channels summed to master bus

- ▶ *Tip: Setting the right levels for recording and mixing can make a big difference to your overall sound. Pay careful attention to input and output gains at every stage and check the levels constantly whilst recording and mixing.*
- ▶ *Tip: Tracking too hot (recording your signal too loud) is a common mistake. Make sure you leave plenty of headroom. It's good practice to ensure your signal stays mostly in the green region of the channel's LED metres with perhaps an occasional peak into the orange section.*
- ▶ *Tip: Working at a bit depth of 32 bit floating point allows additional headroom that prevents clipping when a signal exceeds 0 dBFS. This will come at the cost of increased file sizes and more demand on your computer's CPU (see Chap. 8: Bit Depth (Word Length)). Also, even though your session may be running at 32 bit floating point, your plugins may not be. If the signal clips in the plugin, it will not show on your channel metres. It's a safer bet to work at 24 bit and gain stage all devices properly.*

▶ **Chapter 6 Tasks:** The following tasks will contribute to achieving a successful level across your recording chain.

- Within your recording setup, try adjusting input and output levels across a microphone or instrument to test the analogue gain staging.
- Make a note of the 'sweet spot' where clarity of sound without distortion is achieved.
- Do you need higher input gain or higher output gain to get a successful balanced level in the recording?
- Check the digital signal within your DAW to make sure the digital signal is not clipping by ensuring the headroom above the loudest point of the signal does not exceed −6 dBFS.

Microphones 7

▶ **Learning Outcomes**

By the end of this chapter, the reader will be able to:
- Define the differences between dynamic, condenser and ribbon microphones.
- Summarise different types of polar patterns used in microphones.
- Utilise appropriate microphone positioning to achieve well-balanced recordings.
- Explore recordings of different microphone types and distinguish the proximity effect.

Types of Microphones

There are a few different types of microphones. Understanding the differences between them will help you to choose the right type for a particular purpose.

Dynamic Microphones

Dynamic microphones use electromagnetism to convert sound into electrical signals. They can handle very high sound pressure levels, making them best suited for recording loud sounds such as drums, percussion or a powerful vocalist. Dynamic microphones do not require an external power supply. They are connected to the mic input on your preamp, mixing desk or audio interface by a male-to-female XLR cable (see Chap. 5: Hardware—Audio Cables) (Fig. 7.1).

Supplementary Information The online version contains supplementary material available at https://doi.org/10.1007/978-3-031-40067-4_7. The videos can be accessed individually by clicking the DOI link in the accompanying figure caption or by scanning this link with the SN More Media App.

Fig. 7.1 Neumann KMS 104 Plus dynamic microphone. (Image courtesy of Neumann GmBH)

Condenser Microphones

Condenser microphones, also called capacitor microphones, sound full and rich and capture more detail than dynamic microphones. They do not handle high sound pressure levels very well which makes them prone to distortion. Condenser microphones usually require an external power supply—usually 48 v. This is known as phantom power. Condenser microphones are usually connected to a phantom power box which has an XLR output (Fig. 7.2).

Fig. 7.2 Neumann U87 Ai condenser microphone. (Image courtesy of Neumann GmBH)

Small Diaphragm Condenser Microphones

Small diaphragm condenser microphones, also known as small capacitor or pencil microphones, are great for recording instruments with lots of high-frequency information, such as hi-hats, cymbals and acoustic guitar. Just like condenser microphones, they require 48v phantom power to run (Fig. 7.3).

Fig. 7.3 Neumann KM 185 small condenser microphone. (Image courtesy of Neumann GmBH)

Ribbon Microphone

Ribbon microphones also fall into the 'dynamic' category as they too convert sound into electrical signals through electromagnetism. They sound incredibly smooth which makes them great for recording harsh sounds such as trombones, trumpets, violins and cellos. They are usually bi-directional (figure 8 polar pattern) (see Chap. 7: Microphones—Microphone Polar Patterns) which means they pick up sound equally from the front and rear of the mic. Ribbon microphones require a pre-amp capable of very high input gain. They are also fragile and need to be handled with care. Ribbon mics are the preferred choice of most professional engineers when recording brass, strings or any harsh sounding instruments. Ribbon microphones are usually passive, although active ribbon microphones requiring 48v are available (Fig. 7.4).

Fig. 7.4 Golden Age Project R1 Active Mk3 Ribbon Microphone. (Image courtesy of Golden Age Project)

Other types of microphones are available for more specialised applications. Some of these are:

Shotgun microphones: These are generally used for capturing sounds and voices during film shoots, television broadcasts and other scenarios where the microphone may be required to follow the sound source. They can be mounted on a boom pole, on the camera or handheld.

Lavaliere microphones: These are used mostly in television, theatre and public speaking applications. They are usually clipped onto clothing, most often on a collar or lapel, worn around the neck or clipped onto the ear. They are commonly condenser or dynamic types.

Boundary microphones: These types of microphone are designed to be mounted flush against a surface, resulting in a significant reduction of the effects of comb filtering. Another advantage is an increase in sensitivity of around 6dB.

Microphone Polar Patterns

The polar pattern of a microphone refers to the direction from which it picks up sound.

There are four types of polar pattern: Cardioid, Hypercardioid, Bidirectional (also called Figure Eight) and Omnidirectional. Each is represented by a symbol usually found on the body of the microphone. Some microphones have selectable polar patterns.

Cardioid

A cardioid pattern is symbolised by a heart-like shape with the point of the heart representing the front of the microphone (Fig. 7.5).

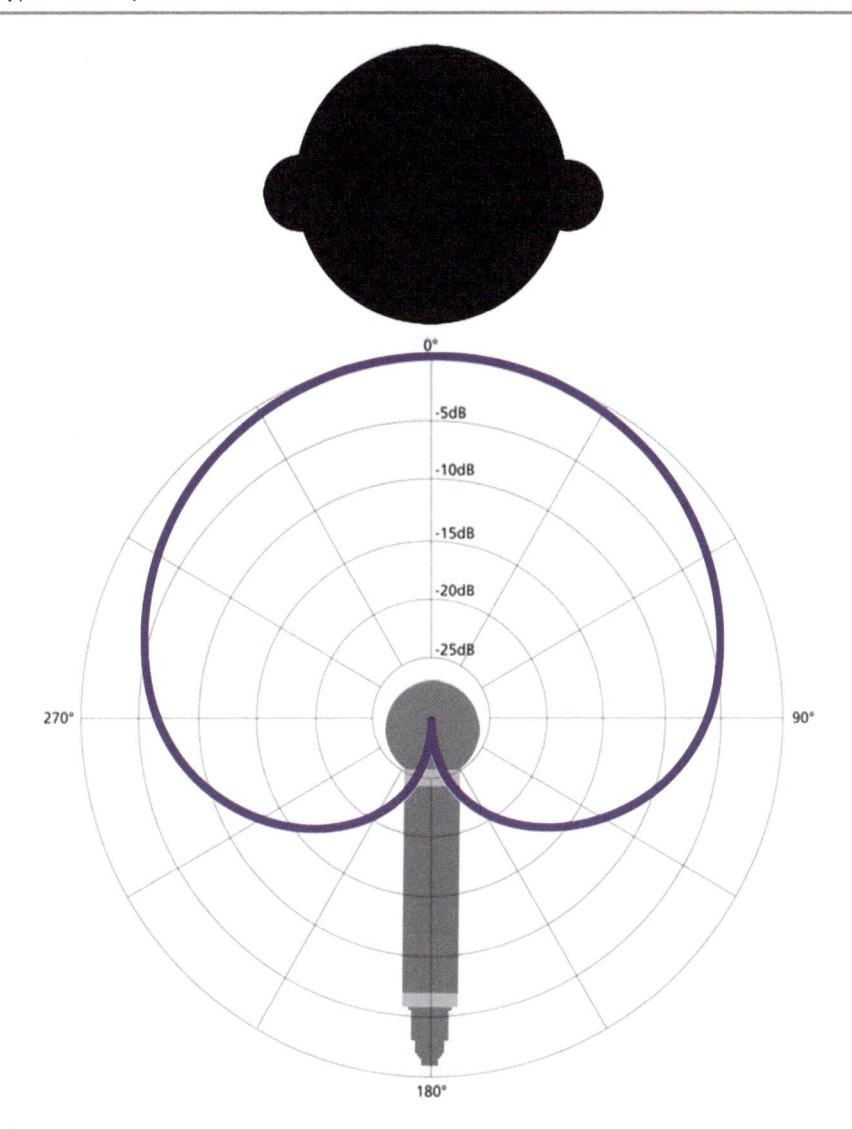

Fig. 7.5 Cardioid pattern

A cardioid pattern picks up sound mostly from the front of the microphone, a little from the sides and virtually nothing from the rear. This pattern is useful if you are recording more than one instrument at the same time and want to avoid spill or bleed from one mic to another. For example, if you are recording a cello and a violin together in the same room, using a cardioid pattern on each microphone will ensure that the cello is not picked up by the violin microphone and vice versa.

Hypercardioid

A hypercardioid pattern is symbolised by an elliptical shape with a smaller circle below. The smaller circle represents the rear of the microphone (Fig. 7.6).

Hypercardioid patterns are much the same as cardioid patterns though much tighter and even better at eliminating unwanted spill from other instruments.

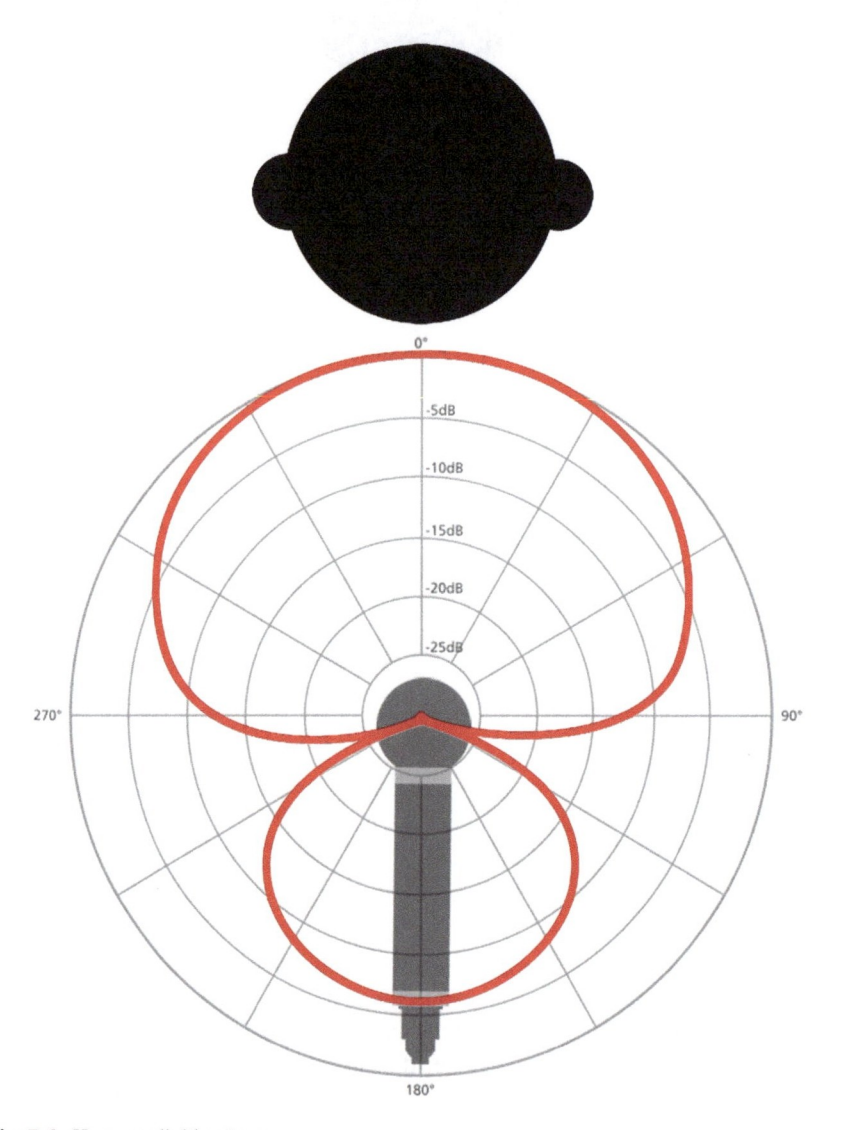

Fig. 7.6 Hypercardioid pattern

Bidirectional (Figure 8)

A bidirectional pattern is symbolised by two circles, one above the other, which looks a little like the number 8, and is also called the Figure 8 pattern (Fig. 7.7).

This pattern picks up sound equally well from the front and the rear but very little from the sides. This pattern can be very useful when recording two voices or instruments at the same time, whilst blocking out any other sound. For example, use this pattern when recording two singers simultaneously, one facing the front of the mic and one facing the rear.

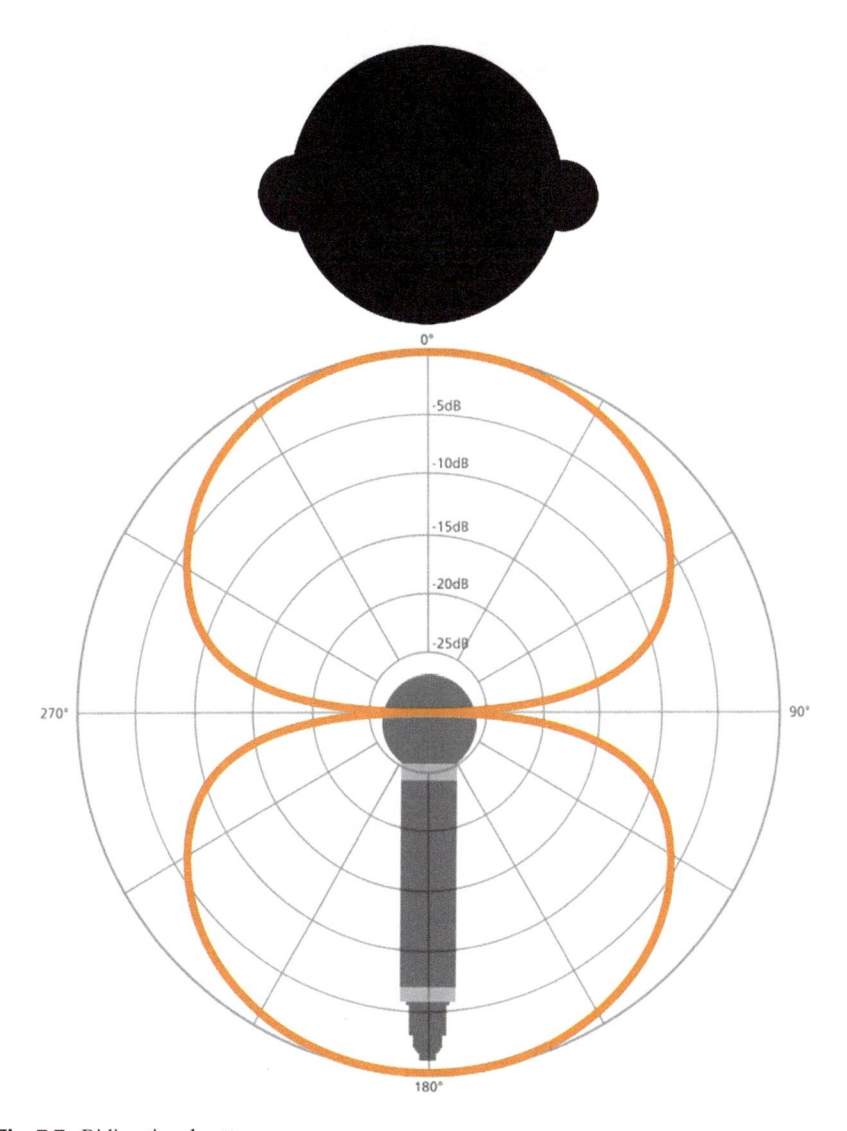

Fig. 7.7 Bidirectional pattern

Omnidirectional

This pattern picks up sound equally well from all directions and is represented by a circle symbol (Fig. 7.8).

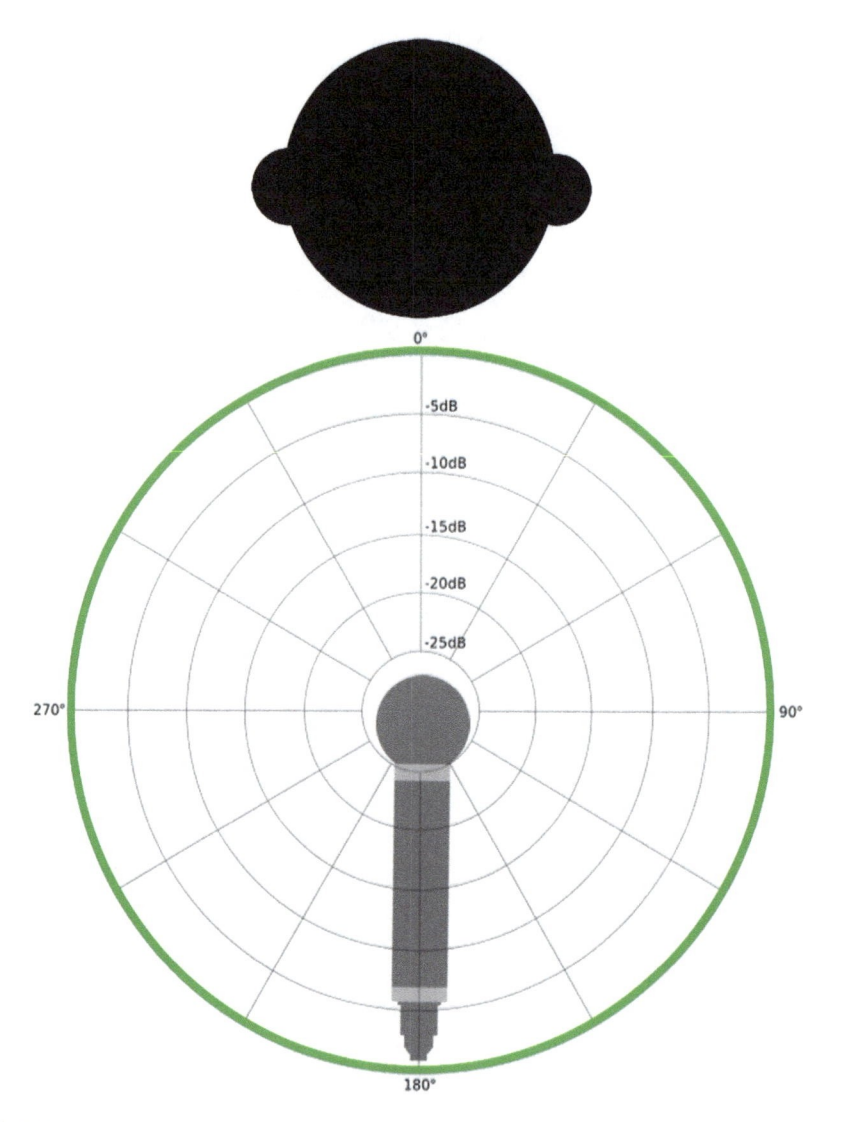

Fig. 7.8 Omnidirectional pattern

Proximity Effect

When a microphone is moved close to a sound source, the low-frequency content it picks up increases. The closer the mic is to the sound source, the more bass frequencies will be captured.

The intensity of the proximity effect is increased or decreased depending on which polar pattern is selected. A figure 8 pattern has the strongest proximity effect, cardioid and hypercardioid patterns have less, and an omni-directional pattern exhibits little or no proximity effect.

The proximity effect can be desirable in instances where more bass frequencies need to be captured, but it can also be problematic when recording a sound source that constantly moves—such as a singer, or when the source sound spans a wide range of frequencies such as guitars—which can go down to 80 Hz or below on the low E string. This can result in a recording that is constantly fluctuating between bass heavy and bass light (Fig. 7.9).

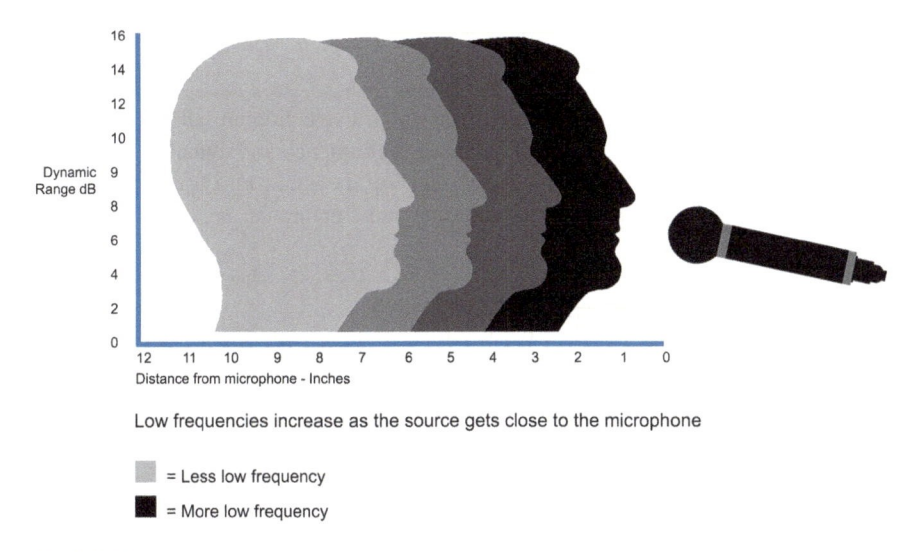

Fig. 7.9 Microphone proximity effect

Whilst the volume level of the source sound has no impact on the proximity effect, the proximity effect does have an impact on the dynamic sensitivity of the microphone. The closer to the microphone the singer gets, the more sensitive the microphone becomes to minute changes in level. If a vocalist is too close to the microphone, the recording will exhibit huge differences between the quietest and loudest parts of the performance, which will then require much heavier compression or limiting to obtain a more consistent level (Fig. 7.10).

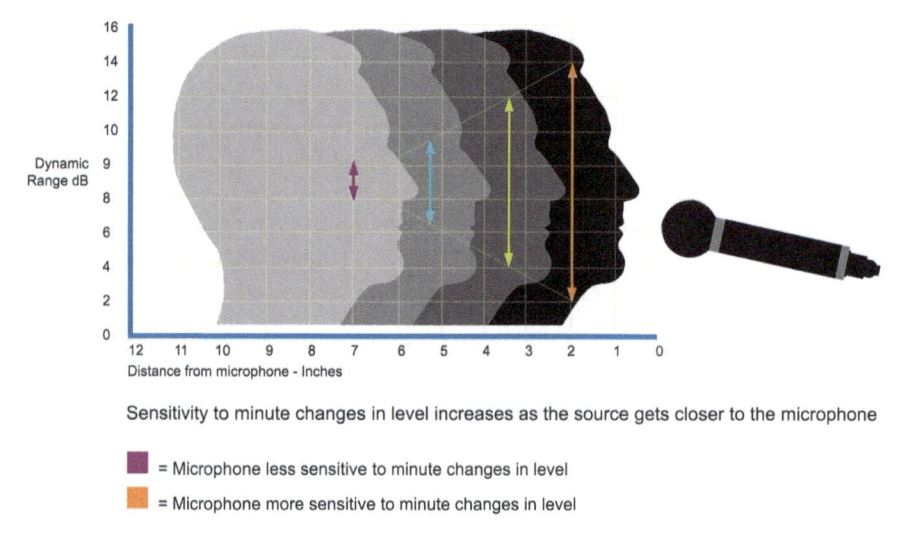

Fig. 7.10 Microphone sensitivity to changes in level

Microphone choice, placement and polar pattern selection are all important factors in capturing a sound that is well balanced in frequency and dynamic range.

When recording with microphones, taking all of the above into consideration will make the difference between a good recording and a great one.

Microphone, Instrument and Line Level

Mic Level

Microphones produce signals with very low voltage. These signals are weak and require a preamp to boost them to line level. The outputs of the preamp can then be connected to the line inputs of an audio interface. It's common for audio interfaces to have microphone preamps built in.

Microphone impedance affects the efficiency of how the signal is transferred to the input of the preamp. High-quality microphones have low impedances and are best connected to low impedance (often abbreviated to Lo-Z) inputs. Low impedance means the current is stronger, therefore giving a better signal-to-noise ratio.

Consumer microphones are often high impedance and should be connected to high impedance (Hi-Z) inputs. High-impedance signals are more prone to interference and noise (Fig. 7.11).

Some condenser mics (see Chap. 7: Microphones) have a high output. When using them with loud sound sources and when phantom power (+48 v) is enabled, they can be plugged directly into a compressor or mixing desk without the need for a pre-amp. Check the manufacturer's specifications for your microphone before connecting it directly.

Microphone, Instrument and Line Level

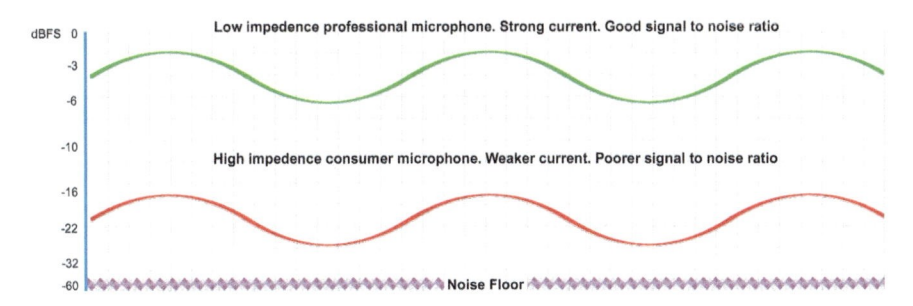

Fig. 7.11 Microphone signal-to-noise ratio

Instrument Level

Keyboards and guitars do not output at the same level as each other. They typically have output signal levels somewhere between microphone and line levels. To take the signal of an instrument to line level, an active DI Box (Direct Injection Box or Direct Input Box) is required. To take the signal of an instrument to mic level, an active or passive DI Box can be used (Fig. 7.12).

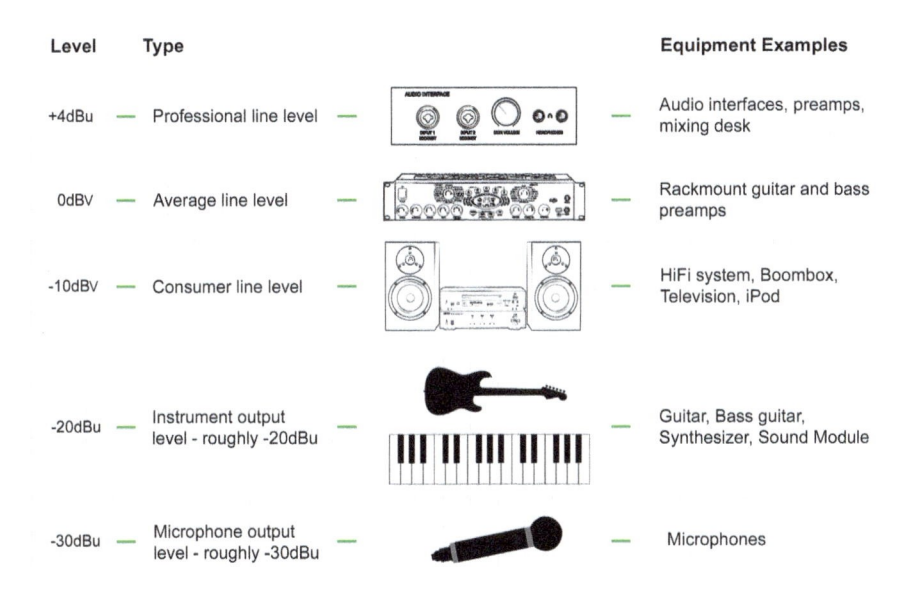

Level	Type	Equipment Examples
+4dBu	Professional line level	Audio interfaces, preamps, mixing desk
0dBV	Average line level	Rackmount guitar and bass preamps
-10dBV	Consumer line level	HiFi system, Boombox, Television, iPod
-20dBu	Instrument output level - roughly -20dBu	Guitar, Bass guitar, Synthesizer, Sound Module
-30dBu	Microphone output level - roughly -30dBu	Microphones

Fig. 7.12 Line, consumer, instrument and microphone levels

Line Level

Line-level signals have a significantly higher output than mic or instrument level. As this signal is stronger, it can be carried over a longer distance. Industry standard is 750 millivolts, which facilitates the interconnection of different devices from different manufacturers.

There are two types of line level:

- Consumer line level is at −10 dBV, used in CD players, cassette decks, etc.
- Professional line level is at +4 dBu, used in mixing desks, audio interface line in and out, preamps, etc.

▶ *Tip: dBu is a logarithmic voltage ratio where 0 dBu has a reference voltage of 0.7746 volts. dBV is a logarithmic voltage ratio where 0 dBV has a reference voltage of 1 volt.*

RCA (phono) connectors are usually −10 dBV. **XLR** connectors are usually +4 dBu (mic level). **TRS** quarter inch jack plugs can be either −10 dBV or +4 dBu.

Direct Injection or Direct Input (DI) Box

DI Boxes convert unbalanced high-impedance signals from guitar pickups and contact microphones into balanced low-impedance signals required by mixing desks and audio interfaces.

Active DI Boxes use electrical circuits to convert the signal and require a power source to run, which is usually a 9 v battery or power adapter. Some can run off phantom power, allow the polarity to be reversed to combat phase issues and have a ground or earth lift switch which allows the user to disconnect the ground cable in a microphone or balanced instrument lead to remove any hum caused by ground loops.

Passive DI Boxes use a transformer to convert the signal. They do not require a power source and are usually cheaper than active DI Boxes. Most passive DI Boxes will suffer some loss of high frequencies; however, this is often outside of the usual range of operation in all but the cheapest models. A high-quality passive DI Box is a safer bet for live shows, as there is no danger of the battery running out during a performance (Figs. 7.13.1 and 7.13.2).

Connecting a DI Box is pretty straightforward. Plug your instrument or microphone cable into the input and connect a balanced microphone cable from the output to your mixing desk or audio interface.

Fig. 7.13.1 A typical passive DI Box

Fig. 7.13.2 A typical passive DI Box

Recording Vocals

What Type of Microphone Should I Use?

Condenser microphones are generally best for recording vocals. They don't handle high sound pressure levels as well as dynamic mics, but they do sound fuller and richer. Condenser mics also reproduce higher frequencies more accurately than dynamic mics giving them a more detailed and open sound.

▶ *Tip: If you are using a tube condenser microphone, try hanging it upside down. That way, heat rising from the tubes will not affect the diaphragm of the microphone. Changes in temperature to the microphone's diaphragm will alter the captured frequency response.*

Which Polar Pattern Should I Select?

A cardioid pattern is the preferred choice for many recording engineers. With a cardioid pattern selected, the mic picks up sound mostly from the front, thereby eliminating unwanted noise or spill from the rear or sides. This is particularly useful if you are recording vocals at the same time as recording other musicians in the same room, or if you want more of the vocal and less of the room sound in your recording (Fig. 7.14).

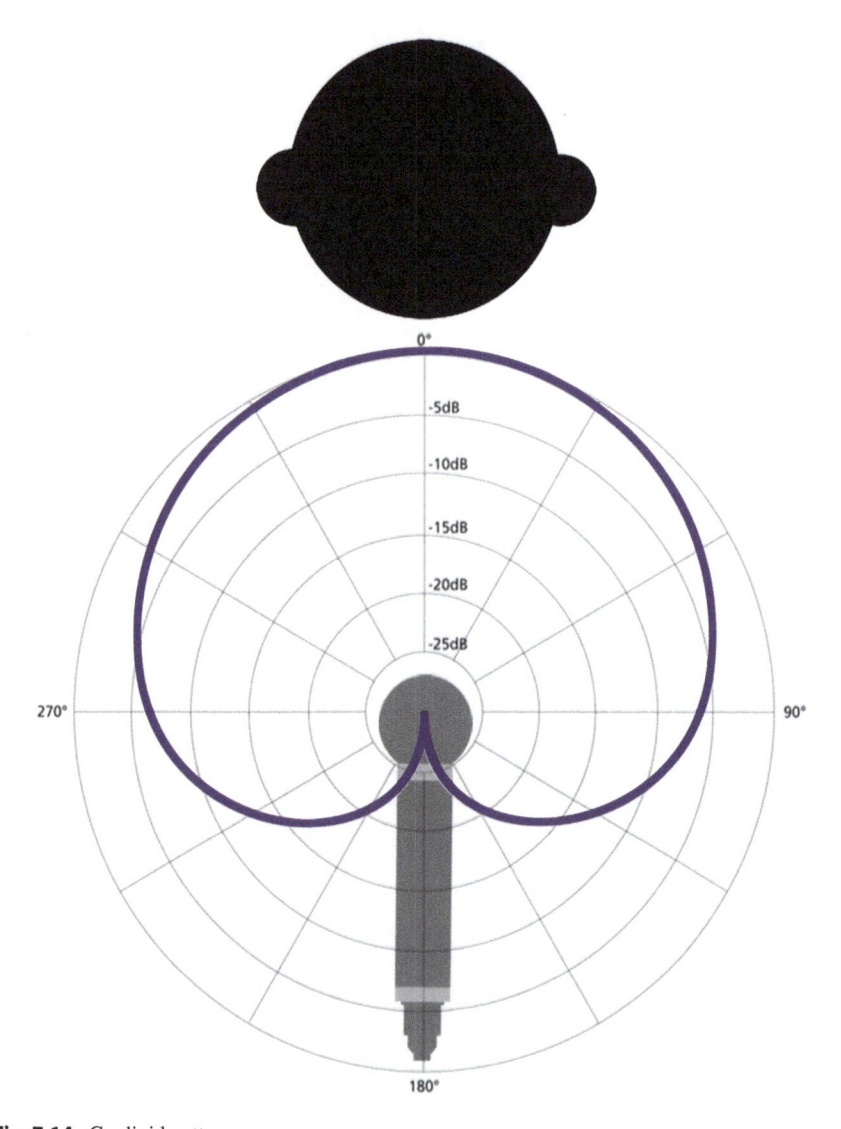

Fig. 7.14 Cardioid pattern

Should I Use a Pop Shield?

A pop shield is a plastic or wire frame covered in nylon which can be placed in front of the microphone. This helps prevent plosives, sibilants and fricatives by absorbing some of the energy of these sounds to some degree. Using a pop shield can make a big difference to the quality of your vocal recording (Fig. 7.15).

▶   *Tip: You can easily make your own pop shield that will be just as good as a professional one. Take a wire coat hanger and bend it to form a circle. Get an old pair of tights and wrap them around the circle so that there is a single layer on each side. Attach it to your microphone stand so that it sits a few inches in front of the microphone's diaphragm.*

Fig. 7.15 Neumann U87i with pop shield. Image courtesy of Neumann GmBH

Microphone Pop Shield

Should I Use a Shock-Mount?

A shock mount is a cradle with an elasticated support that holds the microphone. It's generally a good idea to use one as it will absorb vibrations which would otherwise cause low-frequency thumps and thuds on your recording.

Should I Use the Microphone Hi Pass Filter (HPF)?

High-pass filters (see Chap. 11: Equalisers) are found on microphones, equalisers and some other audio tools such as preamps. High-pass filters commonly denoted as HPF are used to cut off some of the lower frequencies whilst allowing the mids and highs to pass through unaffected. On microphones, the cut-off frequency will usually be fixed. Common cut-off frequencies are usually up to 120 Hz.

It's generally best to avoid using the high-pass filter on the microphone as it can sometimes remove more low frequencies than is necessary. You'll have more accurate control by cutting off some of the unwanted low frequencies later on using an equaliser (Fig. 7.16).

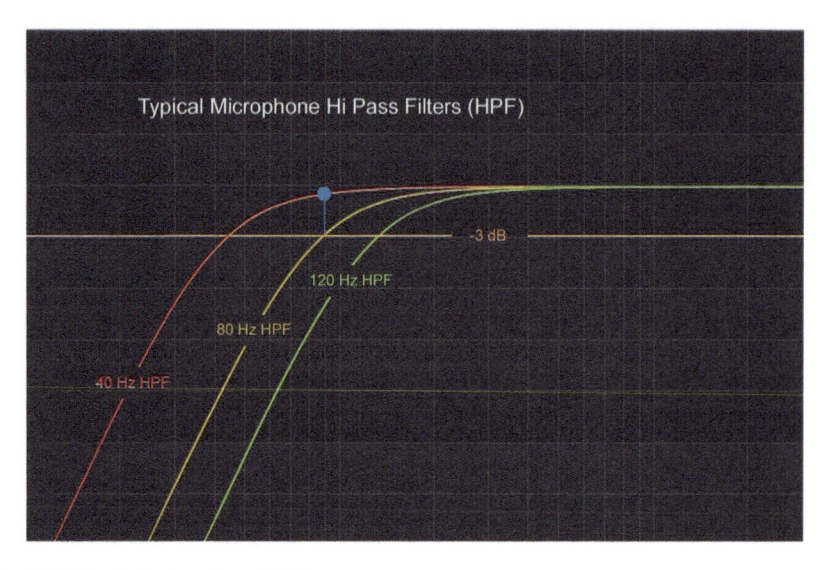

Fig. 7.16 Typical microphone HPF

Before using the high-pass filter, try repositioning the microphone. Moving the microphone a couple of inches higher than the singer's mouth, so that they are aiming their voice towards the barrel rather than directly at the diaphragm, will help to reduce some of the bass frequency content. Conversely, positioning the mic so that the diaphragm is aimed more towards the singer's chest will introduce more bass frequency content (see Chap. 7: Microphones—Proximity Effect).

How Far From the Microphone Should I Stand?

Generally speaking, 15 cm to 30 cm from the mic should be about right. Bear in mind, the closer you get to a condenser mic, the more the low frequencies are pronounced. This is known as the proximity effect (see Chap. 7: Microphones—Proximity Effect) (Fig. 7.17).

In some instances, a bass heavy sound may be desirable, for example, when you want a voiceover to sound more authoritative. Radio DJs often position themselves very close to the microphone for this reason. If you want a more ambient 'roomy' sound, you can try moving the mic further away. Also, the closer you get to the microphone, the more sensitive it becomes to minute changes in level. This will result in a big difference between the quietest and loudest parts which will require a lot more compression or fader automation to get a more consistent level.

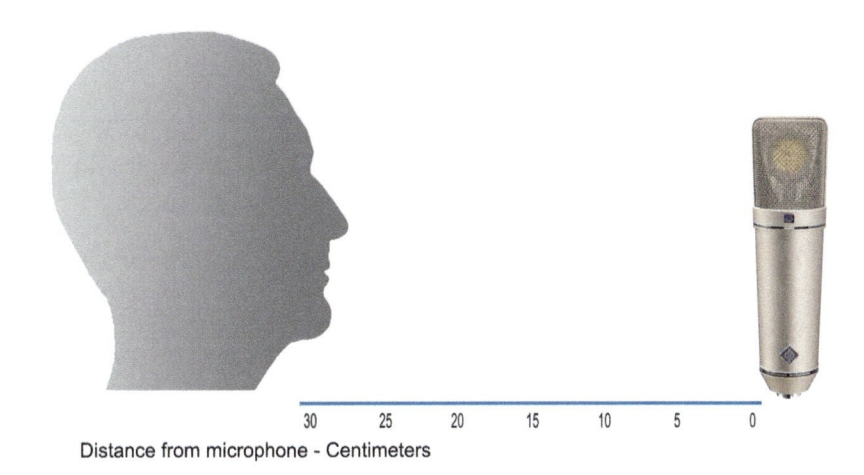

```
                    30      25     20     15    10    5     0
Distance from microphone - Centimeters
```

Fig. 7.17 Distance from microphone

▶ ***Tips from the pros:*** *Be kind to singers. Their art is personal. Be patient and listen to them and gauge their wellbeing. Try and judge when a vocal part has been recorded to completion by being assertive on your own decision making instead of going that "extra take for luck".* **Jonny Amos—Songwriter, Producer, Lecturer and Director at The SongLab.** *Shayne Ward, Jpop Idols EXIT, Miss D, Jackie Paladino, Glow Beets, Native Instruments Sounds. MTV, Sky One and Film Four.*
▶ *Tip 1: A microphone aimed at chest height will produce more bass frequencies than when it is aimed at head height.*
▶ *Tip 2: To help maintain an even level, encourage the singer to move their head back a little from the microphone whenever they anticipate they are about to sing loud.*
▶ *Tip 3: Spend time placing the microphone in different locations in the room until you find the position where the vocal sounds best. Stand 30 cm away from the singer and ask them to sing. Try this in different locations in the room until it sounds best. Place the microphone where you stand relative to the singer.*
▶ ***Tips from the pros:*** *For my backing vocals, I make sure that they are being sung so that they blend with the lead when recording them. Sometimes that means breathier, more smiley, mixed voice, etc. I think this step is overlooked too often, and the emphasis gets put on how to treat them to make them fit. My biggest tip is to sing them so they blend. That in itself is affecting the Eq. Then from there, I tend to keep my vocal busses on the brighter side but not harsh. I keep things panned left and right, and will start to make a bit narrower of a stereo image with them if I need my lead vocal to feel more supported.* **Simone Torres—Vocal Producer, Engineer and Vocalist.** *Normani, Chlöe Bailey, Billy Porter, Anitta, Camila Cabello, Cardi B, Monsta X, Sia, The Backstreet Boys, Dua Lipa, Jessie J and more.*

Recording with Compression

It's quite common to record a vocal through a compressor after the preamp stage. This is known as tracking compression. Use of subtle tracking compression can help to smooth out the recording. Be careful not to overdo it, though, as recorded compression cannot be undone.

▶ ***Tips from the pros:*** *Vocal Processing: Try adding a saturator at 50% wet and a compressor at 30% wet underneath your reverb plugin (100% wet) on your reverb aux chain. The saturator could add a sense of character and depth and the compressor will smooth out the reverb tail. This is a parallel path with serial processing.* ***Jonny Amos—Songwriter, Producer, Lecturer and Director at The SongLab.*** *Shayne Ward, Jpop Idols EXIT, Miss D, Jackie Paladino, Glow Beets, Native Instruments Sounds. MTV, Sky One and Film Four.*

▶ *Tip: A little bit of reverb in the singer's headphones can help them pitch more accurately. How much they require, if any at all, is up to the singer. Do whatever it takes to get the best performance out of them.*

▶ **Chapter 7 Tasks:** The following tasks will improve your knowledge of microphone types and the requirements for achieving a clear signal.

- Listen to the Audio Examples 12, 13 and 14.
- Can you identify differences between the dynamic and condenser microphones?
- Listen to the Audio Examples 15, 16, 17, 18 and 19.
- What are the key differences in tonality and definition within the various polar patterns?
- What changes when the proximity effect occurs?
- Listen to Audio Examples 60 and 61.
- Try your own recording of a vocal with and without a pop shield and identify where the issues are within the phrasing of the voice.

Phase   8

▶ **Learning Outcomes**

By the end of this chapter, the reader will be able to:
- Describe the effects of phase on audio.
- Illustrate the results of phase-based constructive and destructive interferences.
- Utilize methods to remove unwanted phase in recordings.

When recording with more than one microphone, a couple of mics on an acoustic guitar, or several microphones on a drum kit, for example, it's important to be aware of potential phase issues.

Signals entering the preamp can become out of phase when the sound captured by one microphone is overlapped with a delayed signal of the same sound captured by another microphone which is further away from the source. The signal from the second microphone arrives at the input of the preamp slightly later than that from the first microphone. This causes peaks and dips in the frequency response, resulting in comb filtering—a hollow and unnatural sound. Phase issues are most noticeable on low frequencies. A signal that's out of phase will sound thinner than when it is in phase (Fig. 8.1).

Supplementary Information The online version contains supplementary material available at https://doi.org/10.1007/978-3-031-40067-4_8. The videos can be accessed individually by clicking the DOI link in the accompanying figure caption or by scanning this link with the SN More Media App.

© The Author(s), under exclusive license to Springer Nature Switzerland AG 2024
S. Duggal, *Record, Mix and Master*,
https://doi.org/10.1007/978-3-031-40067-4_8

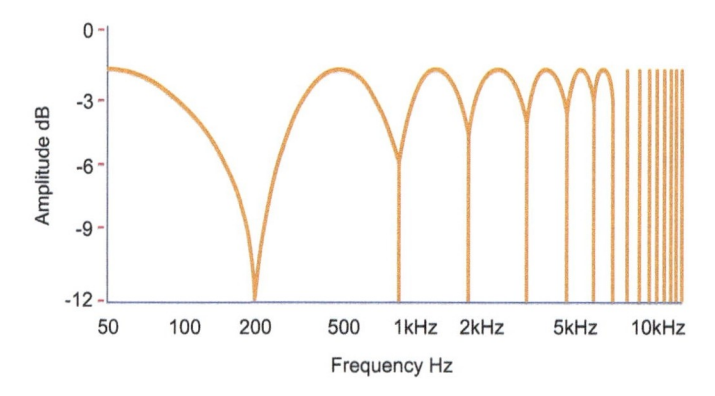

Fig. 8.1 Peaks and dips in the frequency response

Due to the difference in distance between the two microphones from the source, phase cannot be totally eliminated, as the signal will always reach one microphone later than the other.

One way of reducing the impact of phase issues when recording with microphones is to apply the 3:1 rule. This rule dictates that the second microphone should be placed three times the distance from the first mic, as the first mic is from the source, thereby reducing the level of the second mic by enough for any phase issue to be barely noticeable (Fig. 8.2).

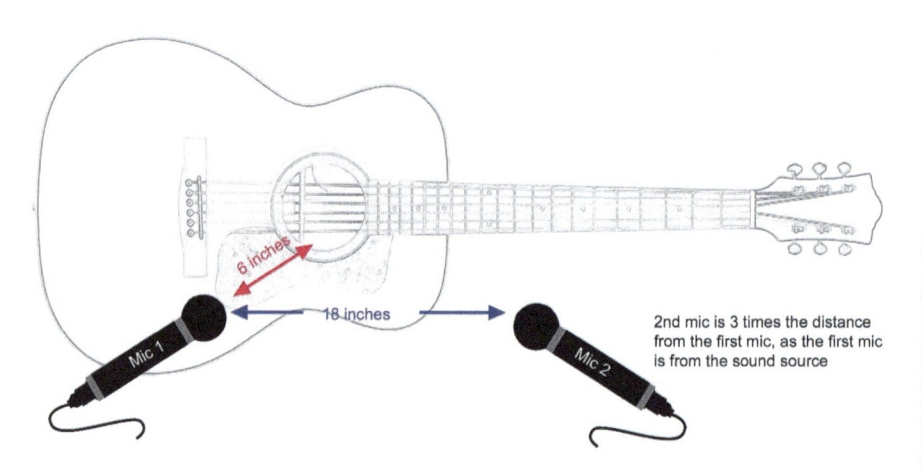

Fig. 8.2 Microphone 3:1 rule

This rule also applies when using multiple microphones. For example, the third microphone would be three times the distance from the second mic, as the second mic is from the source. As with all rules in audio recording, if breaking the rule sounds better, go with it. Ultimately, our ears are the best judges.

You can also correct phase issues inside your DAW. There are plugins available, such as Waves InPhase, that allow you to align the signals from two microphones. In the image below, you can see that the signal captured by Microphone 2 is later than that of Microphone 1. This can be corrected by altering the delay of the second signal until the two signals are aligned (Fig. 8.3).

Phase is measured in degrees. One complete cycle of a waveform is 360 °. A shift of 180 ° would equal a complete cancellation of the signal when added to a duplicate of the same signal that has no phase shift.

Phase issues are not always due to differences in time between signals reaching the preamp. If we take two identical positive sine waves and flip the polarity of one by 180 °, the result will be silence. A positive and a negative sine wave will cancel each other out because the peaks of one signal line up with the dips of the other.

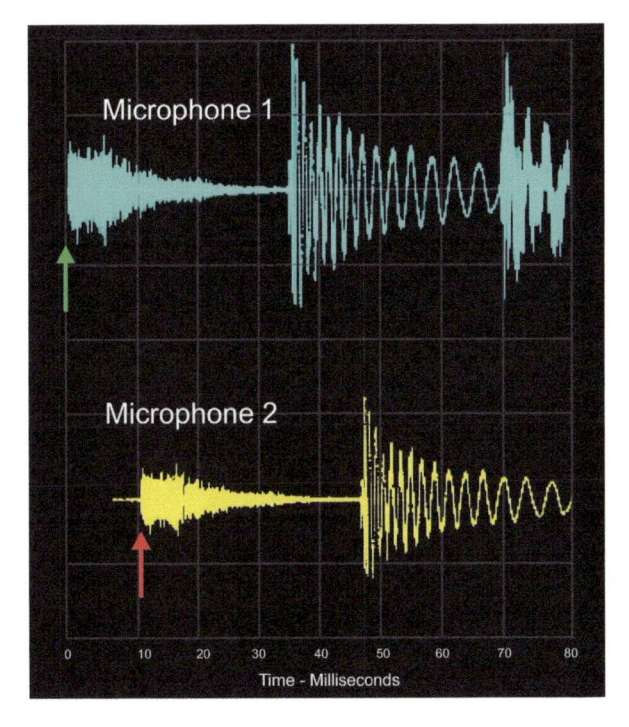

Fig. 8.3 Signal entering second microphone delayed

In the following diagrams, we can see what happens when two positive sine waves are combined and when a positive and a negative sine wave are combined (Figs. 8.4 and 8.5).

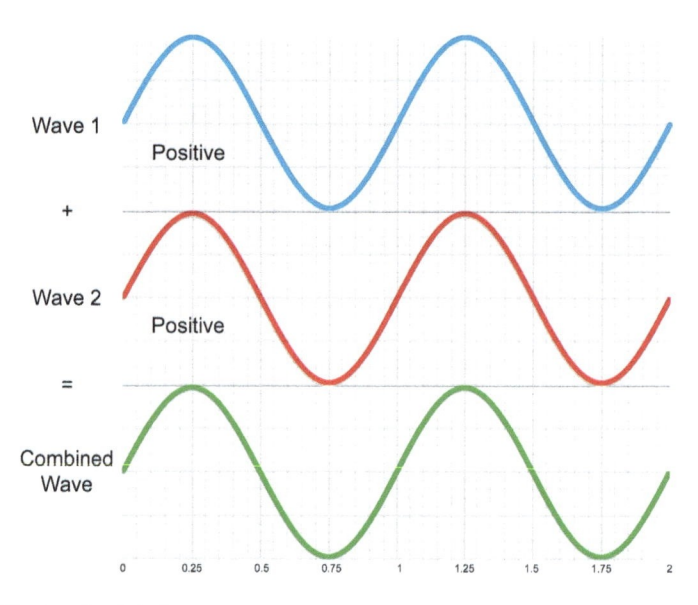

Fig. 8.4 Constructive interference

Fig. 8.5 Destructive interference

8 Phase

Polarity affects the entire frequency range, whereas phase causes only some frequencies to cancel each other out (see Chap. 2: Speakers—Speaker Placement. Also see Chap. 9: Room Acoustics). When complex musical signals and the reflections of those signals from the room's boundaries are involved, phase issues can cause havoc—making it difficult to blend instruments, particularly at low frequencies, together in a mix.

The phase-reverse switch on most equipment flips the polarity by a fixed 180°. Sometimes the problem might be that the signal's phase is out by an amount other than 180°. It could be 15°, 98°, 113° or any amount. In this case, a full 360° rotational phase correction plugin would be required to correct the phase issue by the right amount.

▶   *Tip: When using a 360° rotational phase correction plugin, flip the phase using the phase reverse button. Use the dial to alter the phase until the signal is at its thinnest (most out of phase). Then flip the phase back again. With this approach, it's easier to hear the problem.*

▶   *Tip: Checking your recordings in mono will reveal if there are any phase problems. The sound will become weak and hollow (see Chap. 15: Monitoring in Mono).*

Phase can also be an issue with your speakers. If not set up carefully, frequencies from one speaker may reach your ears slightly later than those from the other speaker. The timing difference between overlapping frequencies would cause comb filtering. There are a few factors that can influence this: the placement of your speakers, reflections off your desk or furniture and SBIR (see Chap. 2: Speakers—Speaker Placement and Chap. 9: Room Acoustics).

▶   **Chapter 8 Tasks:** The following tasks will demonstrate how phase can be both constructive and destructive and improve your ability to notice when phase is occurring.

- Listen to the Audio Examples 20, 20.1, 21 and 21.1.
- Can you describe in words how the recording with destructive interference sounds?
- Using an oscillator, record two identical sine waves into two separate audio tracks in your DAW.
- Zoom in fully to view the sine waves and line them up exactly, with the waveform peaks in alignment.
- Listen to how this sounds.
- Now (with Snap set to samples or ticks), try moving one of the waveforms to the right so it is slightly out of phase and listen.
- Keep moving the second waveform until the sine wave is exactly opposite the first waveform, so the peak of one aligns exactly with the trough of the other.
- Now listen, can you still hear anything?

Room Acoustics

9

Room Acoustic Treatment

▶ **Learning Outcomes**

By the end of this chapter, the reader will be able to:
- Recall the ways in which soundwaves interact with a room.
- Appraise and measure the acoustic suitability of your own critical listening environment.
- Construct an acoustically desirable space to record, mix and master.

In critical listening environments, it is imperative that you get a truthful representation of your audio material through the speakers.

Sound reflecting off the walls, ceiling, floor and furniture arriving at the listening spot within approximately 20 milliseconds of the direct sound from the speakers can cause interference with what you hear. Peaks and dips are created in the frequency response as a result of the reflected sound interfering with the sound from the speakers. This is known as speaker boundary interference response (SBIR).

You can easily hear the effects of SBIR. Walk around your room whilst music is playing. You will notice that bass frequencies are loud in some spots and may completely disappear in other parts of the room. Where they are louder, the reflections are reinforcing the sound, and where they are quieter, the reflections are cancelling out the sound.

Every room has resonant frequencies that occur naturally when excited by any audio source. These are known as room modes. Room modes cause distortion which results in these peaks and dips in the frequency response.

Sound can reflect off the room's boundaries in different ways (Fig. 9.1):

1. Axial modes: The sound wave travels back and forth between two surfaces.
2. Tangential modes: The sound wave travels back and forth between four surfaces.
3. Oblique modes: The sound wave travels back and forth between six surfaces.

© The Author(s), under exclusive license to Springer Nature
Switzerland AG 2024
S. Duggal, *Record, Mix and Master*,
https://doi.org/10.1007/978-3-031-40067-4_9

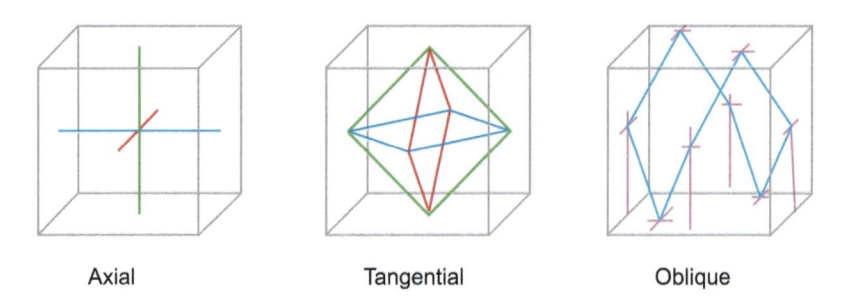

Fig. 9.1 Room modes

When the direct sound from the speakers and the reflected sound from the room's boundaries are in phase with each other (see Chap. 8: Phase), frequencies become boosted. This is known as constructive interference. When the direct and reflected sounds are out of phase with each other, frequencies dip. This is known as destructive interference.

When your speakers are placed at a quarter wavelength distance from the wall for any given frequency, a peak or dip is created at that frequency.

Let's say your speakers are placed 1.075 metres from the wall behind them. This would cause a peak or dip at 80 Hz because the length of an 80 Hz wave is 4.3 metres, a quarter of which is 1.075 metres.

344 (speed of sound in metres per second) ÷ 80 (Hz or cycles per second) = 4.3 metres (wavelength)

Multiples of the given frequency would also see an increase or reduction in amplitude, starting at the lowest notch: 40 Hz, 160 Hz, 320 Hz, 640 Hz, 1280 Hz and so on.

These peaks or dips in the frequency response can be huge, as much as 18 dB or more (Fig. 9.2).

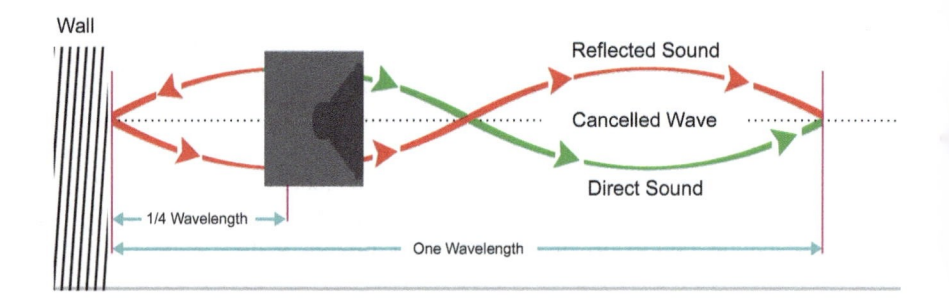

Fig. 9.2 Speaker boundary interference response

Now, let's also consider the distance of your speakers from the side walls, the floor, the ceiling and furniture in the room. Reflections off these surfaces will also cause interference with the frequency response. These reflections combine and cause mayhem at the listening spot as the quarter wavelength calculation applies across the frequency spectrum.

So how does this affect the decisions you make when recording and mixing?

Let's say, for example, you've recorded a bass part and all of the notes in the part sound fine except for one which seems to be much louder. You might try automating the fader to reduce the volume level whenever this note is played, or you might try compressing (see Chap. 12: Dynamics—Compressors) the bassline in an attempt to squash this note back into place.

After spending some time dealing with this troublesome note, you finish your mix and play it in your car or on your Hi-Fi only to find that now you can barely hear that note. The note wasn't actually louder in the first place, it was being reflected off surfaces in your room and combined with the direct sound from the speakers, causing a perceived increase in amplitude at the listening position.

The reflections in the room fooled you into thinking the note was louder, so you reduced its level when you didn't need to. This happens not just with one note in a bass part but at different frequencies right across the spectrum, making it difficult for you to judge anything accurately in an untreated room.

Equally, a reduction in perceived level can occur causing you to turn a particular note, sound, frequency, instrument or voice up because you believe it can't be heard clearly. Once again, your room is deceiving you.

This is a key factor in why your mixes might sound great in your studio but not so great when you play them elsewhere.

Below are some guidelines that will help you create a reflection-free zone (RFZ) where you sit at your mix position, so you can trust that what you hear is a more honest representation of what is actually going on in your recording.

Broadband Bass Absorption

Sound is energy. The deeper or lower the frequency, the more energy it creates. A kick drum will create more energy than a hi hat cymbal, for example.

Low frequencies reflect off the boundaries of your room and bounce back and forth, overlapping each other. These standing waves cause multiple peaks—from constructive interference—and dips from destructive interference—in the frequency response. The result is that some notes appear louder and others quieter than they really are. This is particularly problematic with bass notes.

It's difficult to get rid of this effect known as room modes, though it is possible to even out the sound to an acceptable level by placing broadband bass traps strategically around the room (see Chap. 9: Room Acoustics). Remember, the notes aren't actually any louder or quieter on your recording, they just appear to be because of the effect of room modes. Excessive bass energy needs to be controlled in order to reduce these reflections and to prevent it from masking other frequencies (Fig. 9.3).

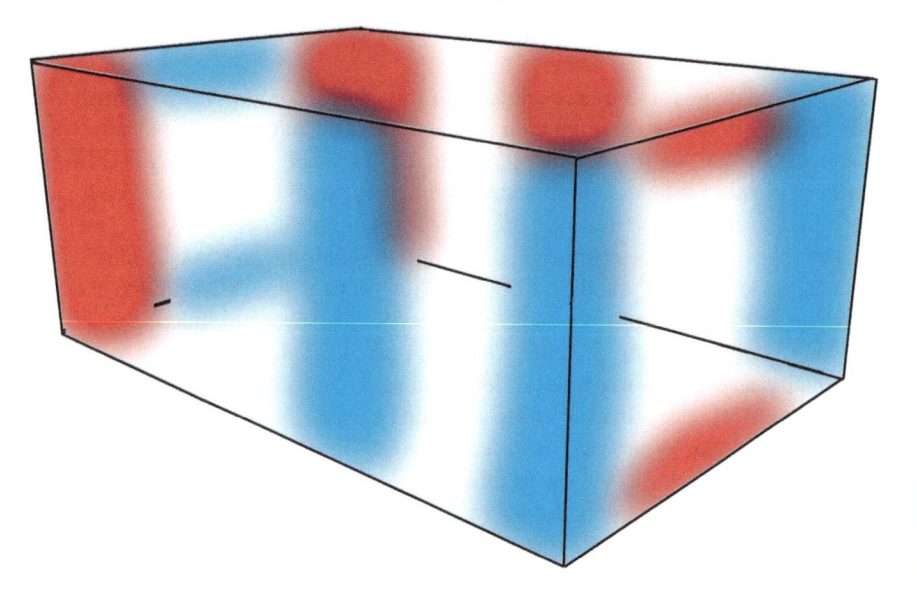

Room Modes - An example of how sound energy builds up in a room.

NB: The different colors are to make it easier to visualise.

Fig. 9.3 An example of how sound energy builds up in a room

Bass energy tends to build up mostly in corners. You can test this out by placing a speaker near a wall and playing some music through it. Placing a speaker directly against a wall will cause low shelving, an increase in the output of bass frequencies. When a speaker is placed near one wall, the increase can be up to +6 dB. When the speaker is placed near two walls, the increase will be up to +12 dB, and when it is close to the floor or the ceiling too, the increase can be as much as 18 dB. That's a lot of low-frequency energy building up.

Broadband bass traps, usually made from a dense absorptive material, absorb this energy by turning it into tiny amounts of heat which gets dissipated, thereby reducing these reflections (Fig. 9.4).

Room Acoustic Treatment

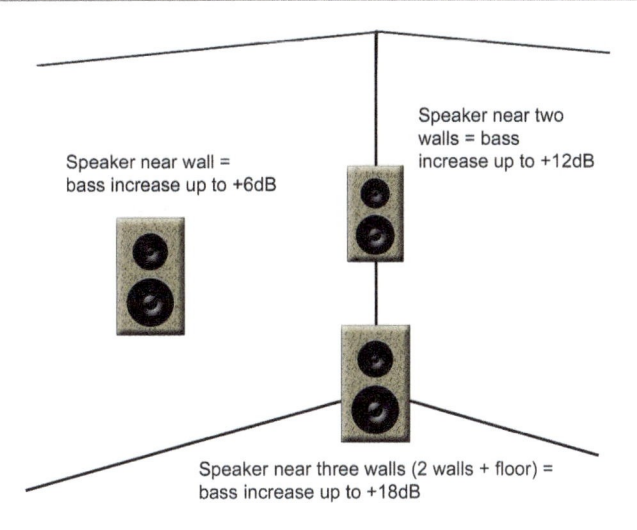

Fig. 9.4 How speaker placement affects low-frequency response

Room Treatment

The first step in treating your room is to place broadband bass traps in as many corners as you can. In a rectangular room, there are 12 corners including where the floor meets the walls and where the walls meet the ceiling. This may not be possible in some places, such as where there's a piece of furniture or a door but treating as many of the other corners as possible will make a big difference. Placing your broadband bass traps so they straddle the corners will increase their effectiveness compared to when placed flat against a wall (Fig. 9.5).

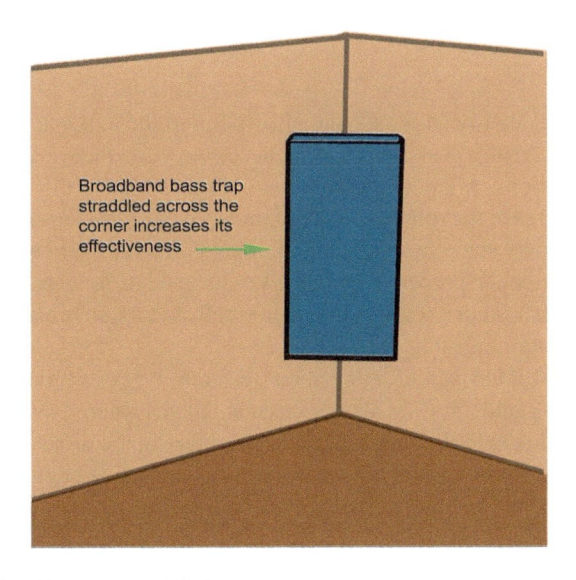

Fig. 9.5 Broadband bass trap straddled across a corner

Early Reflections

Once you have treated your room with broadband bass absorption, you will need to deal with the early reflection points. These are the points on the side walls to your left and right when seated in the mixing position. If left untreated, the sound from your speakers will bounce back and forth between the side walls causing SBIR problems.

▶ *Tip: Ask someone to hold a mirror flat against the wall and move it around whilst you sit in the mixing position. Any position where you can see a reflection in the mirror of either of your speakers should be treated with absorption. Do the same with the opposite wall.*
▶ *Tip: Using broadband bass traps at the early reflection points is a good idea, as reflections from the side walls can extend down into the bass frequency range.*

Low Ceilings

A common problem in small studios is low ceilings. A low ceiling is generally considered anything lower than approximately 2.75 metres. An early reflection is created as sound bounces off the ceiling and reaches the sweet spot soon after the direct sound from the speakers.

An effective treatment is to hang broadband absorbers above the listening position. This is known as a ceiling cloud. 120 × 600 × 10 cm broadband bass absorbers should be used and spaced 10 cm off the ceiling. Cover at least the square area above you from speaker to speaker and to your listening position.

Rear Wall

It is also a good idea to add broadband absorption to the rear wall, the wall behind where you sit at the mix position. Treating the corners and the wall itself will reduce unwanted reflections. Many professional studios also place diffusers on the rear wall so as not to make the room sound unnaturally dead and lifeless. Diffusers break up the reflections by scattering the sound in many directions. However, in order for most diffusers to work properly, they need a distance of at least six feet between them and you. This is not always practical in small studios, so broadband absorption is the preferred option (Fig. 9.6).

There's lots of information online about different types of broadband bass traps from retail to DIY and there are also discussion forums where you can chat directly with experts in this field. Remember, the key to hearing the direct sound from your speakers is to reduce unwanted reflections from your room's boundaries.

Room Acoustic Treatment

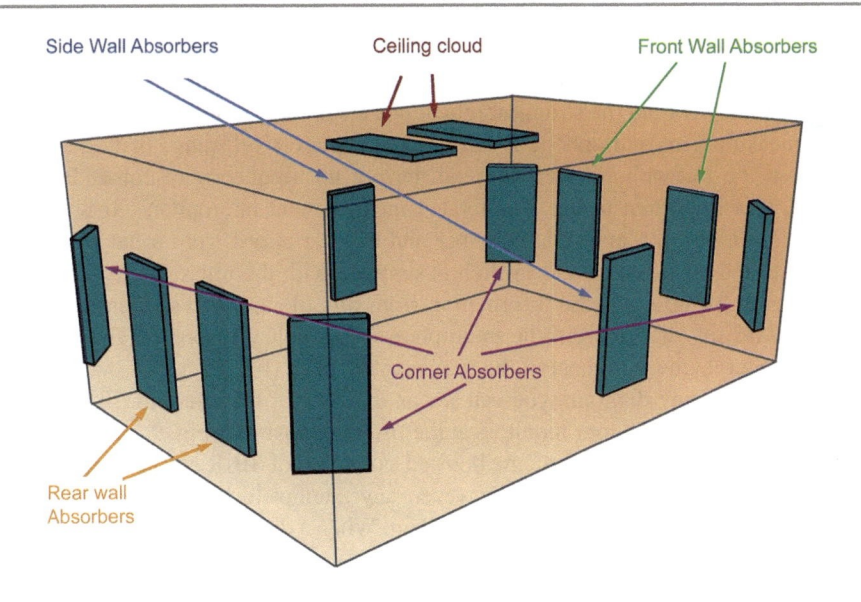

Broadband Absorber Placement

Fig. 9.6 Typical broadband absorber placement

Retail or DIY Broadband Bass Traps?

Broadband bass traps can be bought off the shelf from many pro audio music stores or online. If you are on a budget and have some basic DIY skills, you can build your own for a fraction of the retail cost (see Chap. 9: Room Acoustics—DIY Broadband Bass Trap).

If you decide to buy retail traps, avoid using foam products. They generally do very little for frequencies below ≈500 Hz as they are simply not dense enough to absorb bass energy. Foam bass traps are more likely to suck out a big hole in your mid-frequency range causing you to add this frequency range back into your mixes, making them sound muddy or harsh when played on other systems.

▶ *Tip: When placed in close proximity to the listener, the surface of some bass traps can be reflective at high frequencies. In this instance, applying some foam acoustic tiles on top of the bass trap will remove these reflections.*

Room Measurement

Measuring the frequency response of your room using a calibrated measurement microphone and dedicated software such as Room Eq Wizard, will highlight peaks and dips in the frequency response caused by speaker boundary interference. You will be better equipped to place acoustic treatment strategically around the room once you know where the strongest reflections are coming from.

A measurement microphone is designed to capture a full range of frequencies, however, the microphone itself may not have a flat frequency response. For this reason, it is important to use a calibrated measurement microphone. It will have been measured in an anechoic chamber and any variations from a flat frequency response will be saved to a file which is supplied with the microphone. The measurement software reads the information from this file and makes adjustments to compensate for variations in the microphone's frequency response. This ensures that an accurate measurement of the room can be taken (Fig. 9.7).

In the following diagram, you can see an example of the effect of SBIR on the frequency response of your monitors at the listening position (Fig. 9.8).

Frequencies which have become boosted as a result of SBIR can be attenuated to some degree using equalisation. However, any attempt to boost frequencies that have dipped will only exacerbate the problem. When a dipped frequency is boosted, its reflection is also boosted, thus resulting in the same null.

Fig. 9.7 A typical calibration microphone

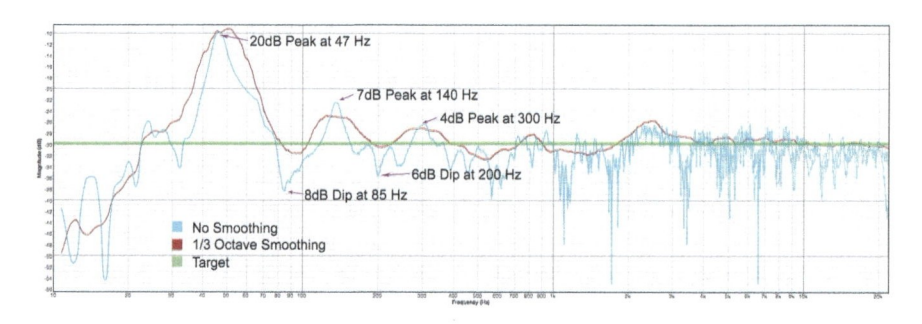

Fig. 9.8 The effect of SBIR on the frequency response

Measuring Your Room

Position your measurement microphone on a stand at head height in the listening spot. It should be aimed towards an imaginary centre line between your speakers. Follow the instructions for your measuring software and take measurements as necessary.

▶ *Tip: Taking measurements at the listening position will give you an idea of which frequencies are affected at that spot. However, it's a good idea to take measurements from multiple points in the room, such as the rear corners, for example, so that you can determine which frequencies have the strongest modes. You can then determine what type of acoustic treatment is best suited to reducing the reflection at that point.*

DIY Broadband Bass Trap

With some basic DIY skills and for a fraction of the cost of retail products, you can quite easily build effective broadband bass traps to tame those offending low-frequency reflections in your studio. The example below is based on a 20 cm deep broadband bass trap, though the same construction method can be applied to any depth bass trap.

Follow the step-by-step guide below to build your bass traps (Fig. 9.9).

To make a single bass trap, you will need the following materials and tools.

Fig. 9.9 A DIY broadband bass trap

Materials

4 × Rockwool RW3, Rocksilk RS60 or Owens Corning 703 Acoustic slabs: 1200 mm (48 inches) × 600 mm (24 inches) × 50 mm (2 inch) with a density of 60 kg/m^3.

4 × 38 mm (1.5 inch) angle brackets.

Pack of 25 mm (1 inch) crosshead screws.

Any breathable fabric such as calico, cotton or hessian to cover the traps with. If you can blow through the fabric without it offering much resistance, then the fabric is suitable for the trap.

2 × lengths of timber 1200 mm (48 inches) × 32 mm (1.25 inches) × 20 mm (0.75 inches)

2 × lengths of timber 546 mm (21.5 inches) × 32 mm (1.25 inches) × 20 mm (0.75 inches)

Tools

1 × saw
- 1 × screwdriver—preferably electric
- 1 × heavy-duty staple gun with a couple of packs of 12 mm (0.5 inch) staples
- 1 × pair of scissors
- 1 × pair of gloves
- 1 × face mask

Step 1

Cut your lengths of timber to size and lay them out on the floor to create a rectangular frame. The shorter lengths at each end should be inside the longer lengths (Fig. 9.10).

Fig. 9.10 DIY broadband bass trap, Step 1

Step 2

Position the angle brackets on the inner side of the frame in each corner and screw them into the timber. If you are using an electric screwdriver, screw slowly to avoid splitting the wood (Fig. 9.11).

Fig. 9.11 DIY broadband bass trap, Step 2

Step 3

Lay some of your material out on the floor and place your timber frame on top (Fig. 9.12).

Fig. 9.12 DIY broadband bass trap, Step 3

Step 4

Fold the material over the edges of the frame and staple it down along each edge (Fig. 9.13).

Fig. 9.13 DIY broadband bass trap, Step 4

Step 5

Trim off any excess material (Fig. 9.14).
Don't worry if the frame looks a little crude at this stage (Fig. 9.15).

Fig. 9.14 DIY broadband bass trap, Step 5

Fig. 9.15 DIY broadband bass trap, Step 5

Step 6

Lay out some more material on the floor and place your 4 × 50 mm (= 8 inches) acoustic slabs on top of the material. Wear gloves and a face mask when handling the acoustic slabs (Figs. 9.16 and 9.17).

Fig. 9.16 DIY broadband bass trap, Step 6

Fig. 9.17 DIY broadband bass trap, Step 6

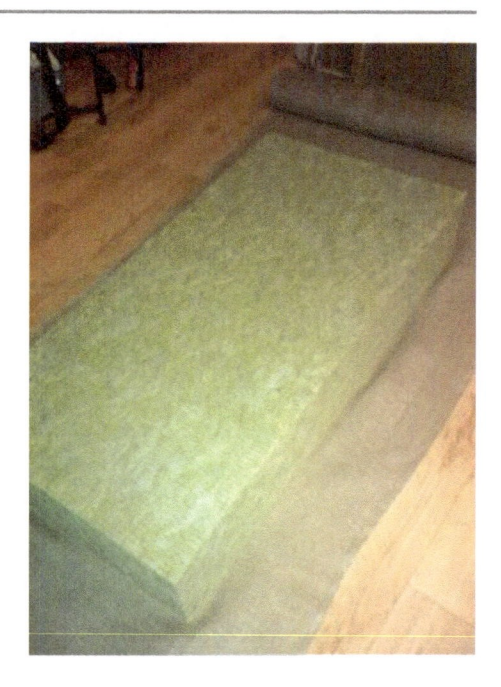

Step 7

Lay your timber frame on top of the acoustic slabs with the front side facing down (Fig. 9.18).

Make sure it lines up at the edges and corners (Fig. 9.19).

Fig. 9.18 DIY broadband bass trap, Step 7

Fig. 9.19 DIY broadband bass trap, Step 7

Step 8

Fold the material up and over the acoustic slabs. Pull it tight and staple it along each edge of your timber frame (Fig. 9.20).

Staple the remaining edges down and trim off any surplus material (Fig. 9.21).

Fig. 9.20 DIY broadband bass trap, Step 8

Fig. 9.21 DIY broadband bass trap, Step 8

Your finished bass trap will look like this from the rear and like this from the front (Figs. 9.22 and 9.23).

Fig. 9.22 DIY broadband bass trap, Step 8

Fig. 9.23 DIY broadband bass trap, Step 8

Position your bass traps where you need them. For details on the best positioning for your bass traps, see Chap. 9: Room Acoustics.

▶ **Chapter 9 Tasks:** The following tasks will contribute to your achieving a well-treated critical listening environment with suitable acoustics:

- Follow the instructions in this chapter to build your own bass trap.
- Position the bass trap in a corner of your room and play some low-frequency sounds through your speakers. Can you perceive an improvement?
- Try moving the bass trap to other positions in the room and listening to the difference in your perception of the bass frequencies.
- Try taking room acoustic measurements with and without the bass trap and compare differences.
- Play some low-frequency oscillator sounds through your speakers and place your head in different areas of the room. Try positioning yourself right in a corner and listening for any increases or decreases in loudness levels.
- Record the sound of a bursting balloon in the centre of your room and load the resulting waveform into your DAW.
- Set your DAW timeline to represent time (rather than beats) and look at the balloon waveform to measure how long it takes to reduce to silence after the initial transient peak. This will give you an idea of the reverberation time of the room.

Recording Tips

10

▶ **Learning Outcomes**

By the end of this chapter, the reader will be able to:
- Apply a range of recording methods to instruments to achieve high-quality sounds.
- Show a working knowledge of vocal recording techniques.
- Define appropriate microphone choices for recording situations.

General

1. When recording anything with a microphone, it's a good idea to leave plenty of headroom to allow for those unexpected loud sounds. For example, if a singer gets too close to the microphone or momentarily sings louder than expected, that extra headroom will prevent the input signal from clipping. −6dB of headroom should be enough.
2. Record in mono with a single microphone. This will help to ensure mono playback compatibility (see Chap. 15—Monitoring in Mono). You can always use effects such as reverb, phasers, flangers or chorus to create stereo width at the mixing stage. If you need to use two microphones, for example, at the front and rear of a guitar cabinet, pay attention to possible phase issues.
3. Spend time exploring microphone positions in the room. Ask the singer to sing and listen to them as though you are the microphone. Move around the room and listen for where it sounds best. That's where you should place the microphone with the singer facing the diaphragm of it.
4. Get the right sound at the source. Make sure instruments are properly tuned and free from rattle or buzzing.

5. Choose the right microphone for the source signal. A dynamic microphone will be better suited to loud sounds, whereas a condenser microphone will capture more detail.
6. Consider the distance of the microphone to the vocalist, instrument or speaker cabinet. When a singer moves closer to the microphone, more bass content will be captured. When a microphone is moved closer to a speaker cabinet, it will capture more of the initial attack of the signal. Experiment with different microphone positions.
7. Try different microphone polar patterns. A cardioid pattern will pick up sound mostly from the front, whereas an omnidirectional pattern will pick up sound equally from all around the microphone. This may be preferable if you want to capture more of the room sound.
8. Label each recording so you can keep track of the best takes and avoid accidentally losing files that have identical or similar names.
9. Record multiple takes of each vocalist or instrument and edit the takes together to make one great take. It may be that the singer gave a great performance, but one word or line spoils the take. You can go through your alternative takes and find the one word or line that sounds best.
10. Use closed-back headphones when recording to avoid headphone spills getting picked up by the microphone.

▶ *Tips from the pros: Have a variety of headphones to choose from. Some musicians play better with the less flattering sounding headphones. It makes them work a little harder to get the tone and balance of their instrument, which translates to a more expressive performance.* **Martin 'Magic' Johnson—Session Drummer, Producer, Mixer**: B*witched, Guthrie Govan, Jo Harman, Sam Fox, Mike Farris, Praying Mantis and more.

Drums

1. Spend some time tuning your drum kit. A kit that's not tuned properly will not sound good, no matter which microphones and preamps you use or where you position your microphones.

▶ *Tips from the pros: Recording live drums, the pre-requisite is...great sounding drums FOR the track, (tuning, dampening, gaffer tape) mic choice and placement and.... then inter-dynamics and balance of the drummer! Dynamic balance, advising a player to play consistently and "self-mix" their own playing in the room is SO CRUCIAL.* **Martin 'Magic' Johnson—Session Drummer, Producer, Mixer**: B*witched, Guthrie Govan, Jo Harman, Sam Fox, Mike Farris, Praying Mantis and more.

2. Use dynamic microphones for the bass drum, snare drum and toms. Dynamic mics can easily handle loud signals.
3. Ensure the drummer has good monitoring. They'll need a comfortable pair of headphones and they should be able to hear the click track and bassline clearly. Adjust the balance of their headphone mix to suit their preferences.
4. When recording with more than one microphone on the same source, pay attention to potential phase issues.

Bass Drum

A microphone placed close to the front head of the bass drum will capture more attack, click and punch than if placed further away. A large dynamic bass drum microphone is a good choice, as it will capture more low-frequency content.

Miking the bass drum from the inside will help to isolate it from the rest of the drum kit.

Snare Drum

Use a dynamic microphone. Placing it close to the head will sound punchier than when placed further away. Point the microphone towards the head. If it sounds muddy, move the mic closer. Small adjustments to the microphone distance from the head will make a big difference in the sound.

Toms

As with the snare drum, the closer the microphone is to the head, the punchier it will sound. Again, small adjustments to distance will make a big difference in the sound.

Hi Hat

Small condenser microphones capture more high-frequency detail than dynamic microphones which makes them a good choice for Hi-Hat cymbals. Use a cardioid polar pattern to capture more of the Hi-Hats and less of the rest of the drum kit. For a darker tone, try a dynamic microphone.

Overheads

Use a condenser mic above the kit, or for stereo, use two—one on each side of the kit. Experiment with height. There's no need to mic each cymbal. Set the polar pattern according to how much room sound you want to capture. Large condenser mics are a good choice for overhead recording. They capture more detail than dynamic mics, and because they have a larger diaphragm than small condenser mics, they will capture a wider area above the kit.

Room Microphone

Use a single large condenser microphone on the opposite side of the room to capture the room's sound. You can blend this in as desired at the mix stage.

> ▶ *Tips from the pros:* Phase check all your primary mics! Use your ears, trust them. Systematically solo 2 mics at time with a Phase invert plug in. Be obsessive about checking the kick, snare, overheads intern with each other. Then the Hi-hats, toms and room mics. This is time well spent. **Martin 'Magic' Johnson—Session Drummer, Producer, Mixer**: B*witched, Guthrie Govan, Jo Harman, Sam Fox, Mike Farris, Praying Mantis and more.

Bass Guitar

1. Direct Injection or Direct Input (DI)—use the instrument input on your audio interface and process your bass guitar using plugins modelled on bass amps.
2. Spend time adjusting the settings on your bass amp to get it sounding great through the speaker. Mic up your bass amp speaker cabinet with a dynamic microphone. The sound will be darker with the mic placed further away from the speaker and will capture more of the attack of the sound when placed closer.
3. Do a test recording to evaluate how bright or dark the sound is compared to the sound in the room. Adjust the microphone position as required.
4. Capture the DI input and microphone input at the same time. Record them on individual tracks. Blend the DI sound with the microphone sound in your DAW as required.

Electric Guitar

1. Record your guitar through the instrument input on your preamp or audio interface, then insert a modelled guitar amp plugin in your DAW. Make sure the dry sound is great to start with.
2. Double-track your guitar part. Pan one hard left and one hard right for a wider stereo image.
3. Mic up your speaker cabinet. On axis, with the microphone pointed directly at the centre of speaker will give you the brightest tone.

4. Use a dynamic microphone. Guitar speakers have a high-pass filtering effect, so there's no point in using a condenser microphone to pick up high frequencies that aren't there.
5. Moving the microphone off axis gradually will change the tone significantly.
6. Use two microphones: one in front of the speaker cabinet and one behind. Experiment with positioning. Blend the recorded tracks in your DAW as desired.

Acoustic Guitar

1. Use a small condenser mic for capturing detail in the high-frequency range.
2. Start with the microphone aimed at the 12th fret around 12 to 16 inches away.
3. Moving the microphone towards the sound hole will capture more bass.
4. Experiment with different microphone positions.
5. Use two microphones in an X/Y configuration.
6. When using two or more microphones, be careful to avoid phase issues. Try the 3:1 rule—the second mic should be thrice the distance from the instrument as the first mic is.

Vocal Tips

▶ *Tips from the pros:* It takes time for your voice to feel and sound ready, especially in the morning. In addition to warming up and taking good care of your voice, I find that waking up early enough makes a great difference when you have a 9 am recording session. **Meldra Guza— Managing Director at The SongLab**, Senior Lecturer, Voice Over Artist (Mattel), Session musician, Songwriter.

▶ *Tips from the pros: In some genres your main vocal might consist of 3 double tracked takes; two panned and one in the middle to achieve the dreamy feeling, while for other genres you might focus on getting that one, very personal vocal take. Be specific about what result you are looking for.* **Meldra Guza—Managing Director at The SongLab**, Senior Lecturer, Voice Over Artist (Mattel), Session musician, Songwriter.

▶ *Tips from the pros: Preparation always adds an extra layer of confidence which in turn makes the recording sessions smoother and more productive.* **Meldra Guza—Managing Director at The SongLab**, Senior Lecturer, Voice Over Artist (Mattel), Session musician, Songwriter.

▶ *Tips from the pros: Connect to the lyrics and focus on being believable. If you have written the song, you might already feel that deep connection, however, if you are recording the vocal as a session musician, particularly if you are working remotely it is even more important that you carry the intended message with integrity. Unless your performance is believable, it is very difficult for the listener to truly connect to the song.* **Meldra Guza—Managing Director at The SongLab**, Senior Lecturer, Voice Over Artist (Mattel), Session musician, Songwriter.

▶ *Tips from the pros:* Creating too many harmonies or layering the main vocal can take away from the song just as much as it can add. Context is everything. So, in this case, it is not about what We want but what the SONG needs. **Meldra Guza—Managing Director at The SongLab**, Senior Lecturer, Voice Over Artist (Mattel), Session musician, Songwriter.

▶ RECORD TASKS The following tasks are designed to put into practice some of the elements learnt across the 'Record' section of this book. It will enable some 'field recording', 'importing sound' into your DAW, 'setting up audio channels' and 'gain staging'. This will also facilitate discovering the best position within your recording space to set up a microphone for vocal recording.

RECORD Part A—Environmental Sounds

1. Import the stereo Audio Track 21.2 into a new DAW session (project tempo 125 bpm).
2. Listen carefully to how the rhythm is made entirely of environmental sounds.
3. Try walking slowly, outside, for a few minutes and listen intently to every sound which occurs.
4. Note which sounds are nearfield, mid-distance and far away.
5. Consider these sounds as rhythmic ideas.
6. Using a mobile recording device (this could be a smart phone), take a few short recordings of the sounds you encounter.
7. Import the sounds into the DAW session and edit the start and end points to create short percussive elements.
8. Sequence your new percussive sounds in alignment with the existing Audio Track 21.2 Environmental Sounds.wav to add further rhythmic elements to the backing track.
9. Save the DAW session as 'Environmental Sounds'!

RECORD Part B—Voice Recording

1. Plug a condenser microphone into your audio interface.
2. Create a 'voice' **audio input channel** in your DAW alongside the 'Environmental Sounds' rhythm track.
3. Set the gain staging across your audio interface and the DAW input, to ensure a good level from a *spoken voice* soundcheck. Keep your mouth around 8–10 cm away from the microphone and use a pop shield if available (positioned right next to the front of the microphone).

4. Arm the track ready to record and check monitoring levels against the rhythm track in your headphones.
5. Record a spoken voice part along to the rhythm track—you could improvise speech or use an existing text on elements of nature or the environment.
6. Check the recording levels are of suitable loudness and quality and 'save'.
7. Create a **second audio input channel** and prepare this for another voice recording.
8. Mute the first vocal recording channel.
9. Hit 'record' and do another spoken voice recording, but this time try walking around the microphone whilst talking. Move to either side and around the back of the microphone whilst recording. Alter your distance back and forth in front of the microphone also.
10. Listen back to both recordings and compare the qualities of dynamics, levels and clarity.
11. Can you hear the proximity effect occurring when you move closer to the microphone? Can you hear the 'sound of the room' in either recording?
12. Repeat both the voice recordings a few times and try placing the microphone in different parts of the room—in corners, in the middle, towards a wall, close to soft furnishings or curtains. Keep experimenting to achieve as many different qualities of recording as you can.
13. Find the best place in the room to place the microphone to achieve a voice sound that has:

- **Minimum room sound** (no reverberation)
- **Good presence** (clear mid-high frequencies)
- **No accented low frequencies** (no proximity effect)
- **Clear and full sound** (low noise ratio and wide dynamic range)

Part II

Mix

Equalisers   11

▶ **Learning Outcomes**

By the end of this chapter, the reader will be able to:
- Describe the different types of audio equalisers.
- Recall the functions and parameters used within equalisers.
- Show a working knowledge of the use of Eq filters and frequency bands and the relationship between instrumentation, frequencies and pitch.

Equalisers give you control over the tone of a sound. They are much like the bass and treble controls on your Hi-Fi, except they cover a much wider frequency range, usually from around 20 Hz up to 40 kHz depending on which equaliser you use.

They can be used to subtly improve a sound, for example, by making a dull sound a little brighter, a harsh sound a little softer or a weak sound heavier, or to change the character of a sound in order to make it work differently or fit better within a recording. For example, if you want to give a clean vocal recording a telephonic effect, you will need to reduce the loudness of frequencies that are not present when listening through a telephone receiver. Or, if you want to make the vocal stand out in the mix, you may need to boost frequencies that give voices more definition or presence.

There are two main types of equalisers:

Supplementary Information The online version contains supplementary material available at https://doi.org/10.1007/978-3-031-40067-4_11. The videos can be accessed individually by clicking the DOI link in the accompanying figure caption or by scanning this link with the SN More Media App.

© The Author(s), under exclusive license to Springer Nature Switzerland AG 2024
S. Duggal, *Record, Mix and Master*,
https://doi.org/10.1007/978-3-031-40067-4_11

Graphic Equalisers

Graphic equalisers have volume sliders, each of which controls pre-set filters. The bandwidth ('Q'), the amount by which frequencies either side of the chosen frequency are affected, is fixed for each band. The user can either boost or cut the loudness of a given frequency using one of the sliders. This type of equaliser is very easy to use (Fig. 11.1).

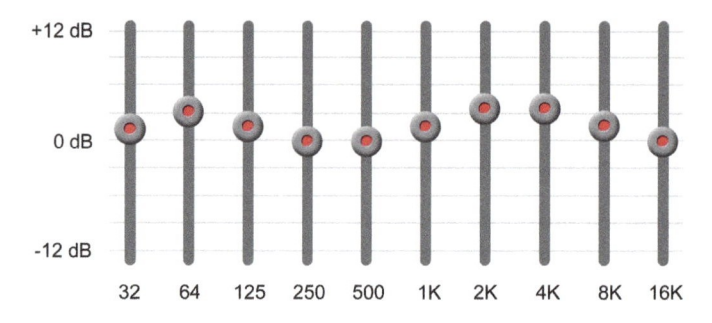

Fig. 11.1 Graphic equaliser

Parametric Equalisers

On parametric equalisers, each band has separate user variable frequency, bandwidth and gain controls. This type of equaliser usually has rotary knobs instead of sliders. There is a knob that allows you to select the desired frequency, one to dial in the amount of bandwidth either side of the chosen frequency, and one that lets you set the desired gain of the frequency. Parametric equalisers give you more precise control over the end result than graphic equalisers (Fig. 11.2).

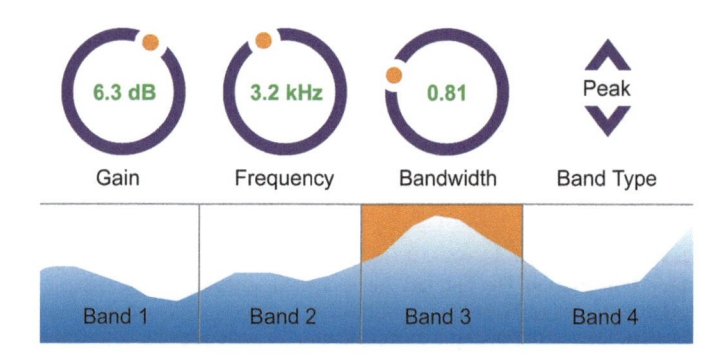

Fig. 11.2 Parametric equaliser

Additive and Subtractive Eq

Whether you are using a graphic or parametric equaliser to change the tone of the sound, you will either be boosting frequencies (additive equalising) or cutting frequencies (subtractive equalising).

There's no right or wrong way to use equalisation. Just be sure to keep an eye on the levels when boosting so you don't overload the output and cause unwanted distortion.

▶ *Tip: Listen to the sound and decide which frequencies are not needed. For example, if the signal sounds muddy, reduce a couple of dB in the 200 Hz to 300 Hz range. If it sounds boxy, reduce some in the 400 Hz to 600 Hz range. You can then use further additive or subtractive Eq to shape the tone as required.*

Types of Equaliser Filters

Low-Pass Filter (LPF)

Low-pass filters cut off a band of frequencies above a selected point, allowing only low frequencies to pass through. The slope of the cut-off can be adjusted in steps of decibels per octave—6 db, 12 dB, 18 dB, up to 96 dB depending on which equaliser you use. This is useful for making instruments blend into the track by removing unwanted high frequencies (Fig. 11.3).

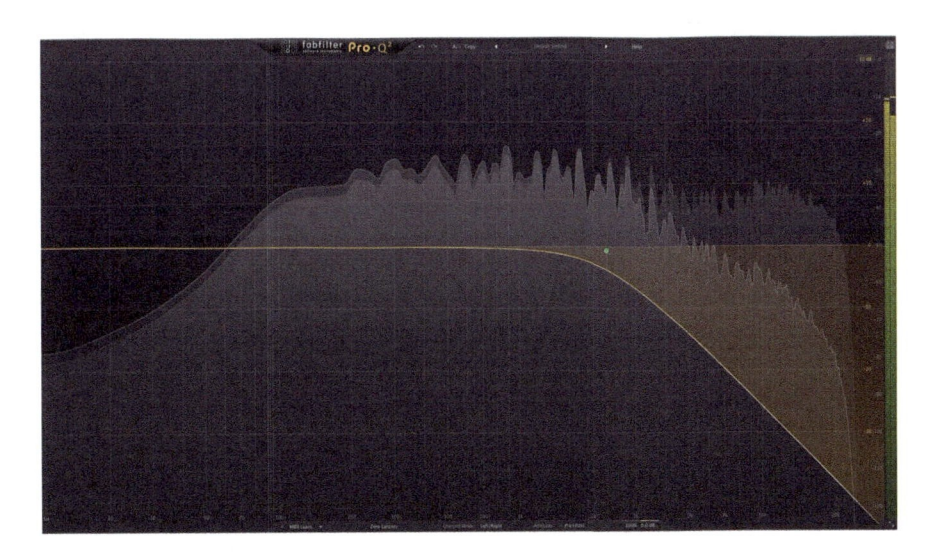

Fig. 11.3 FabFilter Pro-Q2, low-pass filter. (Image courtesy of FabFilter)

High-Pass Filter (HPF)

High-pass filters work in the same way as low-pass filters, except that they cut off a band of frequencies below a selected point, allowing only higher frequencies to pass through. Again, the slope of the cut-off can be adjusted in steps of decibels per octave.

Many signals, such as synths, vocals and guitars, contain unnecessary low-frequency content that interferes with kick drums and bass, causing the low end of your track to sound muddy and ill defined. Sometimes these unwanted frequencies can be as high as 300 Hz or more.

A high-pass filter can be used to remove the unwanted frequencies. Starting at the lowest point, sweep through the low frequencies until you notice the sound starting to change. At that point, stop and back it off a little. This should be the ideal cut-off point. You may find that you need to tweak it a little bit as you progress with your mix.

Many equalisers have a spectrum display which shows the signal and the effect of the changes you make in real time.

Additionally, high-pass filters are great for removing unwanted rumble picked up by microphones, and low-frequency thumps caused by the singer accidentally knocking the microphone stand (Fig. 11.4).

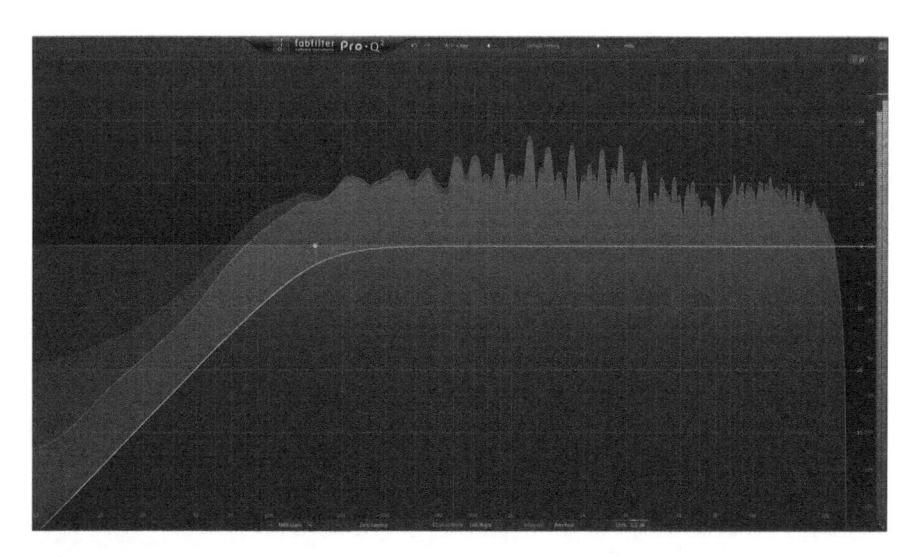

Fig. 11.4 FabFilter Pro-Q2, high-pass filter. (Image courtesy of FabFilter)

Notch Filter

Notch filters allow all bands on either side of the chosen frequency to pass through unaltered. The chosen notch band is attenuated to very low levels. This type of filter is useful for removing problematic frequencies whilst leaving the rest of the signal unaltered. Notch filters generally have a narrow bandwidth (Fig. 11.5).

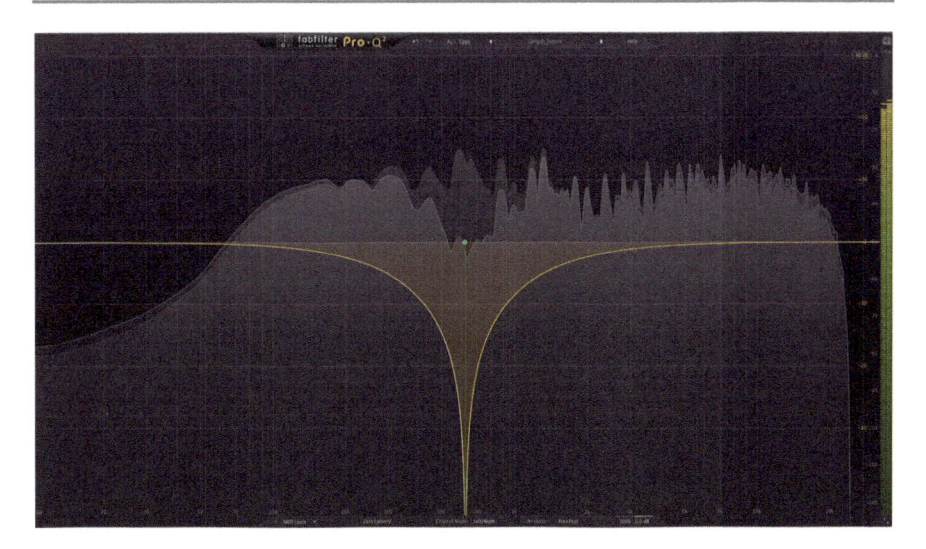

Fig. 11.5 FabFilter Pro-Q2, notch filter. (Image courtesy of FabFilter)

Bell (or Peak) Filter

Bell filters boost or cut a chosen frequency and also affect frequencies either side of it using a bell-shaped curve. The width of the bell shape can be increased or decreased by changing the bandwidth (Fig. 11.6).

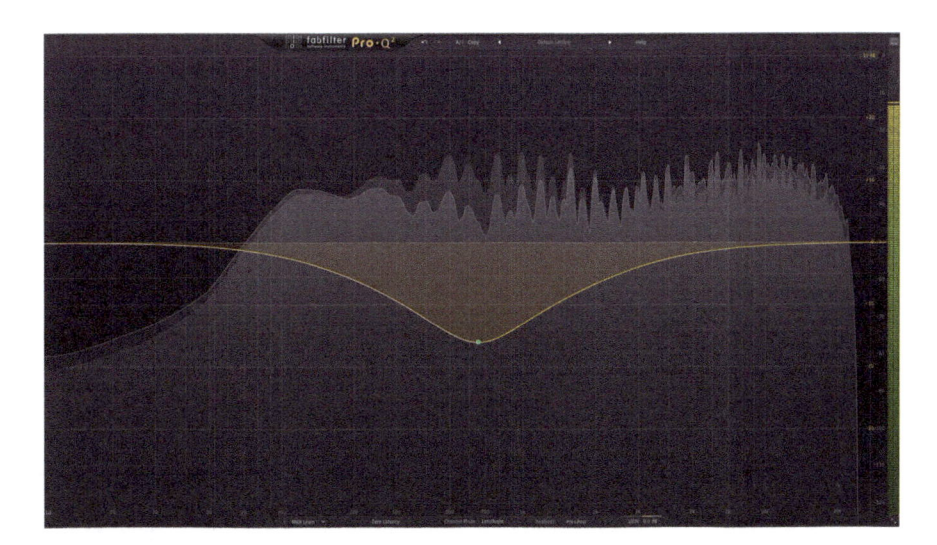

Fig. 11.6 FabFilter Pro-Q2, bell filter. (Image courtesy of FabFilter)

Band-Pass Filter

Band-pass filters allow frequencies between two points to pass through whilst rejecting frequencies either side (Fig. 11.7).

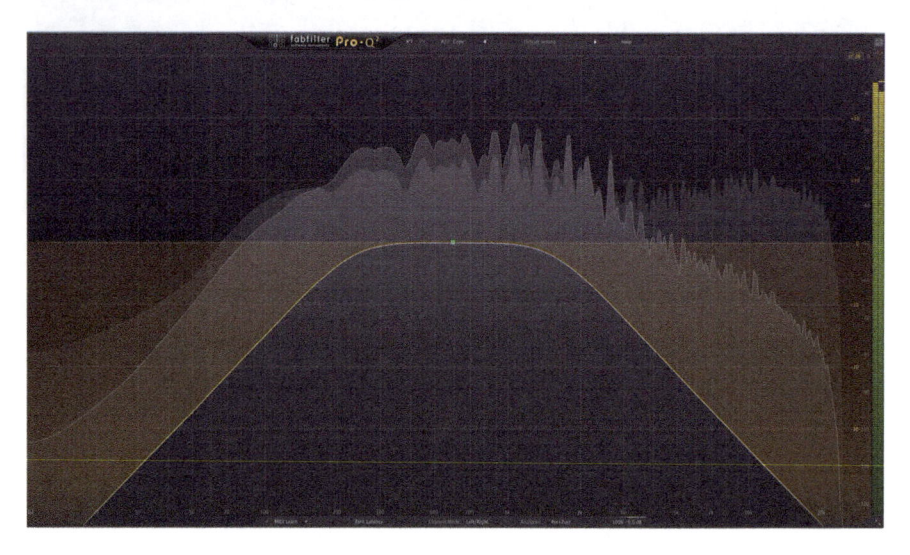

Fig. 11.7 FabFilter Pro-Q2, band-pass filter. (Image courtesy of FabFilter)

High-Shelf Filter

High-shelf filters tilt high frequencies upwards or downwards from a selected point. The tilt can be as shallow or steep as you need and can be tilted upwards to boost frequencies or downwards to reduce frequencies (Fig. 11.8).

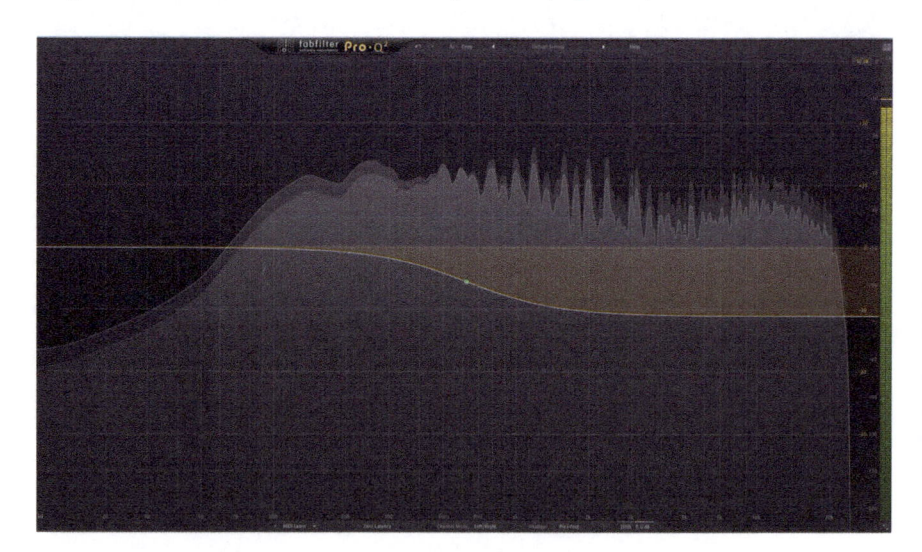

Fig. 11.8 FabFilter Pro-Q2, high-shelf filter. (Image courtesy of FabFilter)

Low-Shelf Filter

Low-shelf filters tilt low frequencies upwards or downwards from a selected point. The tilt can be as shallow or steep as you need and can be tilted upwards to boost frequencies or downwards to reduce frequencies (Fig. 11.9).

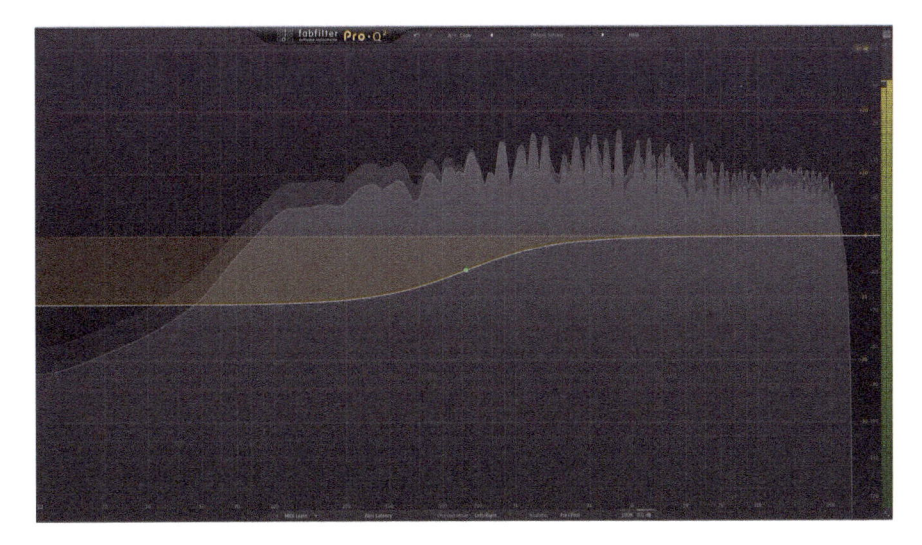

Fig. 11.9 FabFilter Pro-Q2, low-shelf filter. (Image courtesy of FabFilter)

Tilt Eq Filter

A single knob allows you to tilt the selected frequency band by boosting higher frequencies and cutting low frequencies, or vice versa. This type of filter can be useful for broad tone shaping (Fig. 11.10).

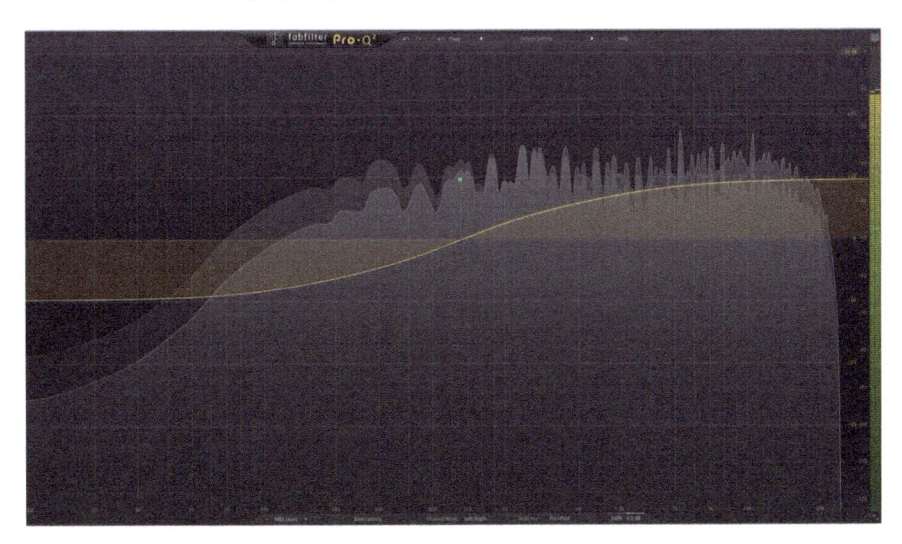

Fig. 11.10 FabFilter Pro-Q2, tilt filter. (Image courtesy of FabFilter)

Q—Bandwidth

When using a band-pass, notch or bell curve filter, you can adjust the Q (bandwidth). This determines the extent to which frequencies on either side of the selected band are affected. The diagram below illustrates different bandwidths from narrow to broad (Fig. 11.11).

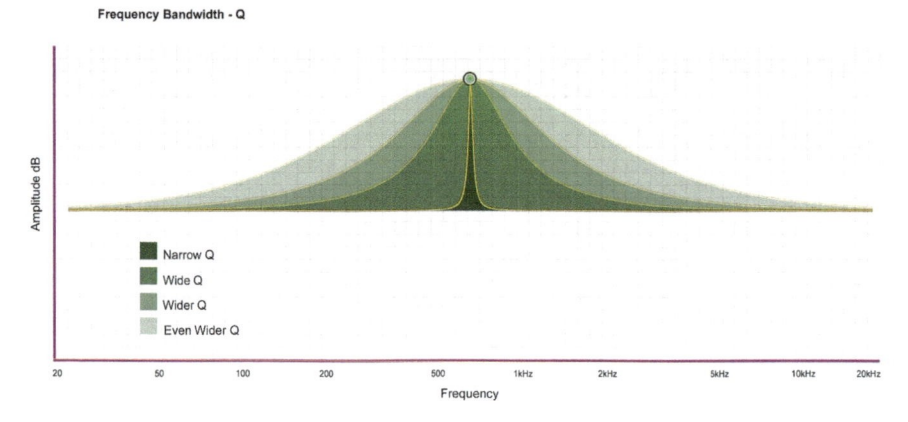

Fig. 11.11 Frequency bandwidth

The symbols in the following diagram represent different filter types (Fig. 11.12).

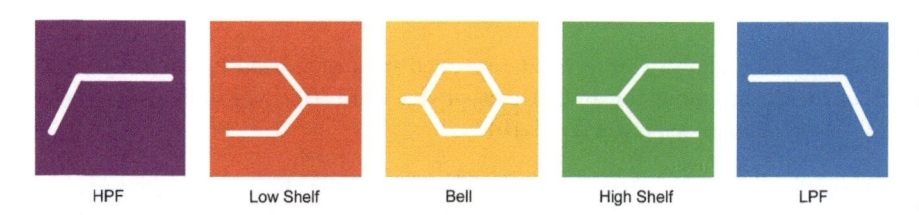

Fig. 11.12 Filter type symbols

▶ ***Tips from the pros:*** *Never be afraid to automate the eq. The singer did not take into account how far they were away from the mic when they were baring their soul.* **Kevin Churko—Producer and Songwriter—** *Disturbed, Ozzy Osbourne, Shania Twain, Five Finger Death Punch, The Corrs, Britney Spears and more.*

Dynamic Eq

Dynamic equalisers have been around for a long time in the form of De-Essers. Essentially, they are a combination of equaliser and multiband compressor (see Chap. 12: Dynamics—Compressors). Dynamic equalisers work in the same way that static equalisers do, except that when a frequency is cut or boosted, the effect will not be applied until the signal crosses the compression threshold. As with a regular compressor, the threshold, attack, release and ratio can all be adjusted for a given frequency band depending on which equaliser you are using. Many dynamic equalisers have automatic attack, release and ratio settings.

Minimum Phase

On an analogue hardware equaliser, when the gain of a frequency band is changed, slight delays in timing occur at that frequency in relation to other frequency bands that have not been changed. Manufacturers design their equalisers to minimise this effect, as it has an impact on the phase of the signal. These types of equalisers are known as minimum phase.

Many plugin equalisers are designed to mimic the behaviour of their analogue counterparts in order to keep latency low (see Chap. 4: Digital—Hardware Buffer Size and Latency) and to deliver a pleasing analogue type of sound. This type of digital equaliser is also known as minimum phase (Fig. 11.13).

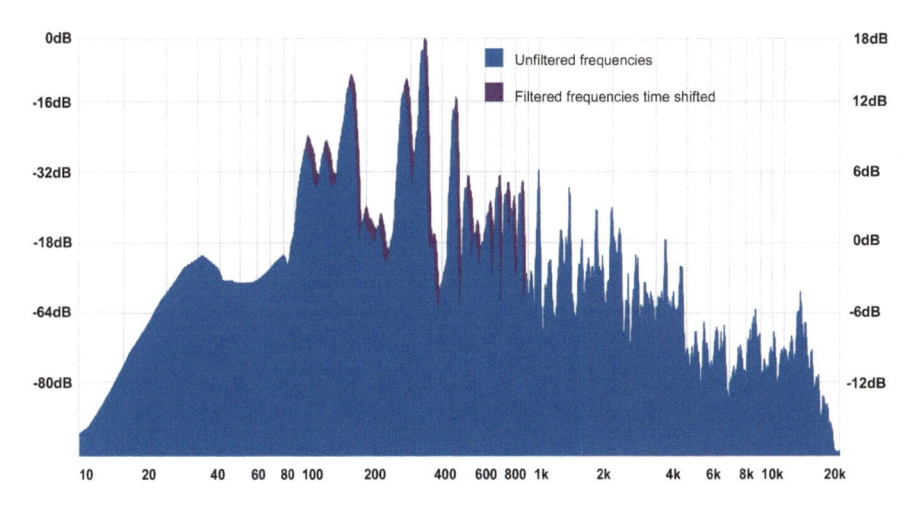

Fig. 11.13 Minimum phase Eq

Linear Phase

In applications where phase correlation (see Chap. 8: Phase) is critical such as in mastering, a linear phase equaliser is the best choice. Linear phase equalisers change the gain of a frequency without any shift in time or phase. The trade-off is that they induce latency. They work by delaying the timing of frequencies that have not been altered to match the timing of frequencies that have been altered. It's this delay that induces latency.

Linear phase equalisers can also introduce pre-ringing. Pre-ringing is a kind of short 'whoosh' that happens before the initial transient of a low-frequency sound when a HPF is applied. It is generally only noticeable on soloed kick drums and bass or other low-frequency content.

> ▶ ***Tips from the pros:*** *If your EQ allows you to "Band Isolate"(e.g ProTools EQIII—Holding Shift and Ctrl when clicking on a knob puts the EQ into Band Isolate soloing just the frequency you are working with) you can isolate harmful resonances and cut them before they hit other processing. Certain Mics and Preamps have "characteristics" which build up e.g SM57 on Guitars usually needs somewhere between 2.5 kHz and 4 kHz massively cutting on a tight bandwidth—use the Band Isolate to find the "hot spot"* **Mike Exeter—Producer, Engineer, Mixer and Composer—***Black Sabbath, Judas Priest, Ronnie James Dio, Cradle Of Filth and more.*

Baxandall Curve

The Baxandall curve is a shelf Eq with an extremely wide bandwidth. It is a minimum phase Eq which was originally designed for use in Hi-Fi. The Baxandall curve has a smooth sweet sound, and is used a lot in mastering or on the mix bus (Fig. 11.14).

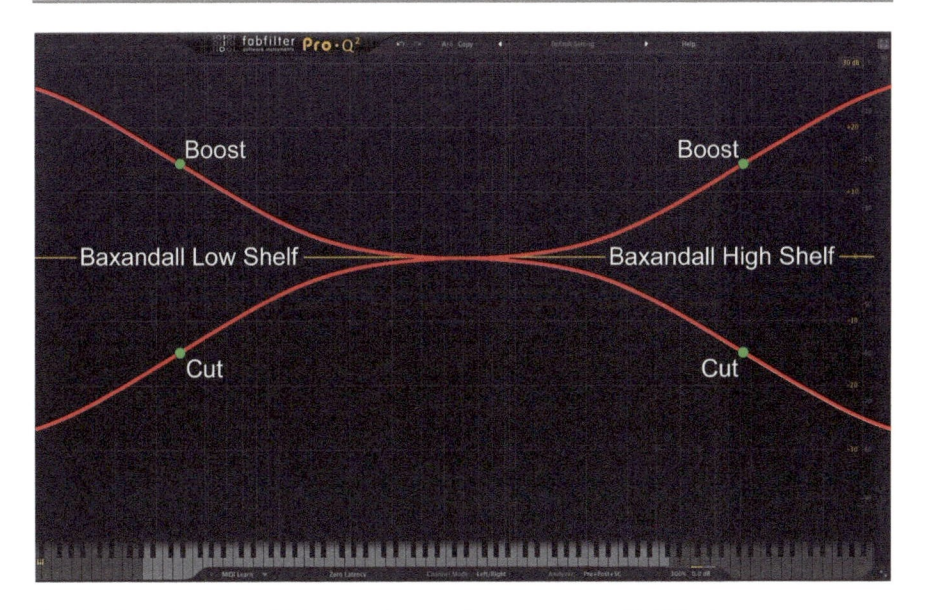

Fig. 11.14 FabFilter Pro-Q2, Baxandall curve. (Image courtesy of FabFilter)

Frequency Range

The following diagram shows the frequency range for each of the following definitions: Sub bass, bass, low mid, mid, high mid and high (Fig. 11.15):

▶ *Tip: Spend some time listening to sine waves for each of the frequency definitions so that you become familiar with what they sound like. For example, sweep through 80 Hz to 200 Hz so that you become familiar with where bass frequencies start and end.*

SUB BASS	BASS	LOW MID
20 - 80 Hz	80 - 200 Hz	200 - 500 Hz
MID	HIGH MID	TREBLE
500 - 2 kHz	2 kHz - 6 kHz	6 kHz - 20 kHz

Fig. 11.15 Frequency range

Equaliser Tips

Frequency	Effect
40 to 60 Hz	Too much in this range can over-emphasise deep low-frequency resonances causing the audio to sound *boomy* and unpleasant. Too little will make the sound weak and less full.
80 to 150 Hz	Too much in this range can make low frequencies sound too hard. Too little will make the sound weak and lack punch and beefiness.
200 to 400 Hz	Too much in this range and the sound will be muddy and blurred making it difficult to distinguish between elements in the mix. Too little will make the sound thin and weak. Getting the balance of this frequency range right will add body to your sound without the muddiness.
400 to 600 Hz	Too much 400 Hz to 600 Hz can make the sound boxy or honky. Reduce a little around 400 Hz if the audio has too much knock. Reduce some at 500 Hz to 600 Hz if it sounds too honky.
800 Hz to 1 kHz	Too much of this frequency range can make the audio sound cheap and unpleasant. Not enough, and it will sound distant.
1 to 2 kHz	Too much in this range can add an unpleasant nasal character to the sound. Not enough, and the voice or instrument may get 'lost' in the mix.
2 to 4 kHz	Too much can make the sound harsh and piercing. Too little can make the sound lack bite. On a mix, over-emphasis of this frequency band can make the recording painful to listen to and cause ear fatigue after prolonged listening.
4 to 6 kHz	This frequency band adds clarity and definition to vocals and instruments. Too little can make the sound dull. Too much can over-emphasise transients.
6 to 8 kHz	This is the 'presence' frequency band. Too little in this range and the audio will sound dull. Too much and it will sound sibilant. This 'presence' band can also emphasise the attack on percussive instruments.
10 kHz	Too much 10 kHz can make the audio sound sibilant. Not enough, and it can sound dull and flat. This frequency is also useful for accentuating the attack on drums, cymbals and percussion.
15 kHz	Adding some 15 kHz upwards to a vocal, instrument or mix can make it sound more natural and real. This frequency band also adds brightness to cymbals, strings and synths.

▶ *Tips from the pros: Don't be afraid to add in some stuff that you feel is missing but listen rather than look at the screen—there is a reason the knobs go from −15 to +15* **Mike Exeter—Producer, Engineer, Mixer and Composer—***Black Sabbath, Judas Priest, Ronnie James Dio, Cradle Of Filth and more.*

▶ *Tip: Cut frequencies with a narrow Q. This way you can remove a problematic frequency without affecting anything else.*

▶ *Tip: Boost frequencies with a wider Q. A narrow Q will cause the frequency to stick out in an undesirable way. Boosting with a wider Q will sound more natural.*

► *Tips from the pros:* When it comes to EQing I try to use subtractive eq rather than additive (cutting rather than boosting)…I'll try to sculpt out a place in the mix so that the main vocal or lead line can occupy its own space… if I need to boost a particular frequency I'll notch out a little just above the boost… this gives the illusion of the boost being more prominent and thus requiring less of it. **Marcus Byrne—Producer and Musician**—Take That, ELO, MIKA, Taio Cruz and more.

Modelled Equalisers

Some equalisers (and other types of plugins) are modelled on vintage hardware units. Often the hardware unit is rare and prohibitively expensive for a home or project studio recordist to acquire, so manufacturers create plugin versions to give the user access to their sound in the digital domain.

With modelled plugins, the analogue circuitry of the original hardware is emulated component by component using complex digital algorithms to recreate the sound. This gives the user the authentic sound of the original vintage unit and the flexibility to use multiple plugin instances across tracks.

The Audified RZ062 equaliser (pictured) is a great example of a plugin that is precisely modelled on a vintage unit. The RZ062 is modelled on the German-designed Klangfilm Eq that was used in mixing consoles in top European studios throughout the 1960s (Fig. 11.16).

Fig. 11.16 Audified RZ062 equaliser. (Image courtesy of Audified)

- *Tip: Use corrective equalisation to fix any anomalies, for example, to remove any unnecessary low frequencies. Follow the corrective equaliser with compression as necessary, and then use another equaliser to shape the tone of the sound as desired.*
- *Tip: Some equalisers have an auto gain feature. This automatically compensates for changes in gain when you boost or cut frequencies. This can be very helpful for judging the tonal changes you make without your perception being affected by an increase or decrease in level.*

Piano Display

Some equalisers, such as Waves H-Eq, have a piano display. This is a great feature that shows you exactly which note a frequency is at. Use the piano display to make some of your equalisation decisions according to the key of the song (Fig. 11.17).

Fig. 11.17 Waves H-Eq. (Image courtesy of Waves Audio Ltd)

Piano Display

▶ *Tip: Use Mid/Side Eq (See Chap. 16: Mid/Side Processing) to equalise the left and right channels of a sound differently. For example, to get more width on a stereo keyboard part, boost some frequencies on the left channel and cut the same frequencies on the right channel. You can do this with the piano display and auto gain engaged if you have these features on your equaliser.*

▶ *Tip: You may not need to Eq the signal at all. If it sounds good, it is good.*

▶ **Chapter 11 Tasks:** The following tasks will demonstrate the effects of equalisation on a range of source recordings and improve your ability to discover problematic areas within the frequency bands.

- Listen through to all the provided Audio Examples from 22 to 28 which demonstrate the variety of Eq types and the effects of boosts and cuts on a signal. What are the noticeable differences between the Eq types?
- Try to develop your ability to identify different frequency ranges by boosting and cutting areas of the frequency spectrum on a stereo mix of a completed song and listening intently to the effect this has on a track.
- Use high- and low-pass filters to remove all frequencies lower than 50 Hz, then all frequencies lower than 200 Hz, then all frequencies higher than 1000 Hz, then all frequencies between 200 Hz and 1000 Hz. For each of these stages, how much audible information in the track is removed when you try this?
- Spend some time comparing notes on the piano display to specific frequencies to build your knowledge of how pitches can help identify problematic frequency issues.

Dynamics 12

Compressors

▶ **Learning Outcomes**

By the end of this chapter, the reader will be able to:
- Explain the function and use of compressors, limiters and expanders in audio processing.
- Recall the settings and parameters of controls used within compressors, limiters and expanders.
- Show a working knowledge of the use of applied settings within compressors, limiters and expanders in application with a range of instruments and voices.
- Explain and utilise noise gates, de-essers and spectral shaping in audio correction.

Compressors are used to obtain a more consistent level by reducing loud parts of the audio material without squashing the peaks, thereby decreasing the difference between the quietest and loudest parts of the signal.

When used correctly, compressors can make instruments and voices sound solid, tight and more powerful by compacting the energy contained within the sound. On static sounds such as programmed drums for example, a compressor can be used to change the envelope—the attack, decay, sustain and release of the sound (Fig. 12.1).

Compressors have the following controls:

Threshold—This is the level at which the compressor is triggered. Any signal that exceeds the threshold will be compressed, and any signal that falls below the threshold will remain uncompressed.

Supplementary Information The online version contains supplementary material available at https://doi.org/10.1007/978-3-031-40067-4_12. The videos can be accessed individually by clicking the DOI link in the accompanying figure caption or by scanning this link with the SN More Media App.

Fig. 12.1 Waves API 2500 compressor. (Image courtesy of Waves Audio Ltd)

Attack—When the signal crosses the threshold, the compressor kicks in. Using the attack setting, you can determine how long it takes before compression is applied to a signal that has crossed the threshold.

Release—This is the time it takes for the signal to be released from a state of compression once it falls below the threshold. This is pretty much the opposite of attack time.

Some compressors give you the option of selecting either electro or opto release behaviour:

Electro releases the signal from a compressed state faster as the gain reduction approaches zero, when it is less than 3 dB. Above 3 dB, the release is slower. This type of release behaviour produces an increase in the average level, which is good for loud signals.

Opto is pretty much the opposite of electro. For signals with less than 3 dB of gain reduction, the release time gets slower as the gain reduction approaches zero. For signals with more than 3 dB of gain reduction, the release time is faster.

Release behaviour	Application
Electro	Produces an increase in average level. Good for loud sounds.
Opto	Good for deeper compression applications where the signal has a high dynamic range such as vocals.

Compressors

Auto release: Some compressors have an auto release function which determines the release time behaviour based on the input signal.

Auto release can be quite effective for signals that are very dynamic, as it tracks constant changes in level and applies the release behaviour accordingly. Fixed release behaviour is better suited to signals that are constant, such as a programmed drum hit that has the same velocity throughout the track.

▶ *Tip: A release time that is set too fast may cause an unpleasant pumping effect.*

Ratio: Ratio controls the amount of gain reduction applied to the signal once it has crossed the threshold. For example, if the ratio is set to 2:1, the signal will be reduced in gain by 1 dB for every 2 dB that exceeds the threshold level. A signal that is 6 dB above the threshold will be reduced in gain by 3 dB (Fig. 12.2).

Compression and limiter ratios are multiplicative. This means that if you compress an audio track with a ratio of say 5:1 and then later compress the same audio track with a ratio of 10:1, the end result will not be a compression ratio of 15:1 (5:1 + 10:1 = 15:1). It will in fact be 50:1 (5:1 × 10:1 = 50:1). This will effectively squash any dynamics right out of your recording, leaving it sounding flat and lifeless.

▶ *Tip: Over compressing audio signals is a common mistake. If you want your audio to sound as good as the professionals, be careful not to overdo it—unless you are using it for deliberate effect. Over compressing will also raise the loudness of any noise content in the audio and can introduce distortion into the sound.*

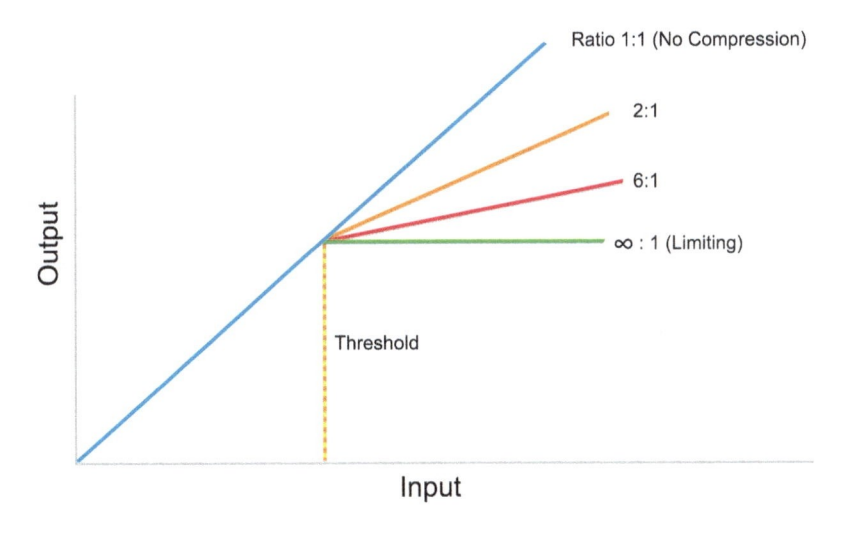

Fig. 12.2 Compression ratio

▶ *Tip: A ratio of 2:1 is considered quite moderate compression. A ratio of 5:1 is medium compression. A ratio of 8:1 is strong compression and ratios of 20:1 and above are limiting rather than compressing.*

Knee

Some compressors give you control over the knee setting. There are two types of knee setting: hard and soft.

Hard Knee

The gain reduction is introduced abruptly when the signal exceeds the threshold. As soon as the signal crosses the threshold, compression is applied at the user-set ratio. Hard knee is the default setting on most compressors and is good for harder sounds like drums.

Soft Knee

The compression ratio increases gradually as the signal level approaches the threshold. Once the signal has crossed the threshold, the full ratio as set by the user is applied. Soft knee is the preference for a lot of producers and mix engineers as it gives a smoother and more transparent sound. This setting works well on vocals, strings and pads (Fig. 12.3).

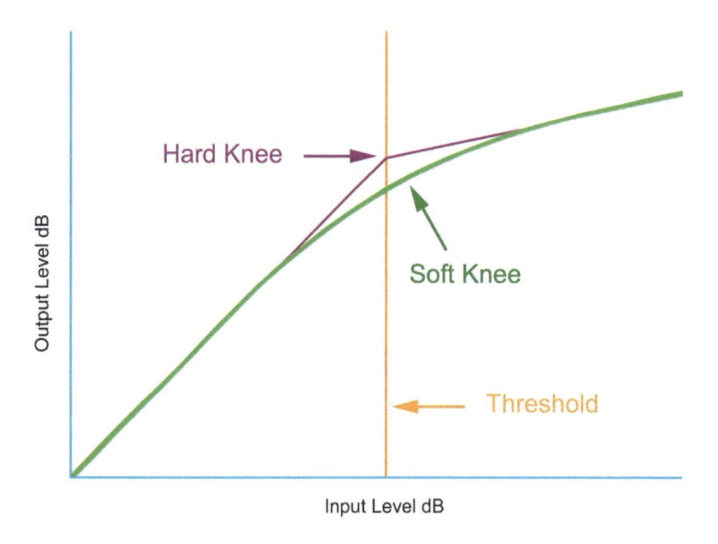

Fig. 12.3 Compression knee

Different Types of Compressor

There are different types of compressor designs. The descriptions below will help you choose the right one for any given application.

FET
FET compressors have extremely fast attack and release response times which makes them suitable for peak limiting applications (see Chap. 12: Dynamics—Limiters). FET compressors use a field effect transistor to control the gain reduction and generally add a lot more colour to the sound which may be quite desirable in some instances. If smooth compression is required, an optical or variable MU compressor might be a better choice.

VCA
VCA compressors use a voltage-controlled amplifier to control the gain reduction and provide smooth compression with control over attack and release response times. VCA compressors are suited to a wide variety of applications from smooth to quite aggressive gain reduction. They are particularly suited to transient (see Chap. 17: Transients) heavy material such as percussion.

Optical/Tube
The input of optical compressors is fed to an LED light which gets brighter as it receives more signal and fades as the signal is reduced. The change in the light's reaction to the input signal is read by a photocell which controls the amount of compression. Optical compressors have a slow attack time and do not respond well to the initial transient of the sound. The release time is quick at first and then slows down. In spite of this, they do sound very musical. Optical compressors are not generally suitable for mastering purposes due to their lack of control over attack and release times.

Variable MU (Variable Gain)
Variable MU compressors use a vacuum tube design to control gain reduction. They are most commonly used in mastering applications. They do not have a separate ratio control; instead, the harder the input signal is driven, the higher the ratio setting becomes. They are not suitable for peak limiting applications as they do not respond fast enough to transients. Variable MU compressors give very smooth results and can add some pleasing colour to the sound.

Compressor Type Summary

Compressor type	Famous compressor models	Compression style
FET	Universal Audio 1176	Very fast attack and release. Great for peak limiting. Adds colour to the sound

Compressor type	Famous compressor models	Compression style
VCA	SSL G Bus Compressor API 2500 DBX 160 & 165	Great for smooth to quite aggressive compression on a wide variety of applications.
Optical/ Tube	Teletronix LA-2A	Slow attack. Not great for transient heavy material. Not suitable for mastering. Do sound very musical.
Variable MU	Fairchild 670 & 660	Not suitable for peak limiting. Used commonly in mastering applications. Smooth results. Adds colour to the sound.

Feedforward and Feedback Processing

In order to understand Feedforward and Feedback style compression behaviours, we must first understand the basics of how a compressor's circuitry works. In the simplest of terms, a compressor receives an input signal which passes through a VCA (voltage-controlled amplifier) which reduces the gain. The resulting signal is then fed to the output (Fig. 12.4).

Fig. 12.4 Compressor circuit

However, the VCA needs to know how much to reduce the gain at any given moment in time. This is the job of the control circuit. An exact duplicate of the input signal is fed to the control circuit. This is the sidechain signal. The control circuit knows when and by how much the sidechain signal has crossed the threshold and uses this information to tell the VCA how much gain reduction should be applied.

With **Feedforward** compressors, the sidechain signal passes through the control circuit before it goes through the amplifier gain reduction stage. This is a modern and common design which can sound punchy and direct. It's generally easier to get a feedforward-style compressor to do what you want it to (Fig. 12.5).

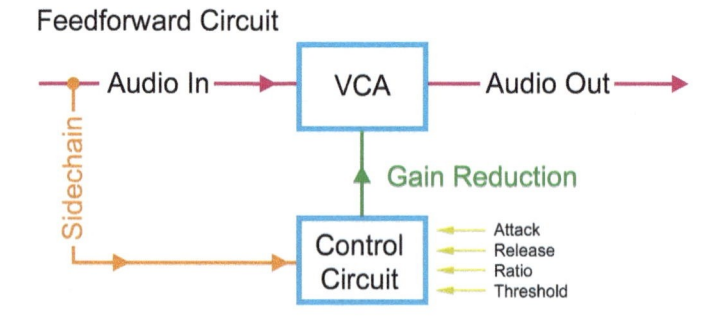

Fig. 12.5 Compressor feedforward circuit

With **Feedback** compressors, the control circuit receives the sidechain signal after it has passed through the amplifier gain reduction stage. This is an older design which can sound softer and more musical. Most classic compressors are feedback design. With this style of compressor, the attack and release are influenced by the amount of gain reduction and the ratio. This affects the way transients are handled which gives a pleasing result (Fig. 12.6).

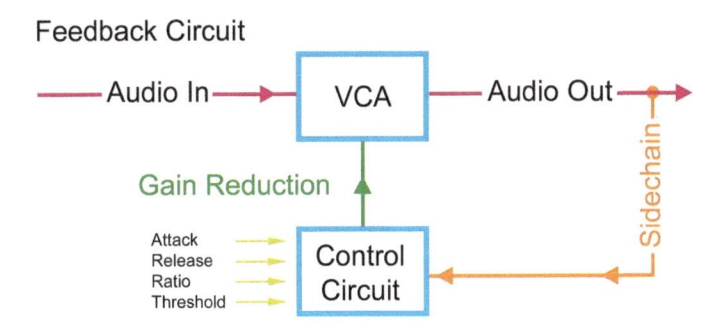

Fig. 12.6 Compressor feedback circuit

How to Use a Compressor

Compressors control the dynamic range of instruments and voices. Correct use of a compressor is a great route to a professional sound.

Whilst randomly fiddling with the parameters of a compressor in the hope of getting a good sound may occasionally yield decent results, the results may not be consistently good, and this approach restricts the musical control you have over the compression sound.

There are some initial settings which will allow you to easily hear the effects of any adjustments you make to the attack and release times. By starting with these settings, you can quickly get the compression sound that you are looking for.

Start by setting the attack time to its fastest, the release time close to its fastest, the ratio to around 20:1 and the threshold to very sensitive.

Having made these initial settings, we can now begin fine-tuning the parameters to achieve the best settings for the particular instrument or vocal you are working with:

1. Play with the attack until you achieve the desired thickness or fatness of the sound. The slower or longer the attack time, the fatter the sound will be. This is because a slower attack will allow more of the signal's transient through before compression is applied. Listen to how the sound changes as you increase or decrease the attack time. Imagine a plectrum striking a guitar string. If the attack is set fast, the string will sound soft, whereas, if the attack is set slow, it will sound thicker (Fig. 12.7).

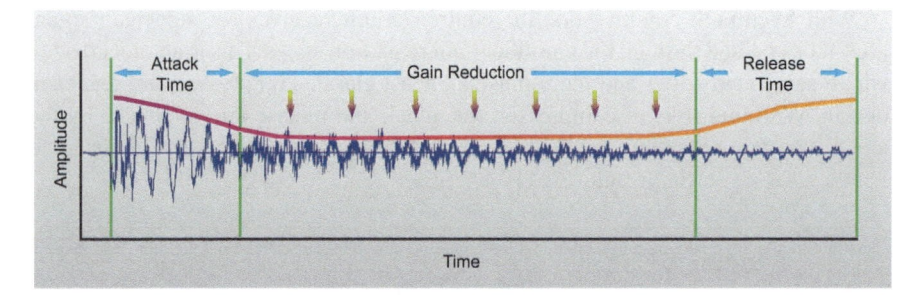

Fig. 12.7 An example of a compressed signal

2. Once you are happy with the thickness of the sound, set the release time so that you can hear the sound bouncing back or rising up as the compression tails off. Try to set this so that it feels right and grooves in time with the song tempo. As the name suggests, release is the time it takes for the compressor to release the sound from a compressed state.

▶ *Tip: Set the release time so that the metres return to zero before the next audio instance, such as a drum strike or guitar pluck. Use the metres as a guide but ultimately trust your ears.*

3. Now, reduce the ratio so that the sound isn't too squashed. A ratio of somewhere between 3:1 and 6:1 should work well for most sounds. Set it so that it feels nice and sounds musical.
4. Reduce the threshold level to less sensitive, so that only the loudest parts of the audio trigger the compressor.

With these settings, you will be able to get great compression results every time.

▶ *Tip: If your compressor only has an input gain control and a threshold control, then the ratio, attack and release times are set automatically. The input level will determine the ratio.*
▶ ***Tips from the pros:*** *Always start with the fastest attack and release, along with a high ratio so you can actually hear what you are doing to the sound. Back them off one by one so you can find out what effect the compressor is having. If it isn't helping, then don't use it—it isn't compulsory!* ***Mike Exeter—Producer, Engineer, Mixer and Composer—*** *Black Sabbath, Judas Priest, Ronnie James Dio, Cradle Of Filth and more.*

Compressor Settings

Use the guide below as a starting point for your compressor settings and tweak as necessary.

Instrument	Attack	Release	Ratio	Knee	Gain reduction
Vocal	Fast	500 ms/Auto	2:1–8:1	Soft	3–8 dB
Acoustic guitar	5–10 ms	500 ms/Auto	5:1–10:1	Soft/hard	5–12 dB
Electric guitar	2–5 ms	500 ms/Auto	8:1	Hard	5–15 dB
Kick & snare drum	1–5 ms	200 ms/Auto	5:1–10:1	Hard	5–15 dB
Bass	2–10 ms	500 ms/Auto	4:1–12:1	Hard	5–15 dB
Horn section	1–5 ms	300 ms/Auto	6:1–15:1	Hard	8–15 dB
Stereo mix	Fast	400 ms/Auto	2:1–6:1	Soft	2–10 dB

▶ *Tip: If you have multiple backing vocal tracks, for example, applying an individual compressor to each one would use up valuable computer processing power. Instead, route all of your backing vocal tracks to a bus and insert a single compressor on it. An added advantage is that you'll only need to adjust the parameters of a single compressor, rather than several instances (see Chap. 14: Subgroups).*

▶ ***Tips from the pros:*** *Knocking off transients with a subtle amount of saturation before compression can lessen the damage caused by badly used compressors.* **Mike Exeter—Producer, Engineer, Mixer and Composer**—*Black Sabbath, Judas Priest, Ronnie James Dio, Cradle Of Filth and more.*

In the following images, you can see the difference between an uncompressed, compressed and limited audio file (Figs. 12.8, 12.9, and 12.10).

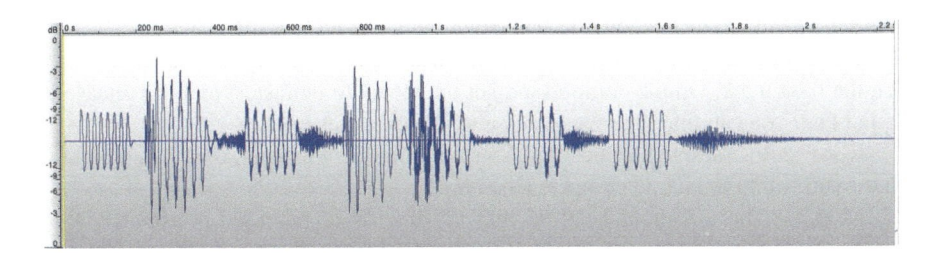

Fig. 12.8 A mix before compression

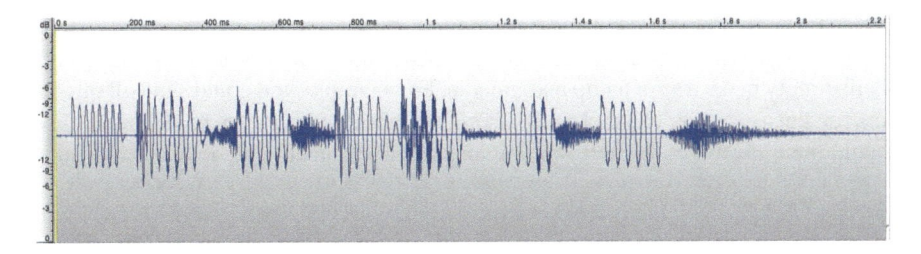

Fig. 12.9 A mix after compression

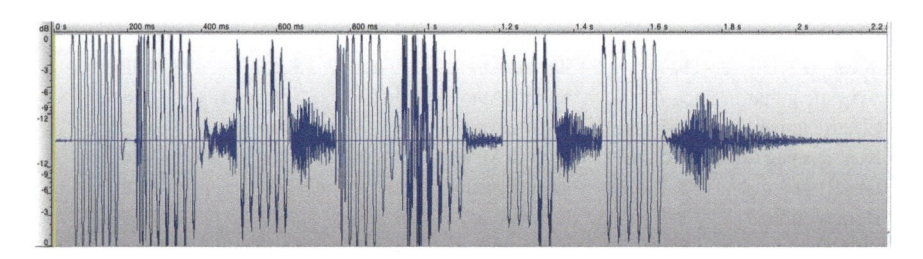

Fig. 12.10 A mix after limiting

Sidechain Compression

Sidechain compression is a technique used to make one track in your mix trigger the compressor on another track. For example, you may want the kick drum to trigger the compressor on the bass track so that every time the kick sounds, the bass gets a reduction in volume. This is a common trick on electronic dance tracks as well as a useful mix tool for whenever one track needs to push another track out of the way momentarily.

Sidechain compression is also used a lot in broadcast applications, for example, whenever a radio DJ speaks the level of the music is reduced, so that they can always be heard clearly.

How to Use Sidechain Compression

Start by inserting a compressor on your bass track. Next, set its key input to bus 1. On the kick drum track, assign a send to bus 1. This will bring up a bus fader. Set the send level on the bus fader to pre-fader and the level to 0 dB.

Press play, and you should see the signal from the kick going into the compressor on the bass track. On the compressor, set the attack to its fastest and the release to quite fast. You can fine tune the attack and release times later.

Now, set the ratio to around 10:1. You can fine-tune this later, depending on how hard you want the kick to compress the bass.

Next, set the threshold level so that the bass is compressed constantly. Now adjust the release time so that the kick and bass work together rhythmically. A faster release time will make the compressor 'pump' more (Fig. 12.11).

Sidechain Compression Setup

Sidechain compression can be used on any instruments or vocals when you need to subtly nudge one part out of the way of another. It can also be used as an effect to deliberately make tracks pump and breathe. For example, you could send all of your instruments to a bus channel and all of your vocals to another bus channel. You could then insert a compressor on the instrument channel, which is sidechained to

Compressors

Fig. 12.11 Sidechain compression setup

the vocal channel. This would allow you to slightly compress the instrument channel when the vocal is playing, which will make sure the vocal is always sitting slightly above the instruments, ensuring it is always heard. This type of sidechaining is common on voiceovers in TV commercials.

Sidechain Eq Filter

Some compressors have a sidechain equaliser. A high-pass filter is inserted in the sidechain signal path. Adjusting the high-pass filter gradually upwards from minimum makes the compressor less responsive to low frequencies, allowing them to pass through uncompressed while the rest of the signal is compressed. This is useful for preventing an unwanted pumping sound which can be caused by low frequencies being over compressed (Fig. 12.12).

Feedforward Circuit with High Pass Filter

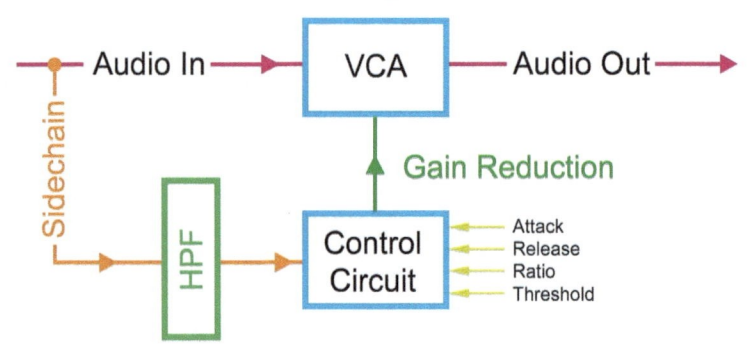

Fig. 12.12 Sidechain Eq filter

Parallel Compression (Parallel Processing)

Parallel compression, also known as New York compression, is a technique used to increase the harmonic content of the audio material by blending in a heavily compressed copy of the sound with the original dry signal.

How to Use Parallel Compression

Send all of your drums—kick, snare, hats, etc.—to a bus channel. Now, duplicate the bus channel and insert a compressor on it. Mute the first bus channel so that you are only hearing the duplicate with the compressor inserted.

Next, compress that channel heavily. Try a ratio of 10:1 or more with fast attack and release times. You can tweak the attack and release time later according to taste. Now adjust the threshold so that the channel is heavily compressed.

Insert an Eq plugin after the compressor and boost low frequencies, around 100 Hz and the high frequencies around 10 kHz. Pull down the fader and unmute the previous bus channel. Whilst playing the drum track, slowly increase the level of the duplicate bus channel until you get the desired blend. Some compressors have a mix control which allows you to blend the compressed sound with the dry sound, eliminating the need to create a duplicate track; however, in this case, you cannot add an equaliser to the heavily compressed signal.

▶ ***Tips from the pros:*** *Parallel compression is a fantastic way to set and forget vocals. Lightly compress one and slam the other. It saves a lot of automation time.* **Kevin Churko—Producer, Engineer and Songwriter—***Disturbed, Ozzy Osbourne, Shania Twain, Five Finger Death Punch, The Corrs, Britney Spears and more.*

Parallel compression/processing can be used on anything, not just drums. For example, you could duplicate your bass track, insert a distortion plugin on the

Compressors

Parallel Compression

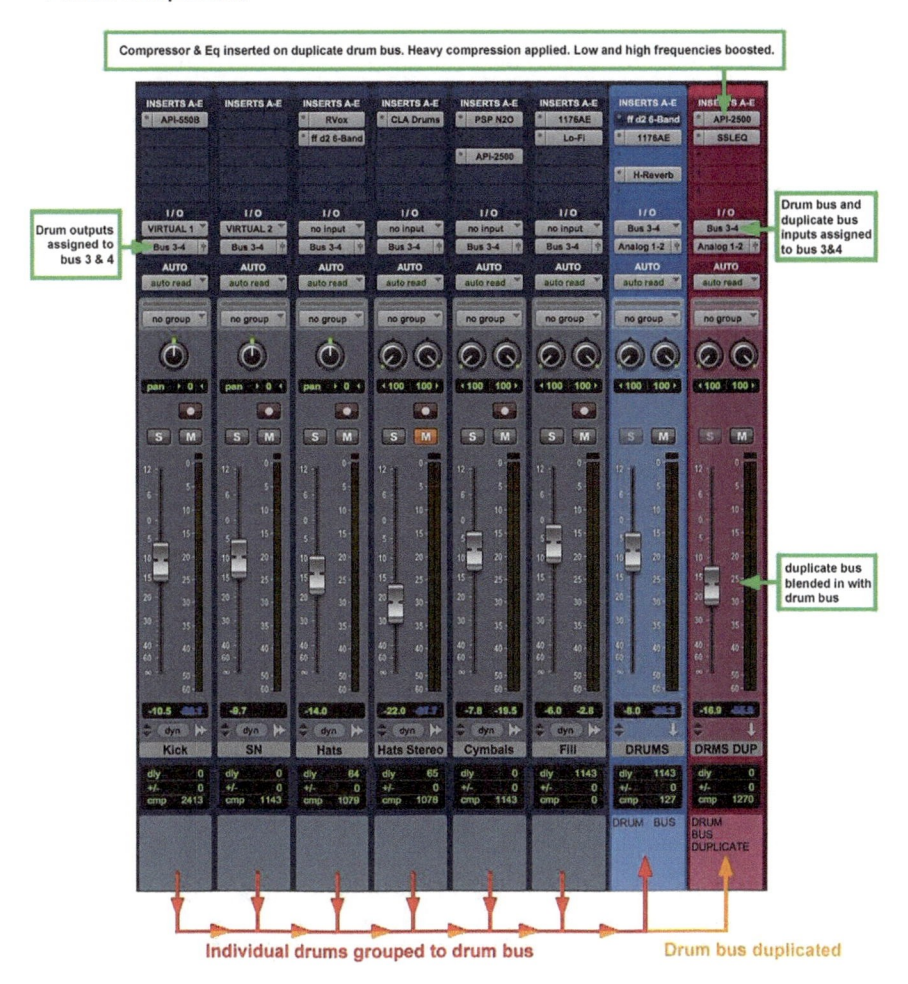

Fig. 12.13 Parallel compression setup

duplicate and blend it in with the original track just as we did with a compressor on the drum tracks. You can achieve some great results with parallel compression (Fig. 12.13).

▶ *Tips from the pros: Duplicate your lead vocal track with the same compressor and eq. Now increase compression settings heavily on the duplicate track and blend underneath the original lead vocal track for a lead vocal that jumps out the mix.* **Diamond Duggal—Producer and Songwriter**—*Shania Twain, Apache Indian, Erasure, The Beat, Maxi Priest, Swami and more.*

Multiband Compressors

Multiband compressors split the signal into different frequency bands, usually low, low mid, high mid and high, and have separate compression parameters for each band. Attack, release, ratio (or range) and threshold controls are the same as a regular compressor, with additional control over the gain (level) of each band.

These compressors have crossover (Xover) parameters, which allow you to set the frequency range for a given band.

Multiband compressors usually have a solo button for soloing a selected frequency band, so you can listen to it in isolation from the other bands. They also have a bypass button for bypassing the selected band whilst listening to all of the other bands (Fig. 12.14).

Approach multiband compressor settings in the same way you would with a regular compressor, the difference here is that you will adjust attack, release, ratio and threshold for each band.

Multiband compressors are usually used in mastering applications, on the stereo master bus and on grouped instrument busses. There are no rules, however, so if you

Multiband Compressor

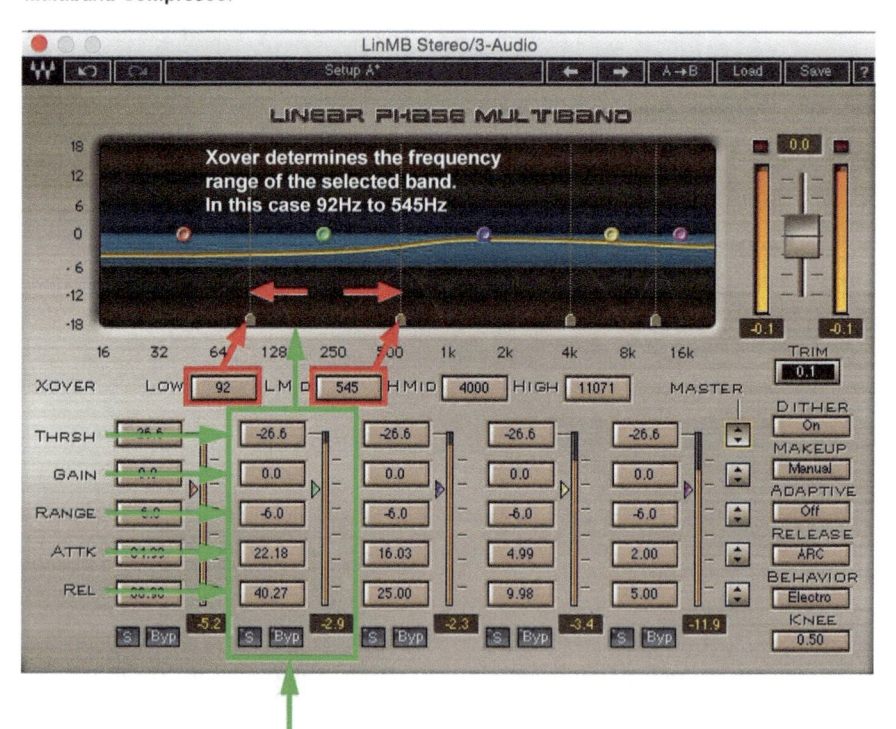

Each section is an individual compressor for the selected frequency band

Fig. 12.14 Waves LinMB multiband compressor. (Image courtesy of Waves Audio Ltd)

find that a multiband compressor gives you the results you want on an individual instrument or vocal track, go ahead and use it.

▶ *Tip: Compression on the master bus can help glue your mix together. Use a VCA compressor such as Waves SSL Comp or Waves API 2500 compressors. Approximately 2 dB of gain reduction should be enough. Be careful not to over compress. Try an attack setting of around 3–10 milliseconds and set the release to auto. Tweak as needed.*
▶ ***Tips from the pros:*** *You can't undo compression, so be gentle—especially during tracking.* **Mike Exeter—Producer, Engineer, Mixer and Composer—***Black Sabbath, Judas Priest, Ronnie James Dio, Cradle Of Filth and more.*

Limiters

Limiters are much like compressors. They both process dynamic levels in the same way. The difference though is that limiters have a much greater ratio. A typical compressor has a ratio of 20:1 or less, whereas a limiter usually has a ratio of between 10:1 and 100:1 (Fig. 12.15).

Unlike compressors, which are best used for obtaining a more consistent level by reducing louder parts of the recording without squashing the peaks, limiters are best used for reducing peaks in the recording without affecting anything else.

Signal peaks crossing the threshold are attenuated, and a maximum output ceiling can be set. On a regular limiter, the attenuated signal can still sometimes exceed the maximum output ceiling to some degree. If an absolute output ceiling is required,

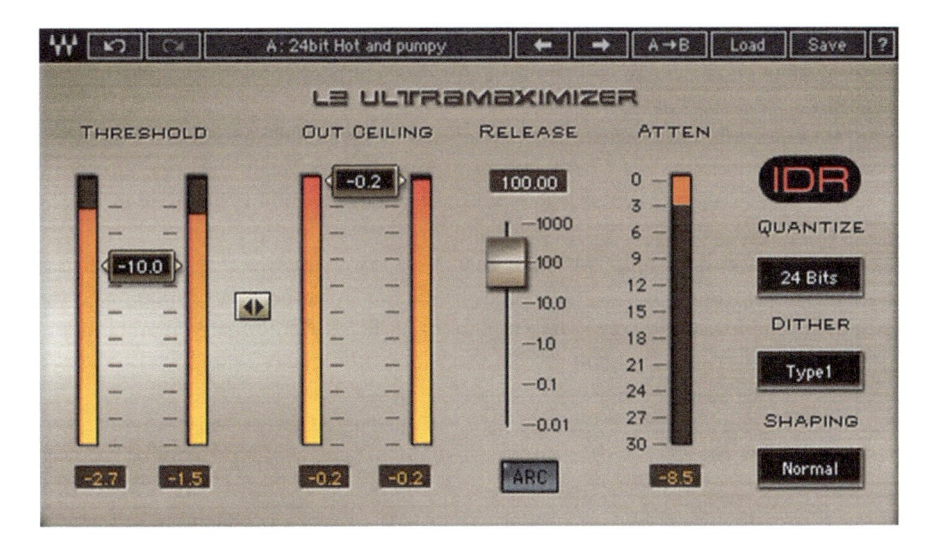

Fig. 12.15 Waves L2 ultramaximiser limiter. (Image courtesy of Waves Audio Ltd)

Audio Before and After Limiting

← Peaks in the audio material →

Before Limiting

← Amplitude of peaks reduced →

After Limiting

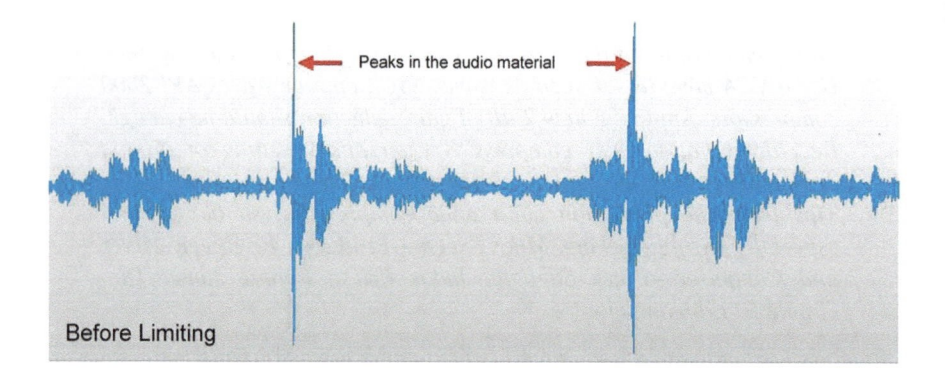

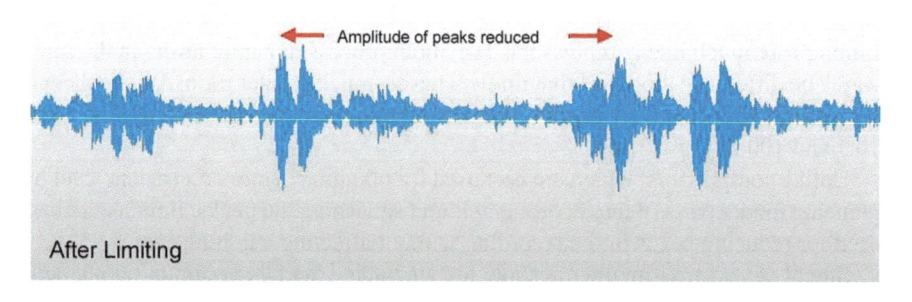

Fig. 12.16 Signal before and after limiting

a brick wall limiter should be used. As the name suggests, a brick wall limiter will absolutely prevent any signal from exceeding the output ceiling (Fig. 12.16).

Limiters usually have a ratio of 10:1 to 100:1, whereas brickwall limiters have a ratio of 1: Infinity. They use a look ahead feature to analyse and process transient peaks, with extremely fast attack and release times. Regular limiters react to signal peaks as they happen, whereas brickwall limiters begin to clamp down on the peaks before they happen, which is made possible by the look ahead feature.

Some limiters have only two main controls. In this case, the threshold control is used to set the trigger level—the level at which the signal becomes limited, and the output ceiling is used to set the maximum output level. Additionally, many limiters have control over the input gain, release time and dither (see Chap. 25: Dither).

▶ *Tip: It's ok to put a limiter on your master bus whilst you mix. Aiming for approximately 6 dB of gain reduction will give you an idea of what your mix will sound like when it's limited at the mastering stage. Remember to remove the limiter before you export your mix.*

Expanders

Expanders increase the difference in loudness between quieter and louder sections of the audio material, making quiet sounds quieter and loud sounds louder. This is called expanding the dynamic range.

Expanders are pretty much the opposite of compressors. They work by turning down the volume when the signal level falls below the threshold and turning it back up when the signal level goes above the threshold (Fig. 12.17).

Expanding is useful when you want to increase the dynamic range of the audio. For example, when you have a noisy recording and want to reduce the volume of the quieter parts so you don't notice the noise as much. A side effect of expanders is that they can change the way sounds decay and can end up silencing quieter parts of your audio that you want to keep. It pays to spend time fine tuning your expander parameters.

There are two types of expansion: downward and upward. Downward expansion, which is more common, reduces the level of signals that fall below the threshold. Upward expansion, which is less common, increases the level of signals that exceed the threshold level.

The main controls on an expander are attack, release, threshold and ratio.

The attack time sets how fast the expander responds to signal levels above or below the threshold, depending on whether upward or downward expansion is used.
The release time sets how fast it reacts when the signal level drops below the threshold.
The ratio determines how much to turn the volume down. A higher ratio results in the volume being turned down more. A high ratio of 12:1 or more is considered a noise gate.
Threshold determines the level at which the signal is either increased or decreased, depending on whether upward or downward expansion is being applied.

Fig. 12.17 Expander

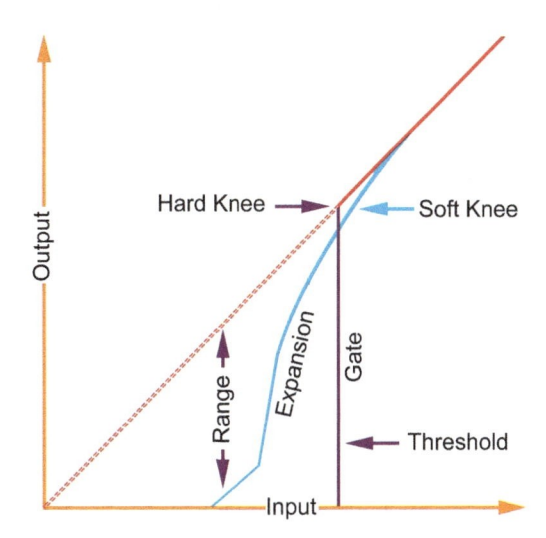

Noise Gates

Noise gates automatically mute the signal during parts of the audio track where the instrument is not being played and unmute again when the instrument is being played. Some noise gates are able to close partially, thereby reducing the level rather than muting the signal altogether.

Noise gates can be set to open and close automatically as needed and most give you control over how long it stays open and the speed at which it opens and shuts.

You may have recorded a great guitar part but during the parts of the song where you are not playing the guitar, the amp hums. A noise gate is an effective solution as it will simply shut during these parts and open again when triggered by the guitar playing again.

A noise gate can also be used as an effect to deliberately open and shut an instrument to create stuttering effects and more.

Noise gates usually have five main parameters: threshold, ratio, attack, hold and release.

Threshold—This sets the level at which the gate opens to let the sound through.
Ratio—The balance between the original sound and the gated sound. For example, instead of using the gate to totally mute the background ambience on a vocal track, you could allow some of the ambience to still be heard if desired.
Attack—Sets the time it takes for the gate to go from a closed state to an open state.
Hold—This sets the amount of time that the gate remains open, after the signal level has fallen below the threshold.
Release—Use this to set how long it takes for the gate to go from fully open to fully closed. A fast release quickly cuts off the sound, whereas a slower release is more like a fade out. Beware not to set the release too fast as it can induce a clicking sound.

▶ *Tip: Avoid using a gate whilst recording. If it's not set up properly, it can spoil the recording. It's best to use a gate when mixing as an insert on the channel so that you can adjust the settings at any stage of the mixing process.*

De-Essers

De-Essing is the method of reducing the loudness of frequencies in vocal recordings that are accentuated when an 'ess or shh' sound is made. This is called sibilance. Sibilance can also occur when a 't' sound is made. It is an unpleasant sound and can spoil an otherwise good vocal recording.

Sibilance is usually exhibited somewhere between 4 kHz and 14 kHz depending on the singer, the compression settings or the recording environment. Sibilance can also be problematic on individual instruments and even an entire mix.

Sibilance can be the result of:

- over compressing a vocal
- recording a vocal in a poor acoustic environment
- Wrong choice of microphone
- Poor mic positioning
- boosting frequencies that cause sibilance
- a singer who has a naturally sibilant voice.

There are a few ways to de-ess or reduce the effects of sibilance:

Automation

In your digital audio workstation (DAW), you can manually go through the vocal track and draw in automation to reduce the volume level on each occurrence of sibilance. This can be time consuming, but is very effective and does not cause the rest of the vocal to sound dull (Fig. 12.18).

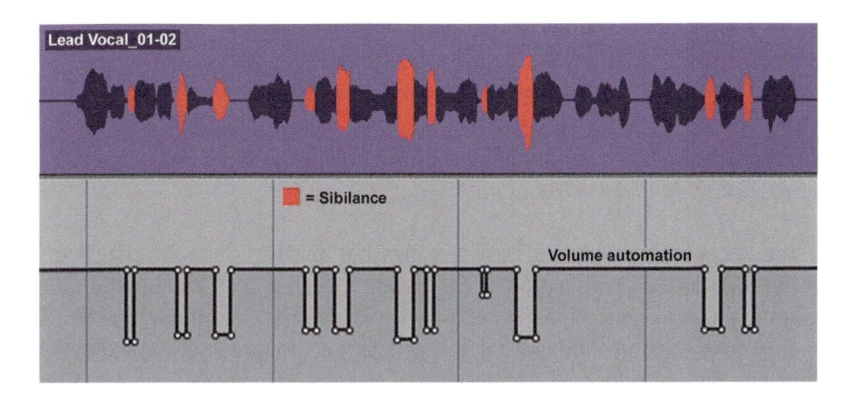

Fig. 12.18 Automating a reduction in level on sibilant parts of the signal

De-Esser Plugin

A De-Esser plugin is a type of equaliser/sidechain compressor that only reduces the loudness of a selected frequency when it crosses the threshold. Dial in the offending frequency, set the threshold and let the De-Esser do its thing. Most De-Esser have a solo button, which lets you hear just the frequencies that are being reduced. This is useful for fine tuning exactly where the offending frequency is.

Fig. 12.19 Waves De-Esser. (Image courtesy of Waves Audio Ltd)

▶ *Tip: Automate the threshold so that the amount of De-Essing changes according to the severity of the sibilance.*

There are occasions when a De-Esser may not totally reduce the effects of sibilance. In this case, a combination of De-Essing, equalising and automating may be necessary. There are also times when two De-Essers may be required as the vocal recording may exhibit sibilance at more than one frequency. For example, ess sounds may be too pronounced as well as fricatives—eff sounds (Fig. 12.19).

Dynamic Eq

Use dynamic equalisation (see Chap. 11: Equalisers) to reduce the loudness of the sibilant frequency. A parametric dynamic equaliser will allow you to pinpoint the sibilance accurately. Use a narrow Q (bandwidth) to zoom in on the offending frequency.

Sidechain Compression

Duplicate your vocal track and equalise the copy so that only the sibilance can be heard. Insert a compressor on your original vocal track and set its key input to bus

1. Assign the insert send on the equalised track to bus 1 and set the send level to 0 dB. Adjust the parameters on the compressor so that the signal from the equalised track triggers the compressor.

Separate Track

Edit the sibilant parts of the vocal onto another track and then equalise that track or reduce its level to reduce the intensity of sibilance (Fig. 12.20).

It may be that the sibilance problem is caused by a constantly moving resonance. In this case, try using a dynamic resonance suppressor (see Chap. 12: Dynamics—Resonance and Spectral Shaping) or a dynamic equaliser (see Chap. 11: Equalisers).

▶ *Tip: It's best to try and avoid sibilance at the source. Spend some time positioning the microphone in relation to the room boundaries and the singer. Increase or reduce the height of the microphone. A microphone aimed towards the singer's chest will result in more low-frequency content. When aimed at the singer's mouth, it will sound brighter. Try changing the angle of the microphone or try using a different one (see Chap. 7: Microphones—Recording Vocals).*

Fig. 12.20 Editing sibilant parts of the signal on a separate track

Resonance and Spectral Shaping

When there's a problematic resonance at a particular frequency that is consistent throughout the track, it can usually be corrected with equalisation. However, when the problematic resonance is dynamic—changing throughout the track, it will be difficult to pinpoint as its frequency band is constantly moving (Fig. 12.21).

Let's say you have recorded a great vocal performance but when you come to the mix, you notice a particularly annoying resonance in the higher frequency range. You try to equalise the resonance out with a narrow notch filter (see Chap. 11: Equalisers) but you are unable to pinpoint exactly where it is. This is because the problem is not static throughout the track. Sometimes there are multiple resonances at different frequencies, making the job of fixing the audio a lengthy and tedious task.

This is where spectral shaping comes in. Spectral shaping is a way of applying dynamic processing across the frequency spectrum automatically according to user-set parameters. It applies compression and equalisation uniquely to selected frequency bands without crossing over to other bands. It's a bit like having multiple De-Essers (see Chap. 12: Dynamics—De-Essers) or dynamic equalisers all in one (see Chap. 11: Equalisers).

A great example of a dynamic resonance suppressor is Soothe by Oeksound. It is a spectral shaping processor designed for suppressing mid- and high-frequency resonances. It works by automatically detecting resonances in the audio and then applying a gain reduction that matches the input signal (Fig. 12.22).

Designed primarily to be used on vocals, it can be great for solving problems in many other applications too such as transparent De-Essing and removing fretboard noises on acoustic guitar. The processing does not induce crossover artefacts or pre-ringing.

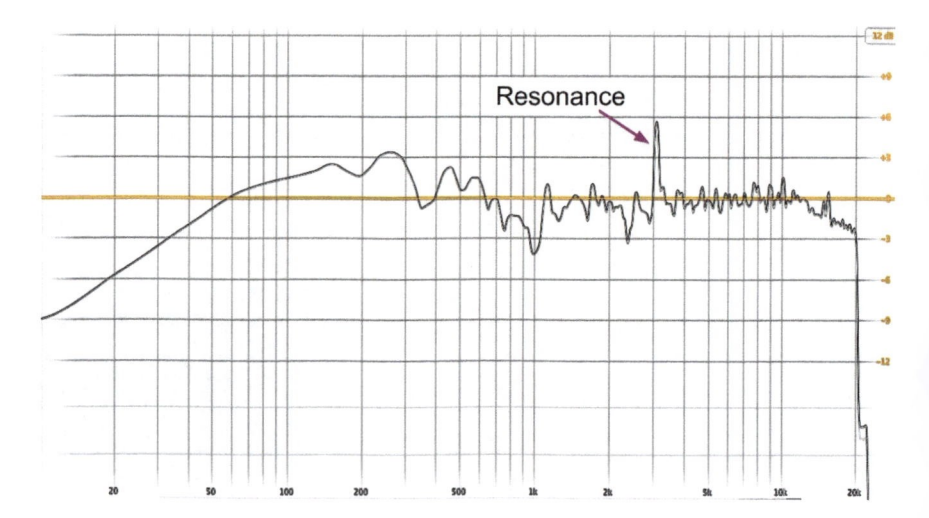

Fig. 12.21 Resonance

Resonance and Spectral Shaping

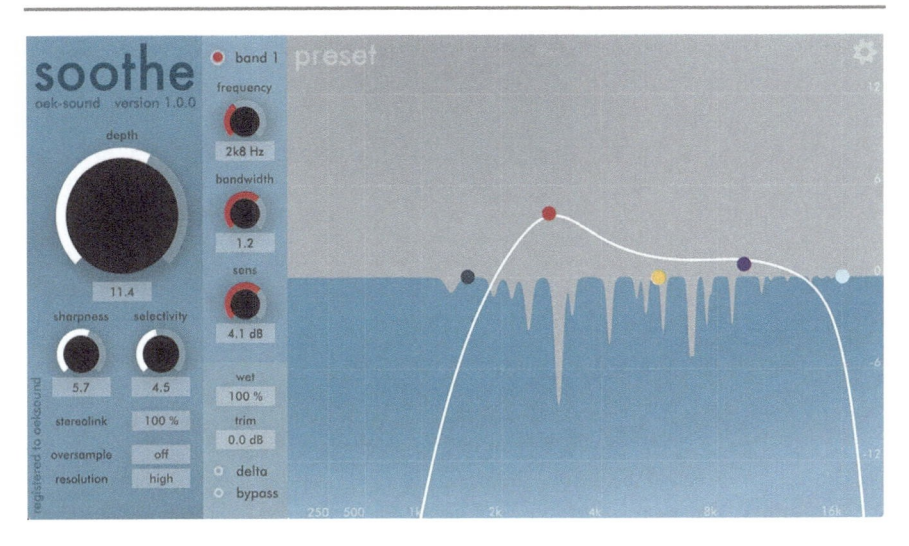

Fig. 12.22 OEK-sound Soothe—dynamic resonance suppressor. (Image courtesy of OEK-sound)

A dynamic resonance suppressor is a very handy tool to keep in your arsenal of plugins and, most likely, one that will get used quite often.

▶ **Chapter 12 Tasks:** The following tasks will enable a deeper understanding of how dynamic processing can alter a recorded sound.

- Listen carefully to the Audio Examples 29 to 45.
- Can you describe the effects that an extreme limiting has on the audio signal?
- What do you think are the benefits of sidechain compression on a drum track, for example?
- Try recording a vocal track and applying a De-Esser before and after a compressor/limiter chain. What works best?
- Apply settings from the Guide to Compressor Settings in this chapter and do some A/B comparisons of the bypassed sound compared to the compressed sound. Set the make-up gain so that the resulting volume levels are the same; this will enable you to more accurately hear the difference the compressor is making.

Effects

13

▶ **Learning Outcomes**

By the end of this chapter, the reader will be able to:
- Describe the functions of audio effects processing for reverberation, delay/echo, modulation (phasers, flanger, chorus) and distortion/saturation.
- Recall useful settings and parameters of controls used within effects processing.
- Show a working knowledge of the use of applied settings within effects processing.
- Recall the function, parameters and use of pitch correction in audio processing.

Reverberation (Reverb)

Reverb is created when multiple, fast, complex echoes are merged together. The resulting sound is a type of ambience that the listener hears as one effect.

In recording and mixing scenarios, reverb is used to recreate the natural ambience of different rooms and spaces without having to physically record in those spaces. Reverbs can also be used to deliberately create weird, unnatural and crazy spaces. Some reverbs are created using digital algorithms whilst convolution reverbs use impulse responses—samples of actual physical spaces (Fig. 13.1).

There are five categories of reverb type:

Supplementary Information The online version contains supplementary material available at https://doi.org/10.1007/978-3-031-40067-4_13. The videos can be accessed individually by clicking the DOI link in the accompanying figure caption or by scanning this link with the SN More Media App.

Fig. 13.1 Waves H reverb. (Image courtesy of Waves Audio Ltd)

Reverb type	Reverb sound
Hall	Large concert halls have typical reverb times of around 1–4 seconds. Hall reverbs simulate the sound of these spaces. Some plugins emulate the reverberation characteristics of many world class concert halls.
Chamber	Chamber reverbs simulate smaller spaces than halls with typical reverb times of 0.3–1.5 seconds. These types of rooms were used for small chamber orchestras.
Room	Room reverbs are generally shorter, up to 1 second, and simulate the sound of a variety of typical rooms. This can be anything from typical living rooms, bathrooms and even cupboards.
Plate	Plate reverbs have a large metal plate which resonates when the sound hits it. They have transducers at each end. One which emits the sound and the other which picks up the resulting reverberation and feeds it to the output. With plate reverbs, the sound vibrations are two dimensional through a large flat metal sheet, whereas room reverbs are three dimensional vibrations through the air.
Spring	Spring reverbs work like plate reverbs, with transducers at each end. Unlike plate reverbs, the sound is transmitted through metal springs.

Reverberation (Reverb)

In the real world, when we hear natural reverberation, for example, when you clap your hands in a large empty room, we hear the initial sound followed by an early reflection of the sound bouncing off the room's boundaries. This is then followed by the tail or sustain of the reverb and then the decay as it fades away. This has a big impact on how we perceive the size of the room. Understanding this natural phenomenon can help you to create more natural sounding reverbs using plugins in your digital audio workstation.

▶ Tip 1: Reverb can have a big influence on the overall sound of your mix. Spend time choosing the right reverb early on in your mix.
▶ Tip 2: The greater the reverb wet/dry ratio is, the further away the singer or instrument will appear to be in the mix.
▶ Tip 3: Many reverbs have a pre-delay function. Adding a few milliseconds of pre-delay to the reverb will delay its start time in relation to the source signal. This allows the transient (see Chap. 17: Transients) of the sound to be heard without being masked by the reverb sound. Pre-delay can be set so that it is in time with the tempo and groove of the song. Use an app such as MusicMath by Laurent Colson to quickly find the right delay time (Fig. 13.2).

Fig. 13.2 MusicMath by Laurent Colson

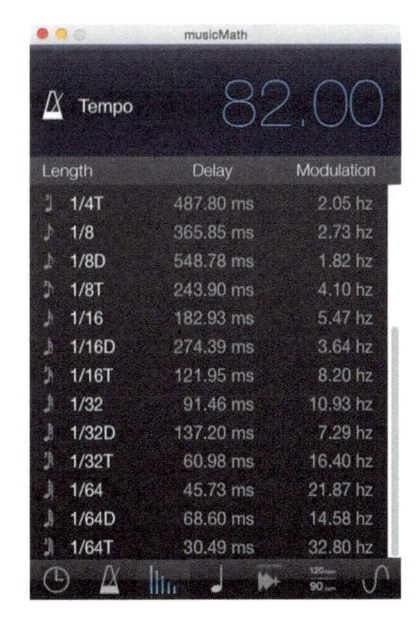

- *Tip 4: Adding a high-pass filter after the reverb to remove unnecessary low frequencies will make it less muddy and easier to hear (see Chap. 11: Equalisers). Note: Some reverb plugins have a high-pass filter built in.*
- *Tip 5: Adding a low-pass filter can help to clean up the reverb. Try low passing down to around 10 kHz.*
- *Tip 6: Experiment with different reverb effects to create unique sounds. For example, try adding a phaser after the reverb to give it a swooshing type sound, or try sidechaining (see Chap. 12: Compressors) the reverb to the kick drum to give it a pumping sound.*
- *Tip 7: Try shifting the pitch of the reverb using an octaver or add a tremolo effect to make it warble.*
- *Tip 8: Print the reverb to an audio track and reverse the audio to create a 'sucking' type of effect. Note: you may have to shift the timing of the reversed reverb track backwards or forwards a little to get it to groove with the send instrument.*
- *Tip 9: Setting the reverb decay time so that it fades out before the next instrument hit will reduce muddiness and masking. For example, set the reverb tail on a snare drum so that it ends before the next snare hit (Fig. 13.3).*

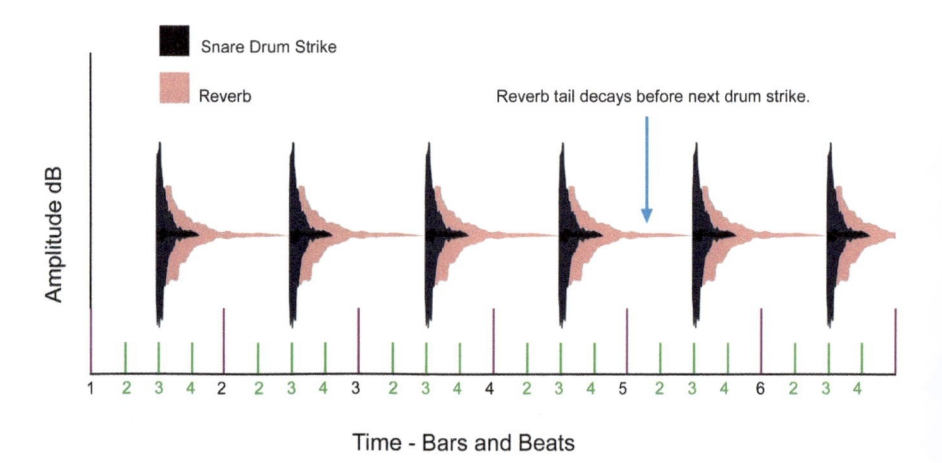

Fig. 13.3 Reverb tail decays before the next drum strike

- *Tip 10: You may not need to add any reverb to the signal. A dry signal will sound closer to the listener.*
- ***Tips from the pros:*** *Sometimes I'll send to the same effect on two different sends. One is static. The other is automated up and down for*

different sections or words. It's much easier to change and adjust without killing your general vibe. Plus, maybe you decide later, those cool delay throws will sound better through or with another effect. The work is already done. **Kevin Churko—Producer, Engineer and Songwriter**—*Disturbed, Ozzy Osbourne, Shania Twain, Five Finger Death Punch, The Corrs, Britney Spears and more.*

Delay and Echo

Delay and Echo are essentially the same thing. The main difference is that echo is a natural phenomenon, whereas delay is an electronic or digital implementation of that effect.

Delay/echo occurs when the source signal is repeated. This can be anything from a single repeat after the initial sound, to multiple, complex, rhythmic, overlapping repeats, or any combination thereof, lasting for several seconds before fading away.

Delay/echo can be used for many applications from creating width on a vocal or instrument, to making crazy otherworldly effects (Figs. 13.4 and 13.5).

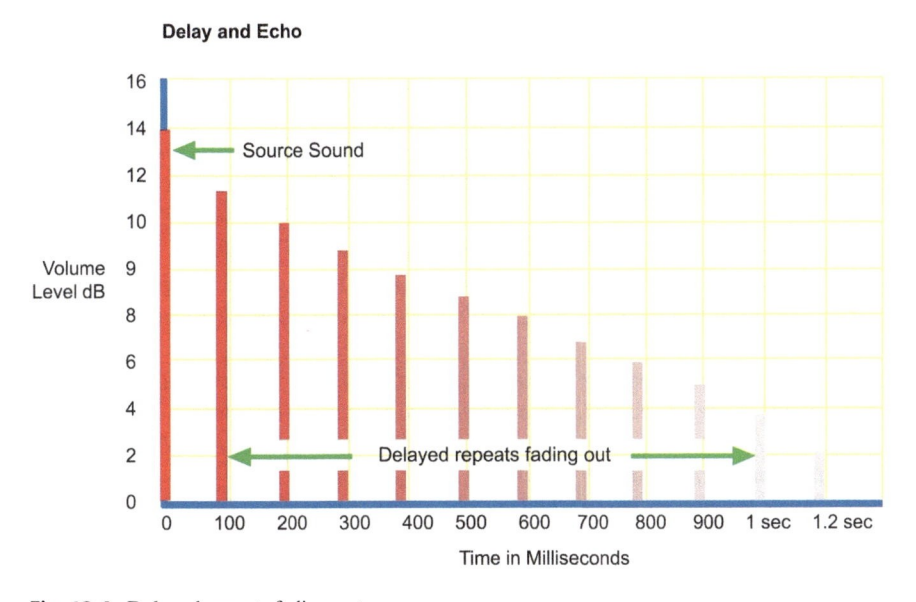

Fig. 13.4 Delayed repeats fading out

Fig. 13.5 Waves H-delay. (Image courtesy of Waves Audio Ltd)

Delay and echo plugins have pretty much the same controls. Typical parameters are:

Delay/echo parameter	Function
Feedback	Sets how long the effect lasts for/the number of repeats
Dry/wet mix	Adjusts the balance between the dry signal and the effected signal
Delay	Sets the note value of the repeats. For example, 1/8th note, 1/16th note, dotted and triplet notes.
Ms	Sets the value of repeats in milliseconds rather than notes
Output	Sets the output level of the effect
Tap	Tap the tempo of the repeats rather than setting by milliseconds or notes
BPM	Locks the tempo of the repeats to a specified tempo
Host	Locks the tempo of the repeats to the current DAW session tempo

▶ *Tip 1: To add width to a vocal, pan it hard left and pan a single repeat delayed by approximately 12 milliseconds, hard right (see Chap. 18: Panning).*
▶ *Tip 2: To add a sense of space and to give character to your lead vocal, pan it to the centre and add a stereo delay with different note values on the left and right. For example, try a 16th note on the left and an 8th note on the right with a wet mix of around 15%.*
▶ *Tip 3: When the delay value is approximate rather than rigid, the result will sound more natural. Set the delay by milliseconds rather than a note value. Use your ears.*
▶ *Tip 4: Delay throws: A delay throw is a triggered or automated delay or echo only on a certain word, note or beat, used to accentuate that part. Most commonly, delay throws have been used in reggae and dub music for decades though there's no reason why they can't be used in any kind of music. Try automating the effect only on certain notes in the phrase. For example, add an echo to the last hit in the bar of a drum part, or the last word in a vocal phrase so that its effect carries over to the next bar.*

Modulation: Phasers, Flangers and Chorus

Phasers, flangers and chorus effects all work similarly by taking the input signal, splitting it into two exact copies and then delaying one copy slightly. The result is then merged back into a single signal (Fig. 13.6).

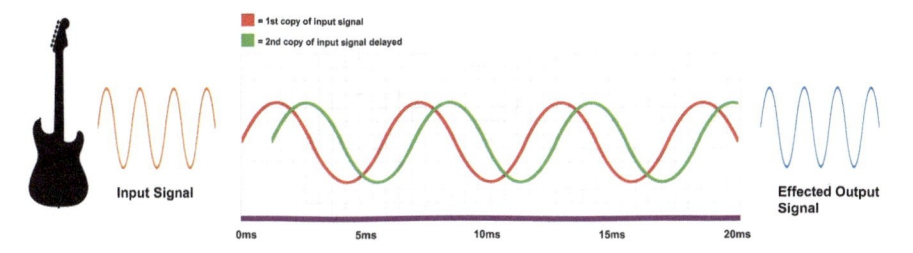

Fig. 13.6 Phaser, flanger and chorus effects

Phasers (or phase shifters), delay one copy of the signal which creates peaks and dips across the frequency response of the input signal. The phaser then sweeps up and down through the frequency range which creates a swelling effect. Phasers usually have control over the speed and depth of the sweep.

Flangers work in the same way as phasers, though they usually have a shorter delay, up to 20 milliseconds, which is constantly fluctuating. Flangers sound more dramatic than phasers.

Chorus effects also split the signal into two and delay one copy. They use a longer delay than flangers and phasers, which creates a more subtle effect. Chorus effects sound great in stereo, creating a 3D type of effect (Fig. 13.7).

▶ Tip 1: Chorus effects can be great for adding depth and stereo width to a signal.
▶ Tip 2: Flanging is a great effect on guitars and even on vocals. It can add movement to the signal as well as vibrato and depth. Experiment with subtle to extreme flanging.
▶ Tip 3: Phasers can add a great swooshing effect that rises and falls. They sound particularly great on guitars, though experimenting with phasers on just about anything can yield some interesting results.

Fig. 13.7 Soundtoys PhaseMistress. (Image courtesy of Soundtoys)

Distortion and Saturation

Distortion comes in many forms. It can be anything from quite subtle to very heavy fuzz. Distortion sounds are created by driving the input stage of an amplifier and overloading the circuit. The harder the input stage is driven, the more distortion is created. An overloaded circuit cannot reproduce higher signal levels which results in the signal's peak getting crushed. This creates either odd or even harmonic overtones. In digital recording, distortion plugins use algorithms to emulate the behaviour of an overloading circuit in order to recreate these odd and even harmonics.

Even harmonics are multiples of the input frequency. For example, if the input frequency is 90 Hz, the first even harmonic would be 180 Hz (2 × 90 Hz) followed by 360 Hz (4 × 90 Hz), then 720 Hz (8 × 90 Hz) and so on.

Odd harmonics are uneven multiples of the input frequency. With the same example input frequency of 90 Hz, the first odd harmonic would be 270 Hz (3 × 90 Hz) followed by 450 Hz (5 × 90 Hz), then 630 Hz (7 × 90 Hz) and so on.

Generally speaking, even harmonics are more pleasant to listen to.

Saturation comes from the old days of recording to analogue magnetic tape. In digital audio, the maximum level at which a signal can be recorded is 0 dBFS. Any signal exceeding this will be clipped (see Chap. 6: Gain Staging). With analogue tape, any signal exceeding the maximum level is handled with less brutality. Magnetic tape is more forgiving of signals exceeding the maximum level, and the result is a pleasant sound that has a combination of compression and distortion characteristics.

▶ **Tips from the pros:** *Saturation is your friend.* **Kevin Churko—Producer, Engineer and Songwriter—***Disturbed, Ozzy Osbourne, Shania Twain, Five Finger Death Punch, The Corrs, Britney Spears and more.*

What are saturation and distortion effects good for? Low-bass frequencies can sometimes disappear when played back on small speakers. Saturation and distortion can enhance the harmonic overtones of bass instruments to make them audible on small speakers and at quieter volumes. Saturation and distortion are not just for low frequencies. These effects can enhance the harmonic overtones of any signal, from guitars to drums and vocals.

▶ *Tip: Try using parallel processing (see Chap. 27: Dynamics—Compressors) to blend in a heavily distorted copy of the signal with the original dry signal. If your distortion plugin has a mix control, you can use this instead of creating a duplicate track. This can breathe life into dull-sounding tracks and add warmth to thinner sounds.*

Inserting Effects

Any effect plugin from reverb to delay, to modulation can be added to a signal in one of two ways.

1. The effect can be inserted directly into the instrument or vocal channel. The effects mix knob can be used to set the wet/dry ratio. Effect plugins would usually be inserted last in the chain unless you specifically want them to be processed with the same compression, Eq or other processing as the input signal.
2. If you want to use the same effect on more than one channel, you can create a bus (see Chap. 14: Subgroups). Insert the effect on the bus channel and set it to 100% wet. You can then send any instrument or vocal channel to the effect by adjusting the channel's send level.

▶ *Tip: The send level can be set to pre or post fader. Pre fader means that the send level is sent before and not affected by the volume fader. If you have a vocal with a reverb send, for example, when you adjust the volume fader, the reverb level will remain the same. When the send is set to post fader, the amount of reverb being sent to the effect will change relative to the volume fader.*

Pitch Correction

Perhaps one of the most essential modern-day tools to have in your arsenal of effects is a pitch correction plugin.

With a pitch correction plugin, it is possible to tune vocals and instrument parts, adjust their timing, level and formants to create flawless takes that are necessary by today's production standards.

At the time of writing, the three most popular pitch correction plugins are Antares AutoTune, Waves Tune and Celemony Melodyne.

Pitch correction plugins can be set to automatically tune the vocal according to user-set parameters such as key, scale and whether and to what extent notes with vibrato should be processed. Processing is usually applied to the audio content of a track in real time.

Correction tools such as Celemony's Melodyne capture the vocal into the plugin so that it can be processed extensively. Once captured, the vocal waveform is displayed on a piano roll, showing the current untuned pitch and unedited vibrato of each note (Fig. 13.8).

Each note of the vocal part can then be moved close to, or snapped to, an absolute note value for perfect tuning. In addition, notes can be split for more precise editing, vibrato can be increased or reduced, lengths can be shortened or extended, gain can be increased or decreased and formants can be changed to compensate for tonal changes or to be used as a deliberate effect. Pitch correction plugins are not just for vocals. You can capture any audio and process it as required. A unique feature of Melodyne Studio is that you can capture chords and then tune individual notes within them. For example, you may wish to capture a guitar part and retune just one of the strings.

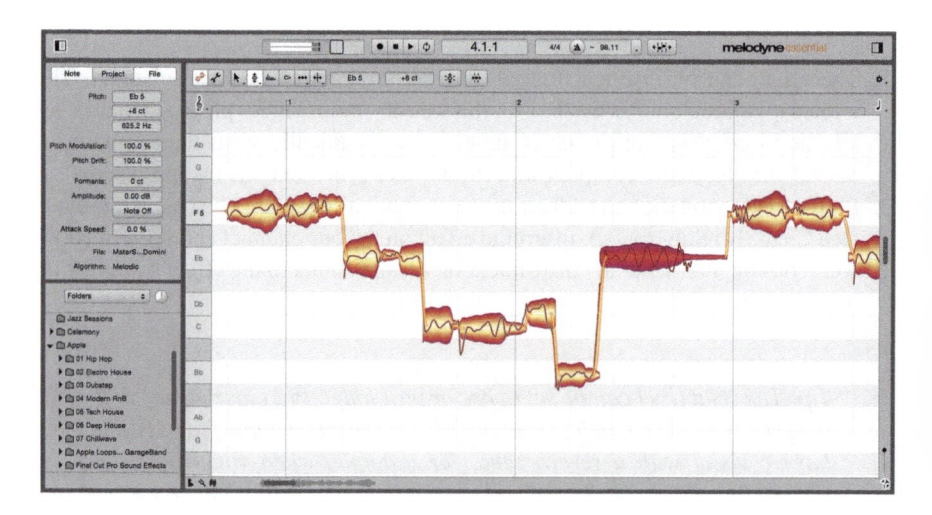

Fig. 13.8 Celemony Melodyne plugin. (Image courtesy of Celemony)

Once you're happy with your edited audio, you can either leave the pitch correction plugin inserted on your track, in case you wish to make any further tweaks later on, and insert any Eq or compression plugins after it, or you can bounce the corrected audio down to a new track and work with it as you would with any audio tracks in your session. Of course, you can also freeze the track if your DAW supports the freeze function.

▶ *Tip: With some pitch correction plugins, you can create some cool vocal effects by playing the desired pitch in real time via your midi controller, and record to a MIDI track in your DAW. For example, duplicate your lead vocal track and insert your pitch correction plugin on it. Create a MIDI track and set it up to send MIDI to the pitch correction plugin. Now you can play a harmony to the lead vocal on the duplicated track and record the notes to a MIDI track. I sometimes do this two or three times in order to create a complete backing vocal just from a single lead vocal. Note, for this to work effectively, you'll most likely need to set the correction amount on the plugin to full.*

▶ **Chapter 13 Tasks:** The following tasks will introduce you to a range of effects and the transformative results these have on recorded sounds.

- Listen to all the Reverberation Audio Examples 46 to 50 can you think of specific examples where the different types of reverbs would suit a voice recording? For example, in what context would a room reverb be more suitable than a plate reverb?
- Listen to the other Effects Audio Examples 51 to 55 and consider what genres of music may be applicable to specific effects.
- Try individually applying each of the effects (reverbs, echo, phaser, flanger, chorus, distortion, saturation and pitch correction) to the same source material and listen to how it alters the perception of the sound.
- Try stacking multiple effects on a single sound source and note the combined results of different combinations.
- Experiment with applying Eq after a reverb effect and note how the reduction of certain frequencies can alter how it sits within a full mix.

Subgroups

14

> Learning Outcomes

By the end of this chapter, the reader will be able to:
- Explain the use of subgroups and VCA channels in routing multiple channels into a separate channel.
- Recall a step-by-step guide to setting up and routing subgroups.

There are times when you need to route the outputs of several channels simultaneously to the input of another channel.

A subgroup is simply an auxiliary channel that is configured to allow the outputs of other channels to be routed to its inputs, much like how all of your channels end up going into one stereo master channel.

Subgroups and VCA

When multiple channels are routed to a subgroup, the subgroup fader acts as a master volume control, turning its input level up or down without altering the individual channel levels. When multiple channels are routed to a VCA, commonly found on mixing desks, the VCA fader acts as a remote control, turning the individual channel levels up or down together by the same amount. A benefit of using VCA is that post fader effect wet/dry balances are preserved when its fader is adjusted.

Sending groups of channels to a subgroup has many advantages.

- Some reverbs and effects require a lot of processing power. Adding a separate plug-in to each drum channel may put a strain on your computer's CPU. Instead, you can send all of your drums to a subgroup and insert a single reverb plug-in on it.

- You will most likely want the entire drum kit to sound like it is in the same space with the same Eq, compression and effects. You can adjust the overall level of the drums in relation to everything else, without affecting the balance of the drums in relation to each other.
- In order to quickly try different Eq or effect settings, you only need to change the parameters of one device.
- You have the added advantage of one fader for the overall level of your selected instruments.

In the diagram below, you can see how individual drum channels have been routed to a subgroup (Fig. 14.1).

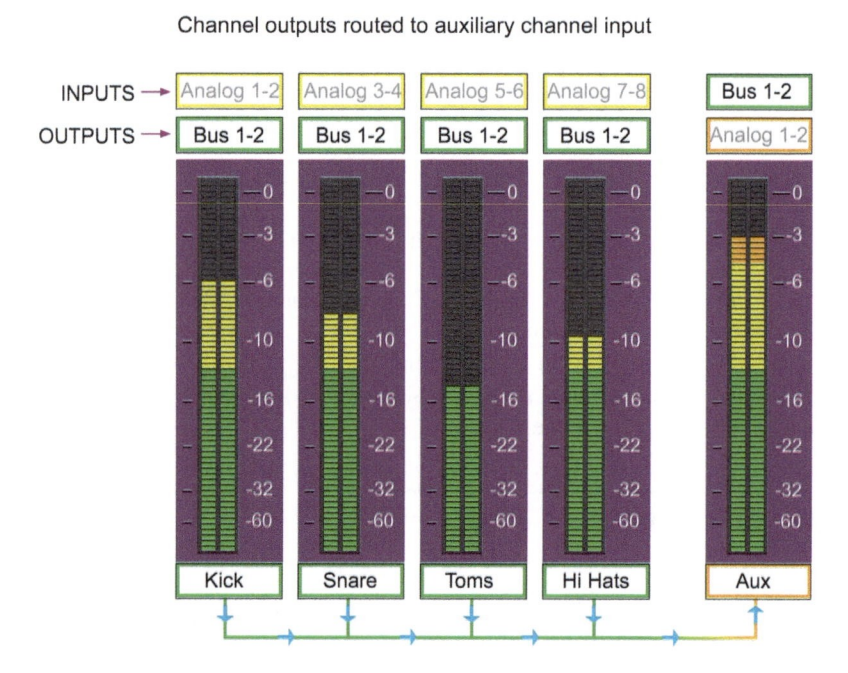

Fig. 14.1 Channel outputs routed to auxiliary input

Step-By-Step Guide to Routing

1. Create a new subgroup channel and set its input to bus 1 for a mono channel or 1 & 2 for a stereo channel. Set its output to 1 & 2 or whichever is your usual output assignment.
2. Set the output of the channel you wish to send to the subgroup to bus 1 (mono) or 1 & 2 (stereo).
3. Repeat step 2 for each channel you want to send to the subgroup.

You can route any combination of channels to a subgroup, and you can have more than one subgroup. For example, you may wish to send all of the drum channels to subgroup bus 1 & 2 and all of your backing vocals to subgroup bus 3 & 4. You could send all the instrument channels, including the outputs of any subgroups to one subgroup and all the vocal channels to another, thereby allowing you to change the vocal to instrument balance with only two faders. You could use the insert sends to send the channel simultaneously to a subgroup with an effect on it, such as reverb. There are many possibilities, and exploring different methods of routing is recommended.

▶ **Chapter 14 Tasks:** The following tasks will provide you with a drum mixing template, utilising and expanding your understanding of subgroups.

- Follow the step-by-step guide to routing in this chapter to build a mix template with multiple channels for a full drum set, along with the VCA auxiliary channel to control overall volume.
- Save this as a drum mix template for future use when a quick template is required to achieve a speedy overall drum mix.
- Add in an extra channel with a pre-loaded compressor in the FX insert as a parallel compression channel.

Monitoring in Mono

15

▶ **Learning Outcomes**

By the end of this chapter, the reader will be able to:
- Explain the benefits and reasons for monitoring in mono.
- Recall techniques to enable monitoring in mono.

The human brain finds it difficult to pinpoint the location of lower frequencies. Lower frequencies are omnidirectional—they travel in all directions—whereas higher frequencies travel directly towards the ear (see Chap. 1: An Introduction to How Sound Works—Sound Dispersion). For this reason, it is common practice to mix lower frequency elements such as kick drums and bass guitar to the centre mono part of the stereo field.

Professional mix engineers monitor in mono as It is easier to judge the relative levels and equalisation of instruments, voices and effects when they are perceived as being on top of each other rather than when they are spread between your speakers. When your stereo tracks are folded down to mono, it will become obvious if there are any phase issues. The sound may become thin and hollow, and elements of it may disappear altogether (see Chap. 8: Phase) (Fig. 15.1).

Balance and equalise your tracks whilst monitoring in mono and you'll have more accurate control over your audio parts. When you switch back to stereo, your mix will sound bigger with greater separation between the instruments.

Pan your audio tracks to the desired positions whilst monitoring in stereo (see Chap. 18: Panning) and then switch to mono to balance and equalize instruments, voices and effects levels.

Ideally, you need to be listening in true mono from a single source point or a dedicated, centrally positioned speaker. If this is not possible for any reason, then

© The Author(s), under exclusive license to Springer Nature
Switzerland AG 2024
S. Duggal, *Record, Mix and Master*,
https://doi.org/10.1007/978-3-031-40067-4_15

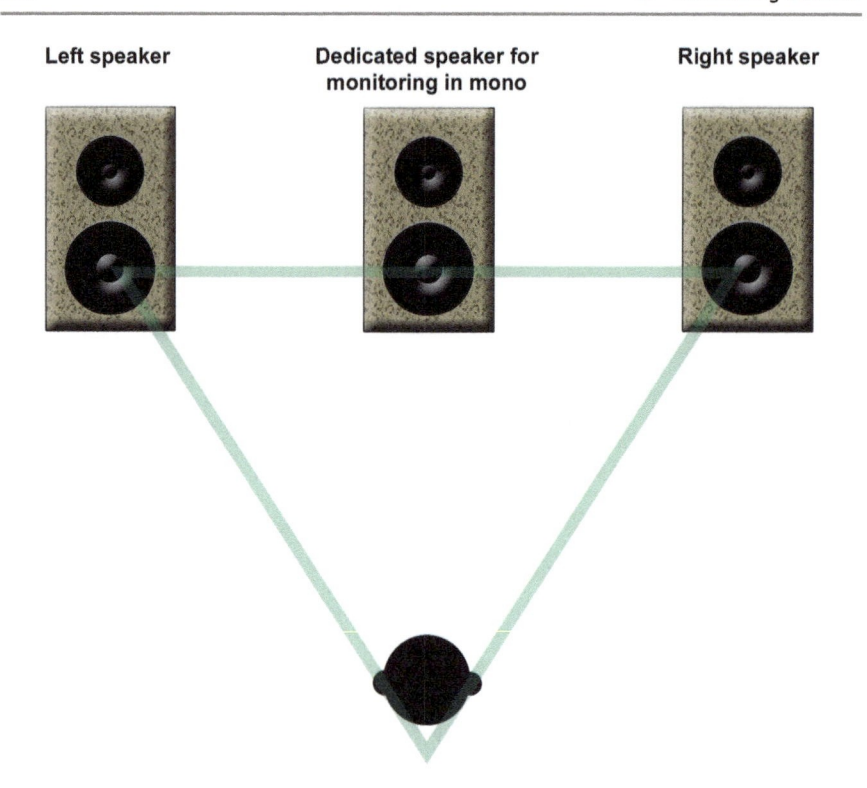

Fig. 15.1 Monitoring in mono

switching your stereo speakers to mono, turning one speaker off and monitoring quietly on the other is a good alternative.

- ▶ *Tip 1: If your DAW or audio interface does not have a mono switch, you can insert a stereo to mono plugin on your master channel.*
- ▶ *Tip 2: Try to record all of your tracks in mono. If you have a stereo virtual instrument part, for example, use only the left side or the right side and use effect plugins to create the wider stereo image. This way, when your track is played back on mono systems, it will always sound solid and balanced.*

- ▶ **Chapter 15 Tasks:** The following tasks will contribute to you creating a mix that will work well on mono systems as well as stereo and improve your knowledge of instrument balance within a mix.

- Import a stereo mix into your DAW that has some wide stereo panning in the instrumentation

15 Monitoring in Mono

- Switch the output to a mono output and check for any anomalies. In particular, can you hear any instruments phasing?
- Ensure your head is located in the 'sweet spot' when listening back.
- As an experiment, execute a mix which places the lower frequency instruments panned hard left and the higher frequency instruments panned hard right.
- How does this sound when played back in mono?

Mid/Side Processing

16

▶ **Learning Outcomes**

By the end of this chapter, the reader will be able to:
- Summarise the benefits and reasons for mid-side processing.
- Apply techniques of mid-side processing to mixing and mastering.

A stereo audio file has two channels, left and right. When these channels play through left and right speakers at an equal level, a phantom centre between the two speakers is created. The phantom centre contains identical information that is present in both the left and right channels—this is the mid part of the signal. Removing this information would leave only the information that differs between the left and right channels—the side information. So, the side information is accessed by subtracting the mid information from the whole signal, and vice versa (Fig. 16.1).

Mid/side processing is the technique of equalising, compressing or effecting the phantom centre part and the left and right parts of the signal separately. Mid/side processing can be used to either boost or cut the mid or side audio information. If the level of the centre part of a stereo signal is increased, the listener will hear more of the mono content of the sound. If the levels of the sides are increased, the listener will hear a wider sound (Fig. 16.2).

A good mix with instruments and vocals placed carefully in the stereo field may not need any mid/side processing. Pay attention to creating width in your mix and use mid/side processing subtly to enhance elements of the entire mix, should you need it. You can also use mid/side processing as a deliberate effect.

Plugins that are mid/side enabled, such as waves centre, must be used to treat the centre and side content separately. The mid/side-enabled plugin will encode the stereo image for processing and then encode the signal output back to regular left and right information once processed (Fig. 16.3).

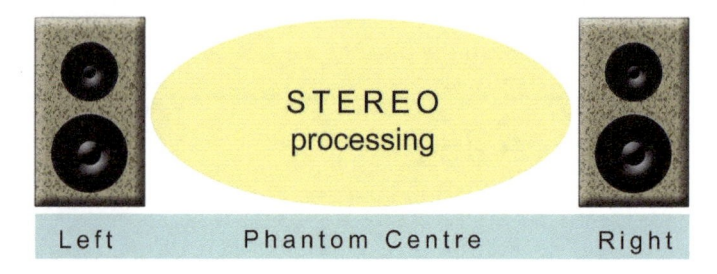

Fig. 16.1 Stereo processing

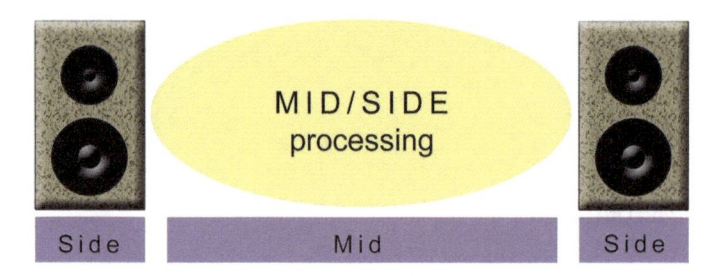

Fig. 16.2 Mid/side processing

Fig. 16.3 Waves centre mid/side processor. (Image courtesy of Waves Audio Ltd)

16 Mid/Side Processing

Mid/side processing can be a great tool for adding solidity and width to any stereo signal. It is also a valuable tool for mastering applications. It can be in the form of equalisation, compression, gating, reverb, delay, distortion and other effects.

▶ *Tip: Try using some mid/side Eq to bring out the mid-frequency information on a stereo keyboard part without interfering with similar frequencies on the lead vocal which would usually be panned in the centre.*

▶ **Chapter 16 Tasks:** The following tasks will contribute to your understanding of creating space within a mix using mid-side processing.

- Insert a mid-side processor onto a track with a stereo synthesiser pad and vocal part.
- Experiment with reducing the levels and Eq on the mid frequencies of the synthesiser and note how this alters perception of the vocal part.

Transients 17

▶ **Learning Outcomes**

By the end of this chapter, the reader will be able to:
- Explain what transients are in relation to an audio recording.
- Illustrate ADSR envelopes to highlight transients.
- Explain how to control transients within the mixing stage.

A transient is the initial attack of a sound—the pluck of a guitar string before the note sustains or the moment a stick makes contact with a drum before the skin resonates.

Transients are very short, have a high amplitude and have no tonal information. They usually contain higher frequencies than the harmonic content (Fig. 17.1).

Sometimes a sound may have too much of a transient which can be painful to listen to, or it can make the sound difficult to compress and place in the mix. Sometimes there can be too little causing the source to sound weak and without impact.

A transient shaper is a dynamic tool that gives you control over the envelope curve—the attack, decay, sustain and release, and transient response of a sound. It can be used to increase or decrease the initial attack of the sound as well as give you control over the sustain.

Transient shapers do not change the dynamic range of the sound in the way that compressors do (Fig. 17.2).

Transient shapers are great for making drums sound punchier, for making guitar string plucks softer, for giving synths more attack or for removing or restoring transients that have been over boosted or cut during the recording process (Fig. 17.3).

Supplementary Information The online version contains supplementary material available at https://doi.org/10.1007/978-3-031-40067-4_17. The videos can be accessed individually by clicking the DOI link in the accompanying figure caption or by scanning this link with the SN More Media App.

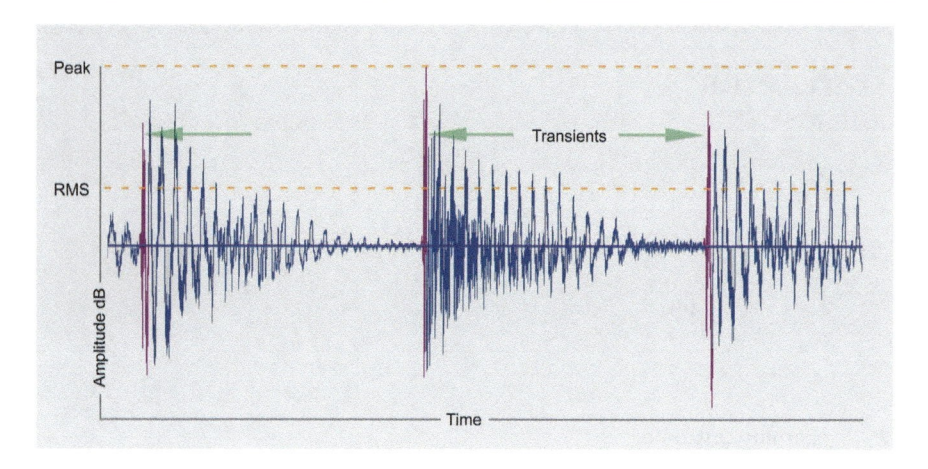

Fig. 17.1 Transients

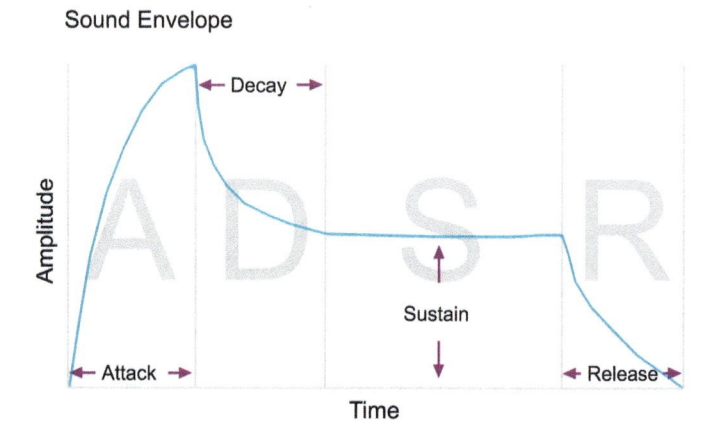

Fig. 17.2 Sound envelope—attack, decay, sustain and release

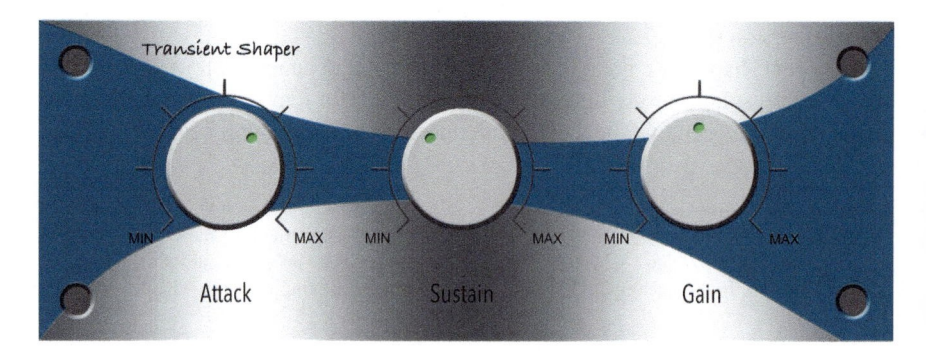

Fig. 17.3 The controls on a typical transient shaper plugin

17 Transients

Of course, a transient shaper is not the only tool available for dealing with transients. If, for example, you wanted to soften the transient on a sound, you could use a compressor such as the UAD 1176 with an extremely fast attack and release time and around ½ dB to 1 dB of gain reduction (see Chap. 12: Dynamics—Compressors). A slower attack time will preserve the transient. Distortion, tape saturation (see Chap. 13: Effects) and clipping are also useful tools for taming harsh transients.

▶ **Chapter 17 Tasks:** The following tasks will improve your understanding of overall sound envelopes alongside your ability to sculpt transients in individual recordings.

- Familiarise yourself with the ADSR envelope.
- Import a single snare drum sample into your DAW and zoom in until you are able to recognise the areas within the snare drum sound that represent the attack, the decay, the sustain and the release.
- Experiment with softening the transient of the snare drum sample using a transient shaper plug-in, or if not available, try using a compressor to achieve the same effect.

Panning

18

▶ **Learning Outcomes**

By the end of this chapter, the reader will be able to:
- Evaluate panoramic placement of sounds in the stereo field from left to right.
- Describe what is meant by the Pan law.
- Recall approaches to creating stereo images with a range of instrumentation and settings.

Panning refers to the panoramic placement of sounds in the stereo field from left to right.

Each channel in a DAW has a rotary pan knob. Some DAWs have single-pan knobs that allow you to move the position of a track from left to right. Others have separate left- and right-pan knobs for each channel, giving you individual control of the left and right sides of the stereo audio channel.

Panning is straightforward. Decide where you want your instrument or voice to be placed in the stereo field and use the pan knob to point it there (Fig. 18.1).

Imagine the pan control knob as a clock. The centre is 12:00, hard left is 7:00 and hard right is 5:00 (Fig. 18.2).

There are no rules to panning. You can place anything anywhere you want in the stereo field. There are some guidelines that will help your mixes sit alongside current production standards:

Kick drums are generally panned at 12:00 in the centre of the stereo field, so that each speaker receives the same amount of low-frequency content. This is also the norm with bass guitar or any other low-frequency content. When the low-frequency content of your mix is spread evenly between the speakers, it will sound solid and balanced.

Supplementary Information The online version contains supplementary material available at https://doi.org/10.1007/978-3-031-40067-4_18. The videos can be accessed individually by clicking the DOI link in the accompanying figure caption or by scanning this link with the SN More Media App.

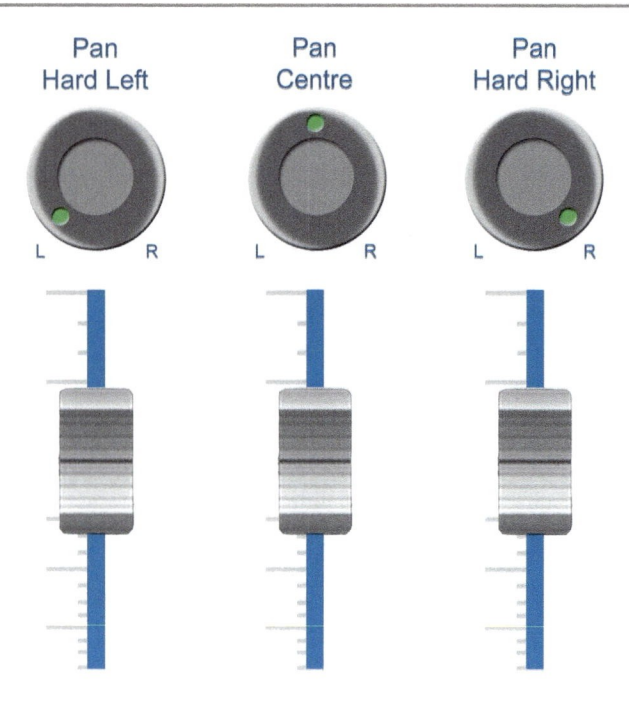

Fig. 18.1 Typical DAW pan controls

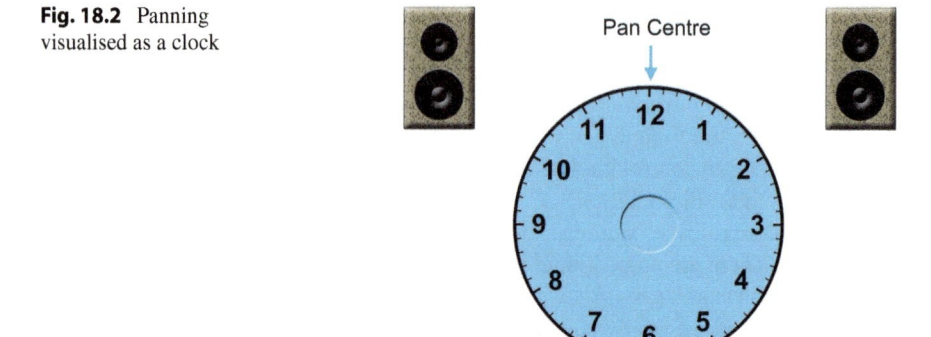

Fig. 18.2 Panning visualised as a clock

Lead vocals are usually panned in the centre too. Moving them just slightly left or right can sometimes help them sit better in the mix, depending on what else is playing at the same time.

Backing vocals: if you have a two-part backing vocal, you may want to pan one hard left to the 7:00 position and the other hard right to 5:00. If you have several backing vocals, you may want to pan them out in a fan-like manner. For example, starting with the lowest harmony, pan one slightly left to 11:00 and the other slightly

18 Panning

right to 1:00. Pan the next harmony parts to 9:00 and 3:00 and the highest harmony parts to 7:00 and 5:00.

Guitars and keyboards: If you have a mono guitar part and a mono keyboard part complementing each other, you may want to try panning them opposite each other. For example, pan the guitar to 9:00 and the keyboard to 3:00, or the guitar to 8:00 and the keyboard to 2:00. With a stereo keyboard part, try panning it hard left and right. With a guitar, you might want to try panning the guitar to 8:00 and the guitar reverb to 2:00.

Panning instruments and effects opposite each other creates balance in your mix, but as mentioned earlier, there are no rules and experimentation is recommended.

Another approach to panning is to visualise where musicians would be on a stage and pan their instrument to that point. For example, the drummer may be in the middle of the stage, so you would keep the drums panned pretty much in the centre. The bass player might be slightly to the right of the drummer, so you could pan the bass slightly to the right. The guitarist may be on the right side of the stage, so you could pan the guitar way over to the right, and the keyboard player may be on the opposite side, so you could pan the keyboard way over to the left (Fig. 18.3).

Whichever approach to panning you take, having an image in your head of where you want things to be will help you to create a balanced stereophonic picture.

▶ *Tip: Some engineers like to pan whilst listening in mono (see Chap. 15: Monitoring in Mono). It may sound weird to try and place elements of*

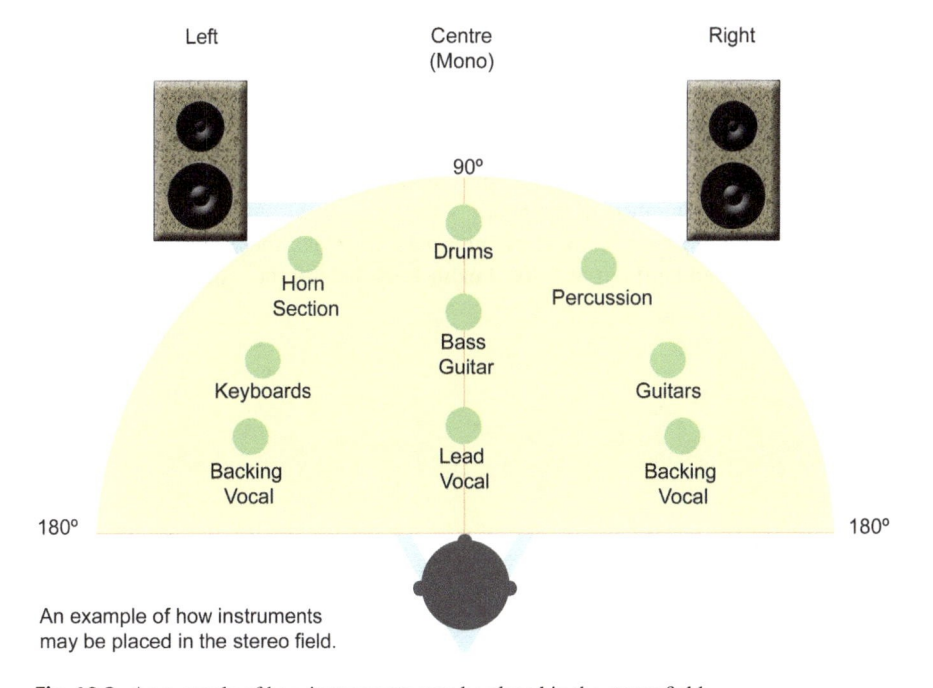

Fig. 18.3 An example of how instruments may be placed in the stereo field

your mix in the stereo field whilst listening in mono, but it can help with the separation of instruments. This is just one approach that can sometimes get you the desired result. Give it a go.

Pan Law

Pan law describes how much quieter a mono audio signal is when it is panned in the centre than when it is panned hard left or right. When a single mono signal is panned hard left or right, its amplitude increases. Pan laws compensate for this change in amplitude by gradually altering the volume as the signal is panned towards the centre, so that the perceived volume remains the same. Many DAWs automatically compensate for this difference in amplitude.

Some DAWs give the user the option to set a preferred pan law. Common pan laws are 0 dB, 2.5 dB, 3 dB, 4.5 dB and 6 dB. If, for example, you choose to set the pan law in your DAW to 3 dB, as you pan your track towards the left or right, your DAW would compensate for the difference between mono and panned levels by gradually reducing the level to a maximum of −3 dB when panned either hard left or right.

▶ **Chapter 18 Tasks:** The following tasks will enable you to investigate stereo positioning to create depth and space within a mix.

- Import a guitar recording into your DAW
- Using automation, write a gradual panning shift from hard left to hard right in the stereo field and then listen back in mono.
- Do you perceive any changes in the sound of the mono guitar as it moves across the stereo field?
- Mix a full track following the example advised in this chapter, where the panning replicates a live iteration of the band.
- Now remix with some radical panning which breaks these rules, such as the drum kit panned hard left and vocal panned hard right, for example.

Plosives   19

▶ **Learning Outcomes**

By the end of this chapter, the reader will be able to:
- Define how low frequencies can create unwanted plosives.
- Apply a range of techniques to reduce plosives.

When a vocalist sings into a microphone, bursts of low-frequency energy are created whenever words that begin with the letters **b** or **p** are sounded. This causes annoying low-frequency thumps on the recording which have to be edited or equalised out. These thumps are called plosives.

In many cases, a high-pass filter can be used to roll off any unnecessary low-frequency content, such as rumble, or the singer accidentally knocking the microphone stand. This usually reduces plosives to some extent too (Fig. 19.1).

If a high-pass filter doesn't reduce the plosives effectively, you can automate a reduction in level for each plosive throughout the vocal take. This can be time-consuming, but it is effective (Fig. 19.2).

Supplementary Information The online version contains supplementary material available at https://doi.org/10.1007/978-3-031-40067-4_19. The videos can be accessed individually by clicking the DOI link in the accompanying figure caption or by scanning this link with the SN More Media App.

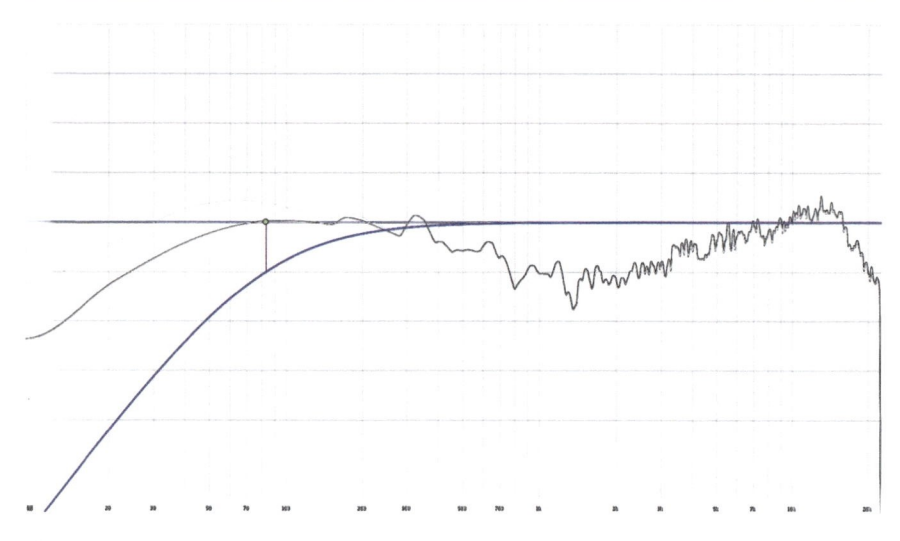

Fig. 19.1 High-pass filter

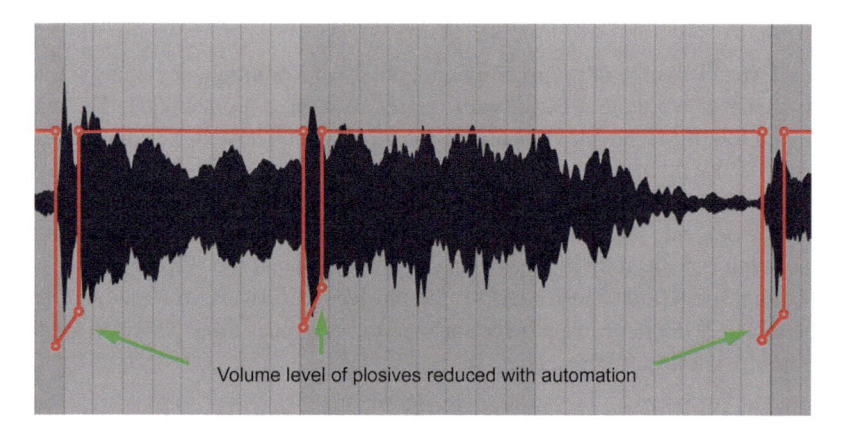

Fig. 19.2 Automating reduction in level on plosives

> ▶ *Tip: Microphone placement, proximity to the singer and polar patterns (see Chap. 7: Microphones) can also have an impact on plosives.*
> ▶ *Tip: A trick for eliminating plosives before they hit the diaphragm of the microphone is to attach a pencil to the front of its barrel. This causes the low-frequency energy from the singer's mouth to be diverted sideways rather than hitting the diaphragm full-on. This can sometimes work well with singers who have voices in the baritone or bass range or when a lyric contains a lot of b's and p's. You can use rubber bands to attach the pencil to the microphone. This can sometimes help reduce sibilance too (Fig. 19.3).*

Fig. 19.3 Neumann U87 microphone. (Image courtesy of Neumann GmBH)

Listen carefully to these two voice recordings. The only difference between them is the use of a pop shield on Audio example 61.

▶   **Chapter 19 Tasks:** The following tasks will give you experience of dealing with unwanted plosives in voice recordings.

- Import Audio Example 60 into your DAW and listen to all the moments where a plosive occurs.
- Using volume automation, reduce the level of the plosive points to smooth the recording and reduce all the plosives.
- If you have no access to a pop shield, try attaching a pencil to your microphone with a rubber band as indicated in this chapter and compare a similar recording of a vocal part without the pencil to the recording with the pencil. Does it improve?

Zero Crossing and Crossfades   20

▶ **Learning Outcomes**

By the end of this chapter, the reader will be able to:
- Explain the benefits of zero-crossing in audio editing.
- Apply crossfade techniques to audio signals to achieve successful edits.

Zero crossing is the point at which a digital audio wave has zero amplitude. From this point, the signal will either rise or fall in amplitude (Fig. 20.1).

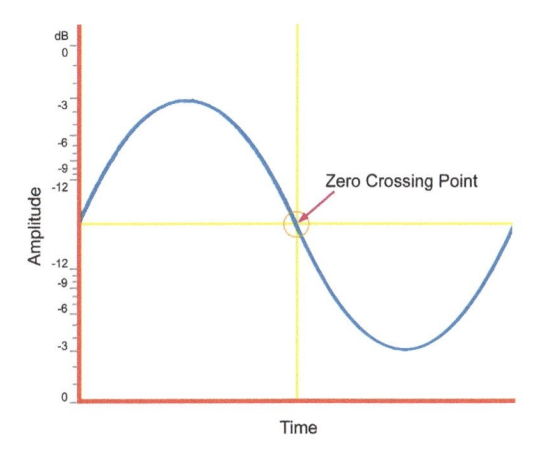

Fig. 20.1 Zero crossing point

Supplementary Information The online version contains supplementary material available at https://doi.org/10.1007/978-3-031-40067-4_20. The videos can be accessed individually by clicking the DOI link in the accompanying figure caption or by scanning this link with the SN More Media App.

© The Author(s), under exclusive license to Springer Nature Switzerland AG 2024
S. Duggal, *Record, Mix and Master*,
https://doi.org/10.1007/978-3-031-40067-4_20

When an audio segment is selected on the timeline to be looped or cut and pasted with another segment, its start and end points should be at zero crossing; otherwise, there will be a jump in amplitude at the loop or edit point which will result in an unwanted click or pop. To loop a selection or edit two sections together smoothly, the audio waveform will have to be zoomed in to sample level (Figs. 20.2 and 20.3).

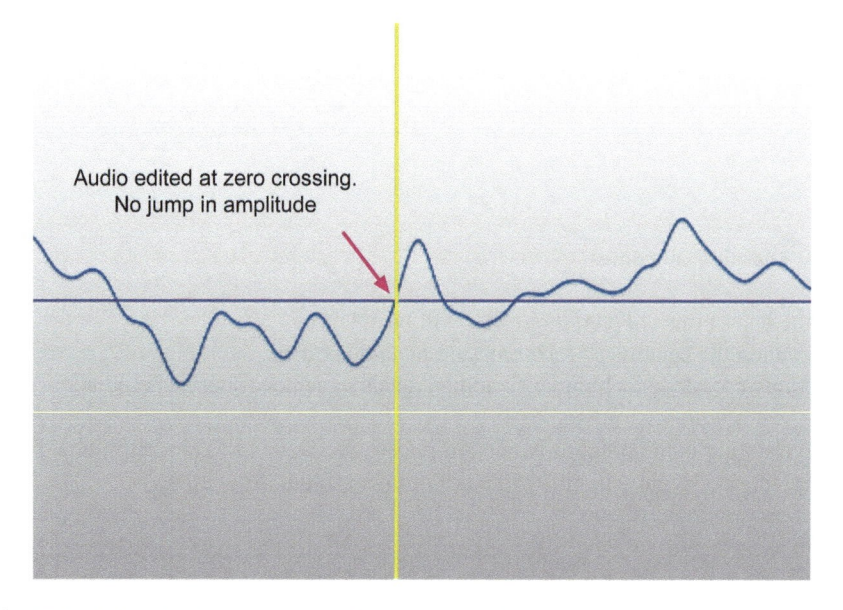

Fig. 20.2 Audio edited at zero crossing. No jump in amplitude

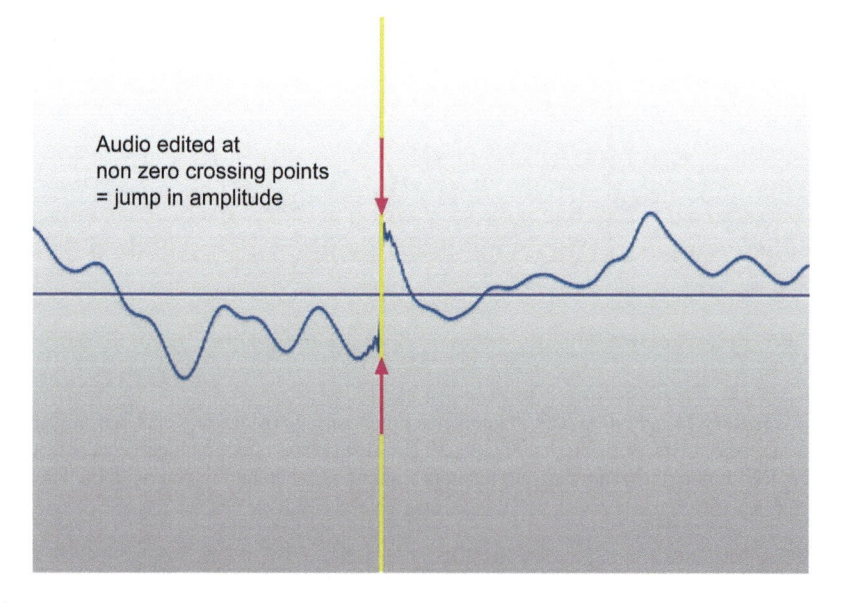

Fig. 20.3 Audio edited at non-zero crossing. Signal jumps in amplitude

> *Tip: For accurate editing at zero crossing, set your DAW's 'snap' to samples rather than beats/bars.*

When it is not possible to cut the audio segment exactly at the zero crossing point, a jump in amplitude can be corrected with a crossfade. A crossfade is a smooth transition from one audio segment to another and ensures that each edit point begins or ends at a zero crossing (Fig. 20.4).

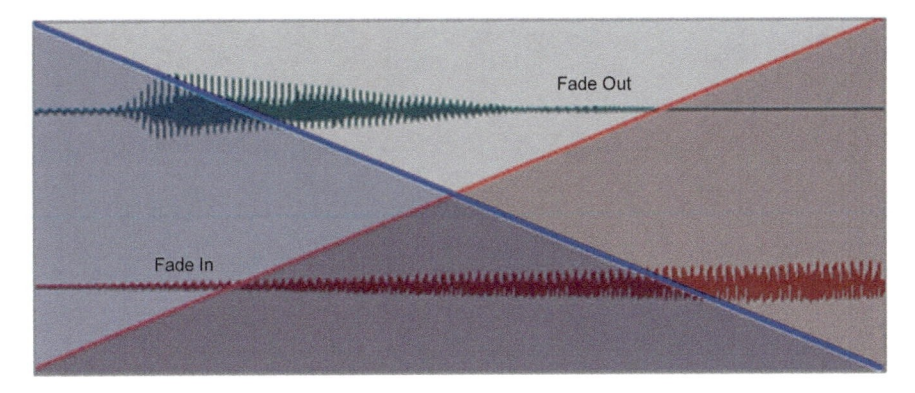

Fig. 20.4 Crossfade applied to edited signal

In the following example, the red and green audio segments will be joined and the section between them deleted. Splicing these sections together will cause a click or pop at the edit point due to the difference in amplitude between the two parts (Fig. 20.5).

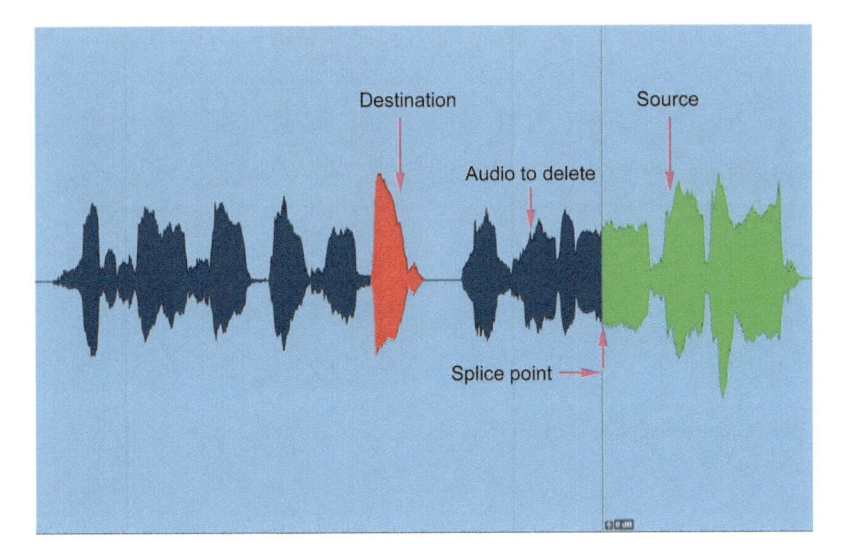

Fig. 20.5 Audio section to be edited

In the next image, you can see the difference in amplitude where the red and green sections have been joined together (Fig. 20.6).

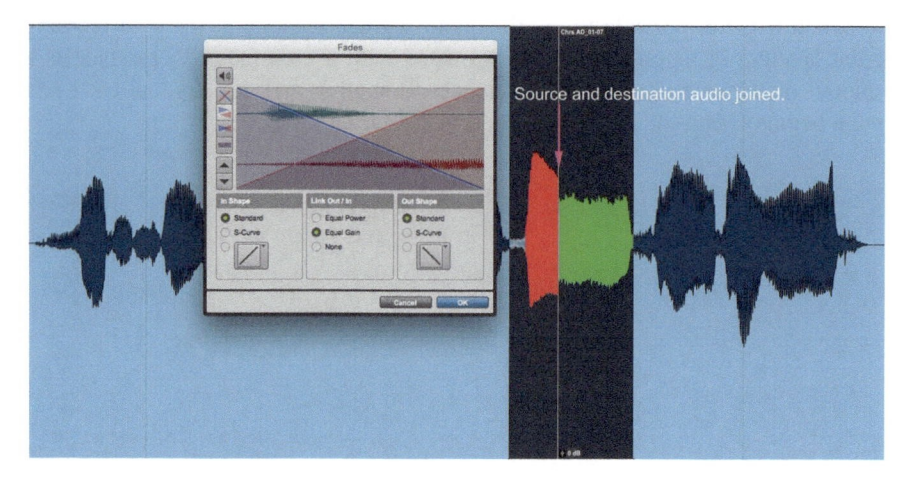

Fig. 20.6 Audio section edited

Using a crossfade, a smooth transition can be created between the two sections. The crossfade gradually fades out in the first section and gradually fades in the second section. The two clips overlap for the duration of the transition (Fig. 20.7).

The result is a smooth edit without clicks or pops.

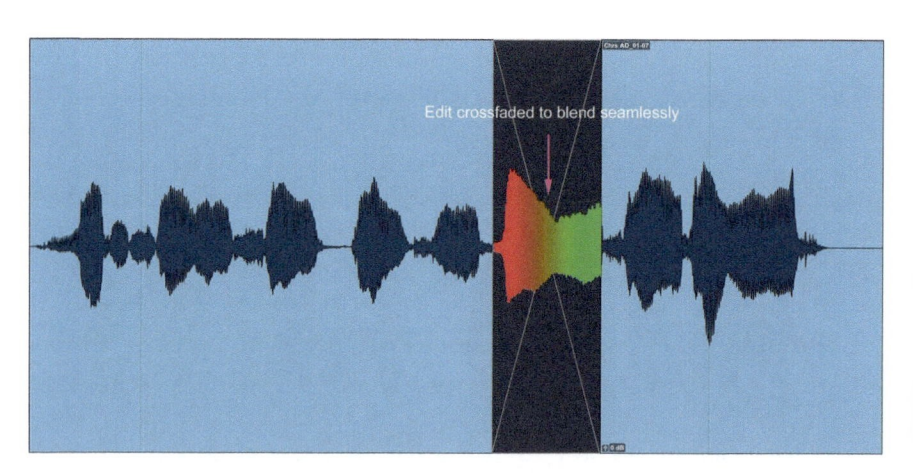

Fig. 20.7 Crossfade applied to edited section

▶ **Chapter 20 Tasks:** The following tasks will improve your ability to create smooth edits when splicing and joining audio.

- Import the Audio Example 62 into your DAW and listen.
- Note the significant difference to the organ part which has been spliced using zero-crossing compared to the part where the audio has been cut and produces a glitch.
- Try zooming in fully to the Audio example and finding the points where the audio was spliced which creates the glitch.
- With 'snap' set to 'Samples or Ticks', use the editing scissors to splice either side of the track around the glitch on zero crossings and then remove the glitch section.
- Join the sections together, employing crossfades to maintain a continuous sound with the glitch removed.

Mixing Tips   21

▶ **Learning Outcomes**

By the end of this chapter, the reader will be able to:
- Apply a range of mixing methods to achieve quality, balanced mixes.
- Recall mixing techniques for individual instruments (drums, bass, vocals, guitars and synths).
- Show a working knowledge of useful effects processing to enhance overall mixes.

Mixing is the process of balancing each recorded part so that its loudness, tone, panoramic position and effect levels blend sonically and musically with each other. The parts are then exported or 'bounced' as a stereo audio file ready for mastering (see Chap. 22: What is Mastering?). The finished master can then be converted into formats that are compatible with consumer playback devices such as CD and MP3 players.

Each mix engineer has his or her own particular style and approach to mixing. However, they all have one thing in common: they know how and when to correctly use all of the audio tools at their disposal (Fig. 21.1).

Fig. 21.1 Mixing desk and hardware effects

© The Author(s), under exclusive license to Springer Nature
Switzerland AG 2024
S. Duggal, *Record, Mix and Master*,
https://doi.org/10.1007/978-3-031-40067-4_21

How you start your mix is a matter of preference. Many engineers tend to start with the kick drum, add the rest of the drums, the bass guitar, and then build the mix from there. This approach is like building a house, you start with a solid foundation—the low-frequency instruments—and build the rest of the mix brick by brick to the apex of the roof—the higher frequencies.

Some engineers prefer to start with the main focus of the song, which is usually the lead vocal or an instrument melody, and then build the mix around that.

> ▶ ***Tips from the pros:*** *The top of the bullet points for your mix should always be, 'what is the impact on the listener?'. Nothing else really matters. Everything else should point towards answering this.* **Kevin Churko—Producer, Engineer and Songwriter—***Disturbed, Ozzy Osbourne, Shania Twain, Five Finger Death Punch, The Corrs, Britney Spears and more.*

Getting Ready to Mix

Make sure each audio track is free from hiss, hums, crackles, pops or any other unwanted noise. Spend some time taking care of any non-creative editing tasks so that the mixing process can be creative and musical. Separating creative and non-creative tasks helps you stay focused for longer.

Monitor quietly. Find a reasonable listening level that's not too loud and stick with it. This way you'll avoid ear fatigue and will remain objective about your mix for longer. (see Chap. 2: Speakers—Speaker Listening Levels). It's important to take periodic breaks. Have a cup of tea, go for a walk, get some lunch, etc. When you get back to your mix, you'll hear things you missed when you were doing that 8-hour, non-stop stretch.

> ▶ ***Tips from the pros:*** *The best tools you'll ever get are already stuck to your head—trust your ears! It's so easy these days to rely on what you see rather than on what you hear, so make sure that you really hear the wonderful-looking thing that you're twiddling with. If you don't hear it, it's probably not there, and certainly not worth it.* **Hans-Martin Buff— Engineer and Producer—***Prince, The Beatifics, Boney M, The New Power Generation and more.*

Periodically monitor in mono from a single source point (see Chap. 15: Monitoring in Mono). It's much easier to balance instruments, voices and effect levels when they are superimposed on top of each other rather than when they are spread between your speakers. For true mono, press the mono switch on your audio interface and turn one of your speakers off, monitor on the other speaker and balance your mix.

Getting Ready to Mix

Use compression (see Chap. 12: Dynamics—Compressors). When used properly, compression will put a limit on the maximum output of the audio signal. This can help maintain an even balance throughout an audio track. For example, you may have recorded a particularly dynamic vocalist who jumps from singing quietly on one word to very loudly on the next. Compression will reduce the gain of the louder word making its volume level the same as the quieter one. Compression will also compact the energy in the track, keeping it sounding punchy whilst maintaining a balanced level.

> ▶ *Tips from the pros:* Monitor at even levels when comparing treated vs untreated materials—ie if you are comparing a compressed kick and an uncompressed kick in the mix—make sure you're not hearing the compressed kick in a higher gain—match their gains to really hear what the compressor does. **Axwell—DJ, Producer & Remixer**—*Swedish House Mafia, Flo Rider, Brandon Flowers, Faithless, Usher and more.*

Use reference material. Periodically refer to commercial recordings in the same style as the track you're mixing. If you are mixing an electro pop track, for example, switch to a track that's current and in the same style. Listen carefully to the levels and Eq of the various instruments and voices. Listen to how effects such as reverb, delay and modulation are used, and generally try to get a feel for how the overall picture was painted (Fig. 21.2).

> ▶ *Tips from the pros: Most of the time we're not mixing to what we like. We're mixing comparatively to similar music. If you think you've just created the biggest, baddest, most bottom heavy rock kick drum of all time that puts all others to shame....you've probably failed. Everybody has tuned their systems to their existing catalog they already know and love.* **Kevin Churko—Producer, Engineer and Songwriter**—*Disturbed, Ozzy Osbourne, Shania Twain, Five Finger Death Punch, The Corrs, Britney Spears and more.*

Fig. 21.2 Mixing desk faders

There are literally thousands of tips and tricks that professional engineers use to get a great sound. The following pages contain a selection of some that I'm sure you'll find very useful.

Note: Bear in mind that high pass filters and big Eq boosts can alter the phase of your signal (see Chap. 15: Phase). Be sure to check the phase of your signal after equalising or high passing.

Drums and Bass

Tip 1: If the kick drum is too subsonic—has too much rumble—use a high pass filter to remove the lowest frequencies (see Chap. 11: Equalisers). Depending on the style of track you are mixing, it's quite common to cut off frequencies below 40 Hz, even up to 80 Hz or more, with a gentle slope. If the kick sounds muddy, try reducing somewhere around 200 Hz to 250 Hz by a few dB with a narrow Q. If it sounds like it has too much 'knock', reduce 400 Hz, and if it sounds boxy, remove some at 500 Hz.

Tip 2: Choosing the 'right' sound minimises how much processing you will need to apply. If you find that you are making huge Eq boosts and cuts, it's probably not the right sound for the track.

▶ *Tips from the pros: If you are spending hours trying to force something in the studio—a mix, a melody or even the right snare sound—once the frustration sets in then develop an ongoing discipline to stop and accept that maybe it isn't going to happen. Go for a walk, down to a cafe for a cup of tea or something to change your scenery (even if it's only 30 minutes). Then head back and try again with a clear head. It's amazing how many times this has worked for me, and usually results in getting it right very quickly once I get back.* **Peter Duggal—Producer/Composer**—*Wolfgang Flür (Kraftwerk), Peter Hook, Midge Ure, Claudia Brücken, Carl Cox, Juan Atkins, Maps and more.*

Tip 3: Sometimes finding the right kick drum sample and tuning its pitch to the key of the song is all that's required to make it sound great in relation to the bass.

▶ *Tips from the pros: The old trick of tweaking EQs on a track without soloing it is still a good one in my opinion. Good to see how things sit in the mix even though they can sound great when solo'd.* **Chris Taylor—CTM Studios, Producer/Musician**—*Ruby Turner, Paul Potts, Robbie Williams, George Ezra, The Shires, Emili Sande and more.*

Tip 4: To add warmth to your snare drum, try boosting frequencies between 125 Hz and 200 Hz. This frequency range will fatten the snare sound. To get rid of any rumble, try cutting frequencies below 90 Hz. To add presence and to hear more of the sound of the stick making contact with the drum, boost between 6 kHz and 10 kHz. If the snare sounds muddy, try cutting somewhere between 200 Hz and 400 Hz.

Tip 5: Try these values as a good starting point for snare and kick drum compression: Attack: 1–5 ms. Release: 200 ms/Auto. Ratio between 5:1 and 10:1. Knee: hard. Gain reduction between 5 and 15 dB.

Tip 6: Unnecessary low frequencies on any instrument or voice can reduce headroom, clarity in the mix, and can cause frequency masking—this is when frequencies that are not needed on one instrument, mask the same frequencies that are required on another instrument. Use a high pass filter to remove unwanted low frequencies (see Chap. 11: Equalisers). Remember to check the phase after using a High Pass Filter (HPF).

▶ *Tips from the pros:* *Try and have an end goal in mind before you go down the rabbit hole. Think about how you want your record to sound, seek out references, immerse yourself in them, study them and pick out what makes them special. Then visualise your take on it.* **Mark Gittins— Producer, Foh Engineer, Mix Engineer, owner of Megatone Studio, Birmingham**—*The Wytches, Youth Man, Robert Craig Oulton, Premier League Productions, BT sports, BBC and more.*

Tip 7: Cutting frequencies on one instrument and boosting them on another will help create space between the two. For example, try cutting 80 Hz on the bass and boosting 80 Hz on the kick. It requires a good understanding of the frequency spectrum to know what needs cutting and what needs boosting, but with a little practice, you should be able to quickly identify areas that need equalising on any instrument (see Chap. 11: Equalisers).

Tip 8: It can be helpful to check the kick and bass low-frequency relationship on headphones. Headphones can reveal more detail in the low-frequency range and are not affected by room acoustics issues.

Tip 9: High-pass filter below 40 Hz on the kick and bass to get rid of unnecessary low-frequency content that would otherwise eat up valuable headroom.

Tip 10: Try high-pass filtering the bass up to around 150 Hz. Eq the mid frequencies until you get the tone you want and then turn off the high-pass filter to put the bottom end back.

Tip 11: The Pultec low end trick—boost and cut the same frequency by the same amount. In theory, this would equal no change to the signal but because the Q is slightly different when boosting compared to cutting on a Pultec equaliser, the result is a nice lift on the low end just where you want it. You can simulate this trick with any equaliser—cut and boost the same frequency by the same amount and then adjust the Q on either the boost or cut.

Tip 12: The Pultec low-end trick actually works on the high end too. Boost and cut the same frequency by the same amount, adjust the Q slightly on either. Give it a go.

▶ ***Tips from the pros:*** *Mixing is an art form. Some of the greatest sounding mixes go back to way before lots of plugins and outboard gear. Many people have asked me "what's the best compression setting or reverb setting? the answer is ... When it sounds right !! Use your ears.* **Richard Taylor—Producer, Songwriter & Musician—Emin, Ronan Keating, Bananarama, XFactor, David Foster, Nile Rodgers, Little Mix,1D, Boyzone, Westlife, James Arthur, Mcfly and more.**

Tip 13: When equalising two elements of the same sound individually, for example, top and bottom snare microphones, use a linear phase Eq to ensure there is no phase shift between them (See Chap. 11: Equalisers).

Tip 14: Automate your drum bus fader throughout the mix to keep them sounding dynamic.

Tip 15: The faster the song, the less sub bass you need on your kick drum.

Vocals

Tip 1: Add some 300 Hz to give a vocal more weight and warmth.

Tip 2: Reduce approximately 3 kHz to make a vocal less harsh and painful to listen to.

Tip 3: Boost a little bit somewhere around 5 kHz to help a vocal cut through the mix.

Tip 4: Double-track your lead vocal twice. Pan the doubles hard left and right. Pitch the left down −12 cents and the right up +12 cents. Blend the doubles in behind the lead vocal for a wider fatter sound.

Tip 5: High pass and low pass filter your backing vocals to help them blend in behind the lead vocal.

Tip 6: It's ok to pin the meters on your compressor to make your vocals slam.

▶ ***Tips from the pros:*** *There is more than one way to turn up a track in a mix. Sometimes, it's better to increase the level of an instrument by using effects such as eq, reverb and compression or by decreasing the level of something else.* **TJ Rehmi—Artist, Composer and Producer—** *Nusrat Fateh Ali Khan, Natacha Atlas, Mumiy Troll, Trilok Gurtu, Cheb i Sabbah and more.*

Guitars and Synths

Tip 1: Pan guitars and synths opposite each other (see Chap. 18: Panning). Panning instruments can help create a sense of width in your mix.

▶ ***Tips from the pros:*** *Recording Guitars—Get the instrument setup, especially intonation and make sure the guitarist has a tuner. No expensive Preamp or Converter can undo the damage caused by a terrible sounding/out of tune Guitar.*

▶ Record a DI (Direct Signal) as well as a mic'd up amp. This can help in many ways during editing and mixing. Move the microphone around on the Speaker until you find the smoothest and fullest sound. You may need to keep recording small sections and playing them back in between moves—it takes time and effort, but it is worth it. **Mike Exeter— Producer, Engineer, Mixer and Composer**—Black Sabbath, Judas Priest, Ronnie James Dio, Cradle Of Filth and more.

Tip 2: Use subtle distortion or saturation to bring out harmonic overtones in the instrument.

Tip 3: High pass below 80 Hz on electric guitars. There's a lot of energy down there that will mask your bass frequencies.

▶ *Tips from the pros:* Every song has a message, and creates an emotion; excitement, heartbreak, having fun, anger, etc.... Your job as an engineer/producer/mixer is to communicate that message and not let the emotion get lost in translation. **Mark Gittins—Producer, FoH Engineer, Mix Engineer, owner of Megatone Studio, Birmingham**— The Wytches, Youth Man, Robert Craig Oulton, Premier League Productions, BT sports, BBC and more.

Tip 4: A slight cut between 100 Hz and 150 Hz on electric guitars will prevent the low mids from masking other instruments.

Tip 5: Phasers and flangers can make guitars sound great. Be sure to experiment with effects on your electric guitar tracks.

▶ *Tips from the pros:* Leaving the room with the track playing in the background can be useful. Have a listen from the other side of a half-closed door or from another room. It's a good way of seeing if anything is sticking out of the mix like the snare being too loud. **Chris Taylor— CTM Studios, Producer/Musician**—Ruby Turner, Paul Potts, Robbie Williams, George Ezra, The Shires, Emili Sande and more.

Tip 6: A slow release setting on your compressor will make your strummed guitar chords appear to sustain for longer.

Tip 7: Roll off some high end to make guitars and synths blend in.

▶ *Tips from the pros:* Mixing with Low Pass Filters. Try automating a low pass filter effect on guitar and keys tracks. It can add interest and texture to an otherwise predictable part. **Jonny Amos—Songwriter, Producer, Lecturer and Director at The SongLab.** Shayne Ward, Jpop Idols EXIT, Miss D, Jackie Paladino, Glow Beets, Native Instruments Sounds. MTV, Sky One and Film Four.

Tip 8: Double-track your guitar part. Pan one hard left and the other hard right.

▶ ***Tips from the pros:*** *Don't get bogged down with creating the 'perfect kick' or 'cutting 500 hz in everything' because some big shot does it on 'every record'. Your audience, the listener, won't care for any of that. Create a vibe that serves the song.* **Mark Gittins—Producer, Foh Engineer, Mix Engineer, owner of Megatone Studio, Birmingham—** *The Wytches, Youth Man, Robert Craig Oulton, Premier League Productions, BT sports, BBC and more.*

General

Tip 1: Try compressing your effect returns a little to thicken them up a bit. You can use a high-pass filter on your effect returns too.

Tip 2: Low pass filters create resonances at the corner frequency. This can be useful for accentuating the tone of the sound. Try boosting a little at the corner frequency.

▶ ***Tips from the pros:*** *Less is more MOST of the time, but sometimes, MORE is MORE!*
▶ **Kevin Churko—Producer, Engineer and Songwriter—***Disturbed, Ozzy Osbourne, Shania Twain, Five Finger Death Punch, The Corrs, Britney Spears and more.*

Tip 3: Wide Eq bandwidths with subtle boosts can sometimes sound more musical. Don't be afraid to use a wide Q (see Chap. 11: Equalisers—Q—Bandwidth).

Tip 4: Use reverb to create a sense of depth. As well as the left, phantom centre and right channel information, a good mix also has front-to-back depth. You can place elements of your mix further back or further forward, depending on how wet or dry it is.

▶ ***Tips from the pros:*** *Don't hang around in solo-mode for too long. I have found that 'the bigger picture'—the final product, the song—is ultimately what really counts. Always refer back to how the isolated part connects with and sits in the entire mix.* **Iwan VanHetten— Producer, Songwriter and Mix Engineer—***Brooklyn Funk Essentials, Sister Sledge, The Pointer Sisters, Candy Duffer and more.*

Tip 5: Ride the faders. To create movement and dynamics in your mix, automate fader levels so that instruments and voices can sometimes come forward or sit back in the mix.

▶ ***Tips from the pros:*** *I like to use my DM 2000 as a fader control surface. It makes riding vocal levels and writing automation much more intuitive than using a mouse. I guess it's because I grew up on analogue consoles* etc. but hovering your fingers over a vocal fader is faster and feels better than mousing. **Chris Taylor—CTM Studios, Producer/Musician**—Ruby Turner, Paul Potts, Robbie Williams, George Ezra, The Shires, Emili Sande and more.

Tip 6: Automate the master fader so that the chorus is 1 dB louder than the verse. This will help accentuate the power of the chorus.

▶ ***Tips from the pros:*** *Don't let ear fatigue spoil the mix! I've found it useful to check the mix first thing in the morning, or whenever you arrive at the studio with rested ears, at low volume and in both stereo and mono.* **TJ Rehmi—Artist, Composer and Producer**—Nusrat Fateh Ali Khan, Natacha Atlas, Mumiy Troll, Trilok Gurtu, Cheb i Sabbah and more.

Tip 7: Check your mix on headphones, in the car and on your home hi-fi. Tweak so that it sounds good on all of them.

▶ ***Tips from the pros:*** *Use your ears rather than your eyes. I've seen so many engineers glued to screens when EQ ing things and adjusting compression etc. It's far too easy to get wrapped up in the GUI of EQ and it can distract you from the actual sound that you're hearing. It's great for finding problem frequencies but sometimes it can make you think you're applying too much EQ when actually you can add more.... or less! I heard someone say once that we are Recording EnginEARS not recording EnginEYES!* **Chris Taylor—CTM Studios, Producer/Musician**—Ruby Turner, Paul Potts, Robbie Williams, George Ezra, The Shires, Emili Sande and more.

Tip 8: Soften harsh transients with a compressor that is capable of extremely fast attack and release times. Set it as fast as it will go and aim for ½ dB to 1 dB of gain reduction.

Tip 9: Even though mixing quietly will allow you to mix for longer, it's still important to take a break and give your ears a rest. Take at least a 10-minute break every hour to protect your hearing and to remain objective about your mix.

▶ ***Tips from the pros:*** *A mix is a yin and yang between screwdriver work and living the song and it's really important to know the difference: If you're in the zone and you're rockin' out, don't get lost in some minute detail. If you catch yourself listlessly raking through great music, give your music spirit a rest and switch from the big picture to necessary mindless work for a while.* **Hans-Martin Buff—Engineer and Producer**—Prince, The Beatifics, Boney M, The New Power Generation and more.

Tip 10: Every once in a while, close your eyes and listen. The sensitivity of your ears becomes heightened when your eyes are closed.

Tip 11: Label and colour code your tracks so you can easily see what's what at a glance.

▶ ***Tips from the pros:*** *If the mix isn't working start again with the vocal and mix top down. You don't have to start with the drums. Try making the vocal and bass sit together then fill in everything from there.* **Steve Osborne—Producer**—*U2, A-ha, New Order, Suede, Paul Oakenfold, Happy Mondays and more*

▶ ***Tips from the pros:*** *Never be afraid to push boundaries—learn the rules then learn to break them. Many of the great production techniques were discovered through creativity and experimentation. Using technology in ways it wasn't originally intended can lead to beautiful sonic journeys.* **Dr Paul Rogers—Producer, Songwriter, Sound designer and University Lecturer**

▶ ***Tips from the pros:*** *During a late-night practice session in the studio, an old teacher from Berklee, Vassilly, could NOT figure out a problem in the studio. He said to me, "The machines can feel energy. If you aren't good, they aren't good. Maybe it's time you go home and rest so the machine can rest too." And of course, the next day the problem disappeared and the solution was so obvious. My Tip: GIVE YOUR MECHANICAL AND MENTAL MACHINES A BREAK.* **Jaclyn Sanchez, Engineer—Jon Batiste, H.E.R., Anderson Paak, Lauren Hill, Common**

▶ Mix Tasks: The following tasks are designed to improve your active listening skills in relation to mixing. Listening and analysing a wide range of mixes in published music can reveal how other producers apply techniques, which will help to develop your own approaches.

Choose a range of songs across multiple genres and analyse the mixing techniques used. Can you identify the following aspects within the mixes:

- What type of reverb is used on the main vocal track?
- Is there a compressor on the vocal?
- Are there any other recognisable effects used on the voice, such as saturation, heavy equalisation and echo delay?
- Can you detect any volume automation across the vocal where the voice is quieter but the perceived volume is the same?
- How are the instruments panned?
- Where in the stereo field have they placed the bass instrument?
- Is there any use of mid-side processing, or double tracking where an instrument appears to exist left and right sides but not in the centre?

- How is the drum kit spaced in the stereo field—is it panned as though perceived by a live audience, or are there other panning techniques occurring?
- Try listening to the track in mono—does it have the same clarity?
- Try listening to just one side of the stereo field—what does this change?
- Is the same reverb used across all instruments or can you hear a range of types?
- How have frequency ranges been exploited in the track—is there sound present in all the main frequency bands?
- Are there any parts of the frequency range which seem louder than others?
- Can you detect any low pass or high pass filtering on any instruments to allow space in the mix?
- Are the kick drum and bass instruments working successfully together?
- Are the mid-range frequency instruments fighting for space, or do they sit comfortably around each other?
- Can you hear any use of side chain compression creating space in the instrumentation?
- Can you hear any equalisation on effects such as reverb?
- Try to re-create some of the mixing techniques discovered in your listening analysis in your own mixes.

Part III

Master

What is Mastering? 22

▶ **Learning Outcomes**

By the end of this chapter, the reader will be able to:
- Explain the key reasons for mastering.
- Recall the main processes used in a mastering chain.

Mastering is the final stage of the audio production process after recording and mixing have taken place. Professional mastering ensures your track sounds sonically good enough to compete with commercial tracks and sounds consistent on a variety of playback systems (Fig. 22.1).

Mastering involves processing your finished mix with a selection of tools (see Chap. 24: Mastering Tools) to enhance clarity, increase the overall level, add width and dither the final output (see Chap. 25: Dither). The process usually requires the use of dynamic compression, equalisation, harmonic excitement, stereo imaging, limiting and clipping (see Chap. 24: Mastering Tools).

Mastering is not necessarily about making the finished track as loud as it can possibly be, although some genres such as EDM and Hip Hop are generally considerably louder than others. Moreover, mastering is about sonically enhancing the program material, so that it has the right balance of frequencies, dynamics, width and depth.

Mastering an entire album involves making sure that each track is sonically similar to the other tracks, excessive silence at the beginning and end of each track is removed and track spacing and sequence is correct if the end medium is a physical format such as a CD.

It also involves permanently embedding metadata and ISRC codes (International Standard Recording Code) into the files, which are used for identifying recorded music.

Fig. 22.1 Waves L3 multimaximiser mastering plugin. (Image courtesy of Waves Audio Ltd)

Before you master, there are some questions you should ask yourself:

1. Do you want your mastered track to be loud or dynamic?
2. What style of tracks will yours be played alongside?
3. Is your track for radio, television, streaming platforms or club systems?
4. Are you mastering for commercial release or for broadcast?

The style of music will have an influence on your approach to mastering. For example, you wouldn't want to master a jazz track so that it's as loud as an EDM track. Determine what you want your track to sound like and what you want your maximum RMS or LUFS level to be (see Chap. 26: Metering) so that you have an end goal in sight. Have a selection of commercial tracks in the same style as your track handy so that you can periodically refer to them.

▶ **Chapter 22 Tasks:** The following tasks will enable you to apply suitable consideration to your audio before getting them ready for the mastering stage.

- Listen to one of your mixes and consider how you want the track to be mastered.
- Would it suit the track to be pushed as loud as possible or would it be better suited with a greater dynamic range?
- Try and identify the style and genre of your track—what style of music will yours be played alongside?
- Consider whether your track is aimed for radio, television, streaming platforms or club systems.

Prepare Your Track for Mastering 23

▶ **Learning Outcomes**

By the end of this chapter, the reader will be able to:
- Prepare a bounce down of a track in the correct format for mastering.
- Illustrate dynamic ranges in relation to noise floor and headroom in an audio track.
- Apply suitable processing to an audio track prior to the mastering process.

Bounce your mix down as an interleaved WAV or AIFF file at the same sample rate and bit depth as your session. If your session was recorded at 48 kHz and 24 bits, bounce your mix down at 48 kHz and 24 bits. Ensure that the master output levels leave plenty of headroom. A mastering engineer might recommend −6 dB of headroom. If your master fader meters are hitting close to 0 dBFS constantly, that won't leave the mastering engineer with much headroom and will make it more likely that clipping will occur when dynamic processing or Eq is used.

Leave a few seconds of silence at the beginning and end of your track. A good habit to get into is to always start your recording sessions a few bars in on the timeline and bounce your final mix down starting at bar 1 and ending several bars after the arrangement has ended. This way, there's no danger of any of your audio getting truncated during any export or editing process.

Leave bus compression on your mix if it's part of your sound but be sure to remove any limiters on the master bus. Limiting is part of the mastering process.

If you are bouncing down stems—sub mixes of your drums, bass, keyboards, vocals, etc., make sure they all have the same start point, sample rate, bit depth and file format.

It's best not to normalise your bounced mix or stems. Normalising is the process of raising the overall level of the audio material so that its loudest peak hits 0 dBfs, the maximum level achievable in digital audio. Normalising has its uses; however, normalised tracks are more likely to clip when processed with Eq and effects, and they have considerably less headroom which doesn't leave the mastering engineer much to work with (Fig. 23.1).

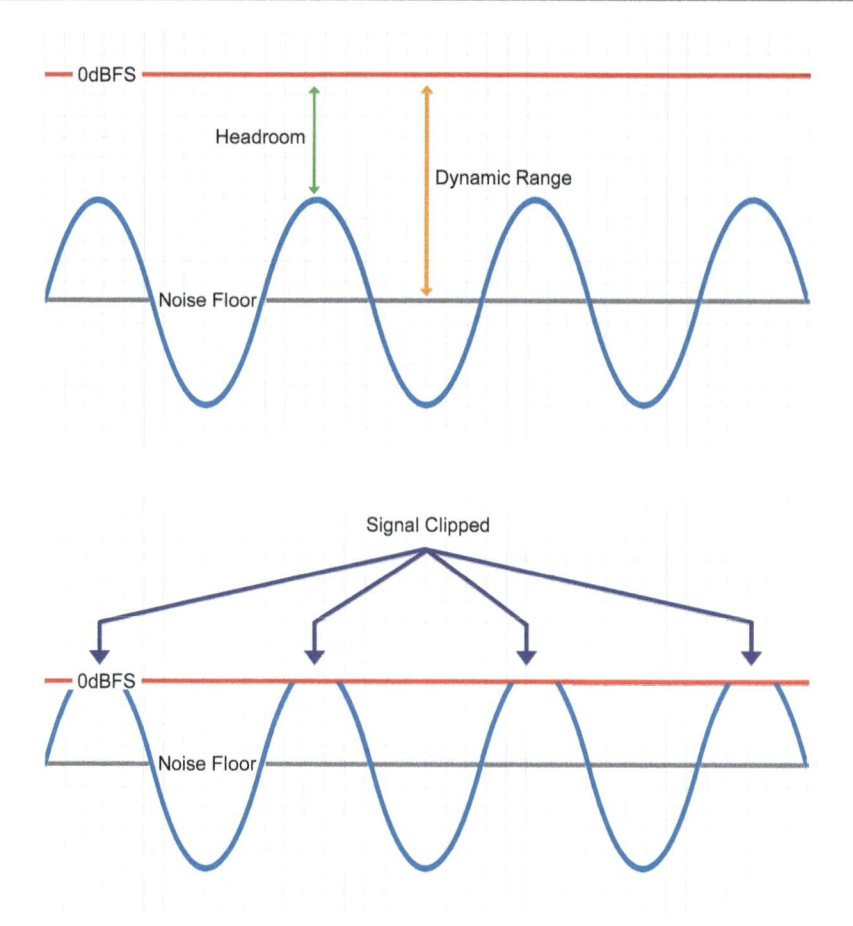

Fig. 23.1 Signal headroom and dynamic range

Normalising can also introduce inter-sample peaks. These are analogue peaks that momentarily exceed the maximum digital level 0 dBfs, and can be introduced during the digital to analogue conversion process. Inter-sample peaks may not be noticeable when using high-quality digital-to-analogue converters but they will cause distortion when your track is played on cheaper consumer CD players and Hi-Fi systems (Fig. 23.2).

Finally, listen to your bounced mix or stems all the way through to check for errors. It is good practice to create a new folder inside your song's session folder and name it something like: 'song title—pre-masters'. Export your song and/or stems to this folder. It's also a good idea to export an instrumental and personal appearance (PA) version of your song too. An instrumental version may be useful for synchronisation purposes. If you are submitting your song for synchronisation use in film, television or to be synchronised with any other type of moving image, your client

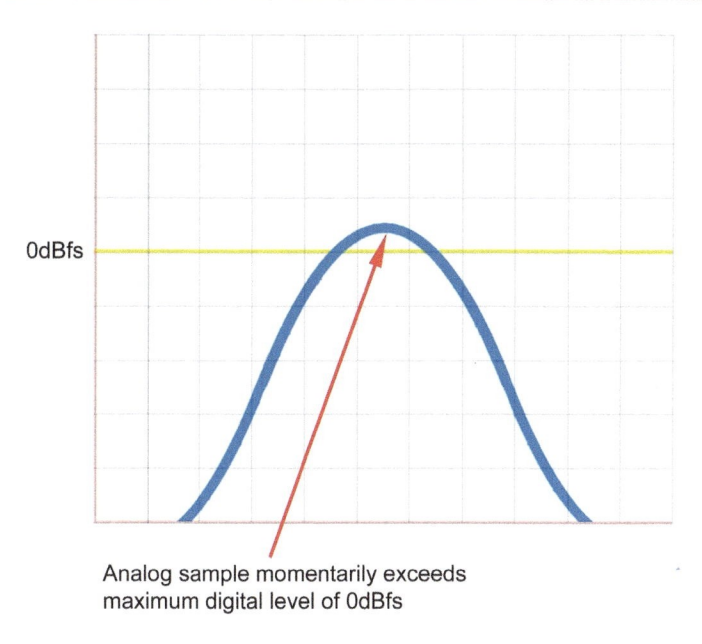

Fig. 23.2 Inter-sample peak

may wish to have the option to use either the vocal or instrumental version. A PA version of your recording usually consists of the full mix without the lead vocal. This is useful if you plan to perform your song using a backing track whilst singing live to it.

Your 'pre-masters' folder will be your safety copy which will contain your original exported audio files should you need to go back to them without having to relaunch your session and export your mixes again. When you are ready to master these files, make a copy of the pre-masters and work on the copy.

▶ **Chapter 23 Tasks:** The following tasks will enable the preparation of your audio in advance of final mastering.

- Bounce down a stereo mix leaving −6 dB of headroom and ensuring there is a few seconds of silence at the beginning and end of the track.
- Also bounce down a version of the track in the same format but without any vocals.
- Make sure you are naming the bounces with 'pre-master' or 'mix' in the file name.
- Listen in detail to the finished bounces on a range of speaker systems and check for errors or artefacts.
- Create a clear folder system for filing the pre-master tracks, so these can always be returned to in the future.

Mastering Tools

24

▶ **Learning Outcomes**

By the end of this chapter, the reader will be able to:
- Describe the functions of the main processes used in a mastering chain.
- Show a working knowledge of where to use compression, Eq and harmonic exciters within mastering.
- Evaluate when to apply reverb and stereo enhancement during the mastering process.
- Recall the differences and uses of limiting and clipping.

Compression

Compression (see Chap. 12: Dynamics) is used in the mastering process to reduce dynamic range and increase energy in the track. Overdoing it with compression can squash the life out of a track, so it's important to use it subtly. Typically gain reduction of 1 to 4 dB should be enough. Multiband compressors (see Chap. 12: Dynamics) can be useful at this stage if you need to compress different bands of frequencies separately. Multiband compressors split the signal into 5 Eq bands, each of which can be compressed separately.

▶ *Tip: Use two compressors in series, each doing less gain reduction than a single compressor. This way, the recovery time of each compressor will be quicker resulting in a more transparent sound. Professional mastering engineers might even use 3 or 4 or more in a chain, adding just 1 dB at a time.*

© The Author(s), under exclusive license to Springer Nature
Switzerland AG 2024
S. Duggal, *Record, Mix and Master*,
https://doi.org/10.1007/978-3-031-40067-4_24

Equalisation

Equalisation (see Chap. 11: Equalisers) is used to fix any sonic anomalies in the track. For example, if the track sounds a bit muddy, you may need to reduce the frequency at around 250 Hz. If it sounds harsh, you may need to reduce the 2 kHz to 4 kHz range. If your track sounds a bit dull, you may want to lift the high end with a shelf Eq from 5 kHz upwards. Don't overdo it with eq.

▶   *Tip: If you find you're making big increases at any given frequency, it's probably best to look at your mix again to find what the problem is. It may be that there's an issue with just one instrument.*

Harmonic Exciter

If you are finding it difficult to get the high frequencies right using Eq, a harmonic exciter might be the solution. Harmonic exciters (see Chap. 13: Effects) increase the harmonic content of fundamental tones and can add sheen and sparkle that is sometimes not easily achieved with Eq. As with compression, it's important not to overdo it. Constantly referencing commercially released tracks in the same style as the track you are mastering will help you maintain an accurate picture of how your track should sound.

Reverb

If your mix sounds a bit dry, a little bit of reverb can add depth and character and can glue your track together. It's not often that you will need to add reverb at the mastering stage but it is a useful tool should you need it. Convolution reverb is best, with a balance of somewhere around 5% to 15% wet. To avoid making your track sound a bit muddy, it's best to high-pass filter the reverb up to around 150 Hz.

Stereo Enhancement

Stereo enhancers can be used to increase or reduce the width of your track. Avoid using single band stereo enhancers as they apply the effect to the entire frequency range. Stereo enhancement is best applied to only high mid and high frequencies, so you will need a tool that lets you select which part of the frequency range to apply the effect to. Mid/side processing can be used for stereo enhancement (see Chap. 16: Mid/side Processing).

▶   *Tip: Avoid adding stereo enhancement to low frequencies. It can make them sound muddy and undefined.*

Limiting and Clipping

Limiters and Clippers prevent the signal from exceeding the maximum output level as determined by the user. Regular limiters typically have a ratio of 10:1 to 100:1. Brickwall limiters typically have a ratio of infinity:1.

Clipping is when signal peaks are squared off. This is called hard clipping. It is used to raise the average RMS level to get the master to sound much louder. Soft clipping is essentially the same thing, though it is eased into rather than being bluntly chopped.

▶ *Tip: Soft clipped signals have rounded tops which sound softer and more pleasant due to less excessive high-frequency content.*
▶ *Tip: The difference between limiters and clippers is that limiters have a release time constant, releasing the signal from a state of compression, whereas clippers act purely on amplitude without any release time constant.*

Careful use of clipping can add character to and raise the loudness of the source material. Be careful though, as misuse of clipping can kill the dynamics in your track and add nasty distortion (Fig. 24.1).

▶ *Tip: Try starting your mastering process at the end of the signal chain. Set your limiter to an approximate gain reduction setting so that only the peaks are being limited. Next, go to the first compressor in the chain and adjust its settings as required. Adjust the settings on the second compressor if you are using one and then apply corrective equalisation as necessary. You may or may not need to follow the Eq with a harmonic*

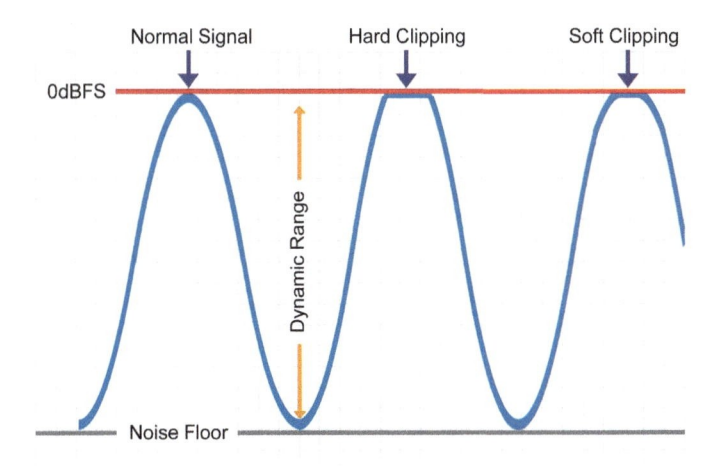

Fig. 24.1 Hard and soft clipping

> *enhancer and a stereo enhancer. From this point, tweak your settings as required. Finally, fine-tune your limiter settings.*
> *Note. There is no strict order of plugins for a mastering chain in the box. You may find that you need to use an Eq first, followed by a multiband compressor, a harmonic exciter and then a limiter. Or, you might find that a multiband compressor followed by a stereo enhancer and a limiter works best. Only you can judge exactly what plugins are needed and in what order.*

> **Chapter 24 Tasks:** The following tasks will get you started on your own mastering and enable some experimentation in exploring what works for your tracks.

- Create a new DAW template dedicated for mastering.
- Insert a plug-in chain in the 'stereo out/master' channel which includes:
- Compressor.
- Equalisation.
- Harmonic Exciter.
- Reverb.
- Stereo enhancement.
- Limiter.
- Clipper.
- Create another stereo audio channel and label it 'reference track'—this can be used to import a commercially mastered track of a similar genre to use as a sonic reference when working on your own mastering.
- Import your mix bounce into your DAW and experiment with the plug-in chain, drawing on advice given in this chapter.
- Experiment with the above plug-ins in different orders in the chain and find what works best for your source material.
- Try adding an equalisation plug-in at the end of the chain as well as at the start of the chain.
- Try experimenting with 2 or 3 compressors, using each one to add a small amount of cumulative compression.

Dither 25

▶ **Learning Outcomes**

By the end of this chapter, the reader will be able to:
- Summarize how quantisation errors can cause problems in file conversion.
- Illustrate how analogue-to-digital conversion can create mathematical errors.
- Evaluate when to apply dithering to a track and recall suitable dither types.

Dithering is the process of adding some very low-level white noise (hiss) to digital audio during bit depth reduction. Why would we want to add noise to our great recording?

Consumer devices, such as Hi-Fi, personal MP3 players and car stereos, playback audio at 44.1 kHz and 16 bits. The professional standard for recording audio is either 24 or 32 bits and often at higher sample rates. This means that at the final stage of mastering, the bit depth and sample rate of the audio material will have to be reduced to be compatible with consumer devices.

When an analogue signal is converted to digital, it is represented as a binary series of zeros and ones. During conversion, mathematical errors can occur resulting in parts of the signal being misrepresented. This is known as a quantisation error. Quantisation errors can also occur when reducing the bit depth which can introduce a harsh gritty sound to the recording (Fig. 25.1).

By introducing very low-level white noise—dither—to the signal, this harshness is smoothed out, making the audio more pleasant to listen to (Fig. 25.2).

Depending on your choice of limiter or maximiser, you may have an option to choose between different modes of dither. Each mode has been optimised to suit different dynamic ranges. Some examples are:

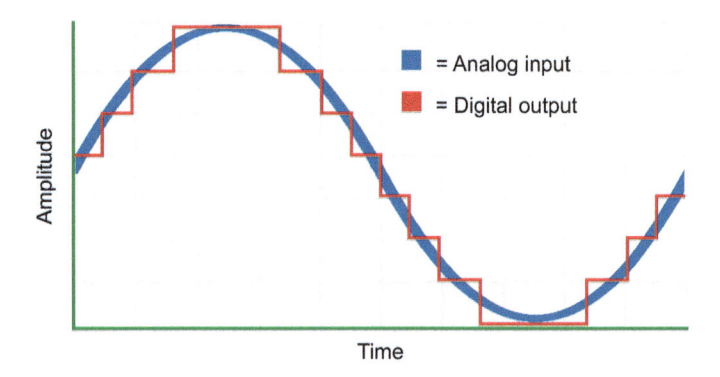

Fig. 25.1 Analogue input and digital output

Dither

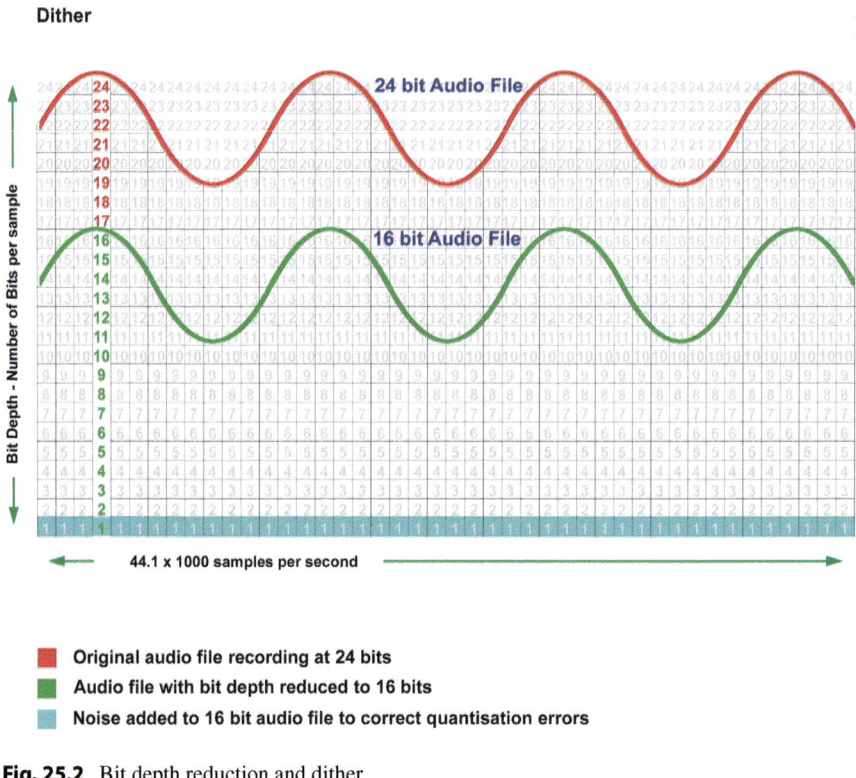

Fig. 25.2 Bit depth reduction and dither

- Original audio file recording at 24 bits
- Audio file with bit depth reduced to 16 bits
- Noise added to 16 bit audio file to correct quantisation errors

25 Dither

POW-r#1 is optimised to suit highly compressed material with a low dynamic range such as EDM.

POW-r#2 may be better suited to less complex material such as a simple guitar and vocal track.

POW-r#3 may be best used on complex highly dynamic recordings such as classical music.

Depending on the plugin manufacturer, these options may be labelled differently, so be sure to refer to your plugin reference manual.

Dithering is the final stage in the mastering process, usually when a 32 or 24 bit file is reduced to 16 bits. It's a good idea to add dither whenever the bit depth of a file is reduced.

▶ **Chapter 25 Tasks:** The following tasks will enhance your understanding and application of dithering audio.

- Experiment with applying different modes of dither to the same source material as you bounce it down.
- Can you hear differences? Which one sounds best?

Metering: Peak, RMS and LUFS   26

▶ **Learning Outcomes**

By the end of this chapter, the reader will be able to:
- Explain the reasons for a range of metering types.
- Recall the Peak, RMS and LUFS metering types and their useful applications.
- Define loudness levels for audio depending on the intended platform outcomes.

The peak of an audio signal is its loudest point. The peak value is a momentary measure of the loudest point.

Root mean square (RMS) and loudness units full scale (LUFS) are measurements of an average signal level based on what our hearing is accustomed to.

RMS is an accurate representation of the average loudness of your mixes though LUFS is considered a more accurate way of measuring perceived loudness. LUFS is the standard by which online streaming services such as YouTube and Spotify measure the perceived loudness of tracks. This is not to force you to listen at any particular volume, but moreover to ensure a relatively consistent level across different tracks (Fig. 26.1).

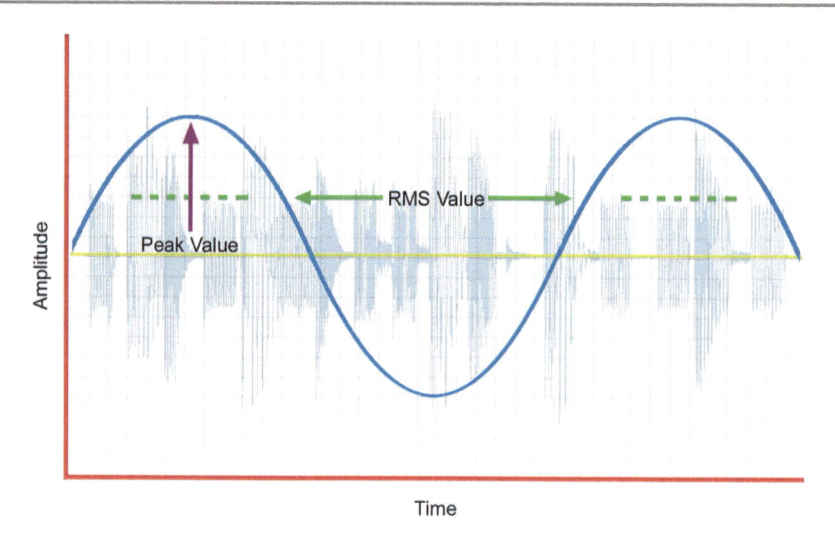

Fig. 26.1 Signal peak and RMS value

There are different types of metres used to measure the level of the signal:

Peak Program Meter (PPM)

PPM metres respond very quickly to sudden changes in level. They are used to ensure the maximum digital level of 0 dBFS is not exceeded, which would otherwise cause the signal to clip. They also give you a view of the dynamic range of the signal, showing the difference between the average and peak values (Fig. 26.2).

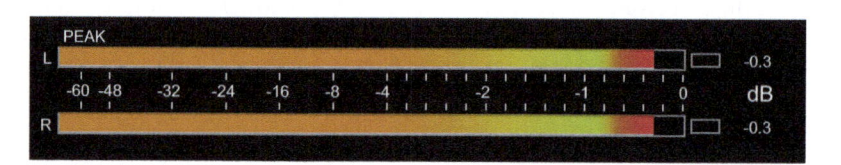

Fig. 26.2 Peak program metres

Root Mean Square (RMS)

RMS metres give you a better view of the average loudness of the signal, much like VU metres on analogue consoles. They display the average level over a short period of time and include any peaks in the averaging (Fig. 26.3).

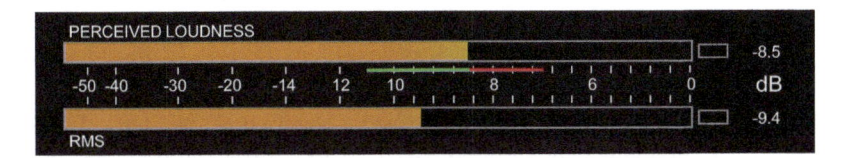

Fig. 26.3 RMS meter

Loudness Units Full Scale (LUFS)

LUFS metres accurately display the perceived loudness of the signal. Spotify, YouTube and other streaming platforms normalise songs using the LUFS metering scale to ensure that all tracks maintain the same volume level. For example, a heavily compressed EDM track would have the same perceived loudness as a more dynamic jazz track, so when listening to a playlist of different recordings, you won't be shocked by a sudden jump in volume on a particular track and you won't have to keep reaching for the volume control.

The integrated LUFS reading is the average perceived loudness, whereas the momentary max reading displays the signal peak (Fig. 26.4).

Fig. 26.4 Loudness units full scale

At the time of writing this book, online streaming services normalise your tracks to the following targets:

Service	Loudness Target
Apple Music	−16 LUFS
Spotify	−14 LUFS
Tidal	−14 LUFS
YouTube	−13 LUFS

When you master your music louder than the target for a given streaming service, the level will be reduced to match the provider's requirements. If you master your music much quieter than the target level, it will be normalised to make it louder. In the case of Spotify at the time of writing this, peak limiting will be applied causing a possible loss of dynamic range in your music. If you are mastering for a specific streaming platform you should aim for their specific LUFS level. Mastering to an average loudness of approximately −14 LUFS with short-term peaks hitting around

−9 LUFS might be the best compromise for tracks intended for release on multiple streaming platforms. The average loudness target for CD is −9 LUFS. Many vinyl records are cut from CD masters, though often more compression is used to reduce dynamic range in order to prevent the turntable needle from jumping. If you are mastering for vinyl only, a loudness target of −9 LUFS is about right. Pay careful attention to dynamics though, particularly in the lower frequency range, as this can have a big impact on whether the needle jumps or not.

▶ **Chapter 26 Tasks:** The following tasks will contribute to your knowledge of metering types and give experience of mastering tracks to a range of levels for commercial release.

- Return to your mastering template and insert a peak, RMS and LUFS metering plug-in to the master output channel.
- Spend some time comparing the metre levels and noticing how they inter-relate.
- Try using the metres to create multiple mastered versions of your track with suitable levels for a range of potential services, such as: Vinyl Release, Spotify Streaming and YouTube.
- Listen to a commercially released track.
- What are the prominent instruments in the track, are some louder than others?
- Monitor the track through a range of metering types—can you detect what levels it is mastered at?
- Is there a wide dynamic range across the whole track or is it fairly consistent?

Mastering Your Song: Things to Consider   27

▶ **Learning Outcomes**

By the end of this chapter, the reader will be able to:
- Explain the importance of monitoring and listening during the mastering process.
- Apply a working knowledge of specific techniques within compressors, equalisers and limiters for mastering.
- Evaluate a mastered audio track using a spectrum analyser.
- Recall the uses of stem mastering.

The most important aspect of mastering is accurate monitoring. Professional mastering studios have dedicated high end speakers that are precise in both the frequency and time domains. This means that they are capable of delivering a flat frequency response and perhaps more importantly, all frequencies reach the mastering engineer's ears at the same time. The speakers are carefully positioned in an acoustically treated room to ensure that SBIR does not interfere with the direct sound (see Chap. 9: Room Acoustics; also see Chap. 2: Speakers—Speaker Placement).

Hiring a professional mastering engineer is a wise move. They will have many years of experience mastering a variety of styles. They will have a fresh set of ears and will listen to your music objectively. Using high end equipment in accurate listening rooms, they will ensure your track sounds great alongside commercially available tracks. Having said that, assuming you have good equipment and a decent listening environment, it is possible to master your own music and get good results.

Supplementary Information The online version contains supplementary material available at https://doi.org/10.1007/978-3-031-40067-4_27. The videos can be accessed individually by clicking the DOI link in the accompanying figure caption or by scanning this link with the SN More Media App.

Listen

The aim of a mastering engineer is to bring out the best in the track, not necessarily to make it as loud as possible. Loudness is important but it comes at the expense of losing some dynamics. This is fine if you're mastering a banging EDM track but not so good if you're mastering a dynamic reggae track.

▶ *Tip: Mastering is all about listening and identifying what the track does and does not need in terms of tone, dynamics and loudness. Use your ears before relying on your metres. Metres are an important tool giving you lots of information about Eq, dynamics and loudness but ultimately it boils down to how it sounds.*

▶ **Tips from the pros:** *The first thing I do is listen to the entire track and memorize everything that sounds strange to me: the balance of the sounds, the equilibrium between low and high frequencies, the resonances, the excessive or needed peaks, the anti-phase zones. Based on the problems that I find, I decide if it is sufficient to use a stereo mastering program or a multitrack DAW to solve some. A DAW is preferred if I need some automations, some cuts of the parts of the structure with musical precision to treat them separately, such as Verse and Chorus but also to treat separately Kick and Bass and the rest of the sounds, for a classic parallel treatment of the file as well, or a mix of all of these. Things that can only be achieved with an excellent DAW capable of handling the various tracks with absolute precision, without any phase shift added.* **Alex Picciafuochi—Mastering Engineer & Producer—***Robert Miles, Luca Agnelli, Claudio Coccoluto, Caneschi and more.*

A good place to start is by choosing a commercial reference track in the same style as the track you are mastering. Listen carefully to it to hear its tone, compression style and volume level. Refer to the reference track frequently in order to maintain perspective on how you would like your track to sound. It helps to write down notes about the reference track. For example, you might notice that the bass end sounds tight and punchy, the cymbals sound silky smooth and the midrange is warm and full, yet each instrument has its own space. Listen to your track and compare how it sounds to your notes.

▶ *Tip: Listen to your track and the reference track at the same volume. If the reference track is louder, you may perceive it to have more bass and treble (see Chap. 1: An Introduction to How Sound Works—Equal Loudness Contours).*

▶ *Tip: Use a spectrum analyser to look at the frequency curve of your reference track and compare it with your track. This will tell you if you're in the right ballpark (Fig. 27.1).*

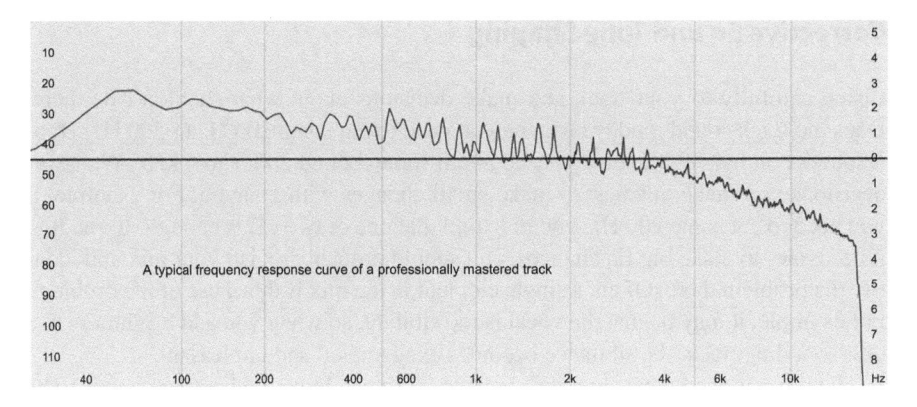

Fig. 27.1 Typical frequency response of a mastered track

Dynamics and Compression

Listen to the dynamics of the track. Does it sound punchy enough? Does the mix sound 'glued' together? Does it need more energy? Multiband compression is a great tool to use here. You can solo each band of frequencies and give each one the right amount of glue and punch as needed (see Chap. 12: Dynamics—Compressors—Multiband Compressors). Use compression sparingly. You don't want to squash the life out of the track and kill the dynamics.

▶ *Tips from the pros: Daily I use: Linear Phase equalizer for surgical corrections, Dynamic Equalizers or Multiband Compressors to contain or emphasize peaks, in narrow band interventions I prefer the Dyn-EQ that is more precise and versatile, in treatment involving a wider band I often choose a Multiband Compressor that is more soften and musical. In my mastering chain there is always also a M/S Eq to reduce to Mono the lower frequencies, this clean and add focus to eventual Kick and Basses, furthermore a monoband compressor to glue or warm the mix. I use another kind of EQ, the more musical equalizers, those purely for mastering, to give a nice curve to the "too much fixed" song to give it more personality. Occasionally I also use Open Reel Recorders when a more analogue sound is required. Finally, to get to the necessary volume, I use Maximizers, Clippers and Limiters, depending on the required target of Loudness.* **Alex Picciafuochi—Mastering Engineer & Producer**—*Robert Miles, Luca Agnelli, Claudio Coccoluto, Caneschi and more.*

Corrective Eq and Tone Shaping

Listen carefully to your track and make decisions about what shouldn't be there. Does the track sound muddy? Maybe you need to cut some 200 Hz to 300 Hz. Does it sound a bit harsh? Maybe you need to cut some around 2 kHz to 4 kHz. Whatever decisions you make, it's best to make small changes with your Eq. For example, if you need to cut some 200 Hz, you may find that one or two dB is enough. If you find it necessary to make big Eq changes, you should probably revisit your mix and identify the problem there. Often, a single element in the mix is the cause of the problem. For example, it may be that the vocal is too sibilant, so when you add brightness to a dull-sounding track, the sibilance becomes exaggerated and unpleasant.

Having removed what shouldn't be there, you can look at what there needs to be more of. Maybe you need a gentle lift on the high end to add a bit of sheen to the track, or maybe it needs more weight on the low end. Dynamic equalisers are a good choice here as they will only apply changes to the track where needed (see Chap. 11: Equalisers; also see Chap. 12: Dynamics—Compressors).

▶ *Tip: Sometimes the balance of the centre mono part of the image needs adjusting relative to side information. You may need to equalise the mid and side information separately (see Chap. 16: Mid/Side Processing). Mid/side processing can be in the form of equalisation, compression, gating, reverb, delay, distortion and other effects.*

Harmonic Enhancement

When an equaliser can't quite achieve the desired result, a harmonic enhancer is a good choice. Harmonic enhancers add odd and even harmonics to the audio material, which can be great for making low-frequency sounds audible on small speakers, and can add presence and sparkle to dull sounding tracks without making the high end too piercing (see Chap. 13: Effects—Distortion and Saturation).

Limiting

Limiting is the last process in the mastering chain and is used to raise the overall level of your audio (see Chap. 12: Dynamics—Limiters).

With all other tools bypassed, start by setting the limiter to an approximate level. You can fine tune your limiter settings later on in the mastering process. For online streaming services, mastering to an average level of around −14 LUFS with short-term peaks hitting around −9LUFS—anywhere close to these numbers—should be about right.

Dither

If the final master is for streaming or CD, the bit depth will have to be reduced to 16 bits (see Chap. 25: Dither).

Mastering Chain

There is no strict order of plugins in a mastering chain. It may vary depending on the style of music and the desired end result. However, a limiter is always the last processor as it is used to raise the overall level of the track to meet final playback requirements.

Stem Mastering

Stems are separate mixes of the drums, bass, keyboard/guitars and vocals. They should all be exported with the same start-point, sample rate and bit depth. Importing these stems into your mastering session gives you much more control than when working with a single stereo mix.

▶ **Master Tasks**

- Import Audio examples 63 and 64 into your mastering template.
- Listen carefully to both versions.
- Does example 64 sound louder than 63?
- Do the instruments sound like the are 'glued' together more in 64?
- Is there greater clarity in the overall sound?
- What else do you think is improved or different about the mastered version compared to the un-mastered?
- Now mute version 64.
- Gradually apply your mastering chain plug-ins to 63.
- Add equalisation, compression, limiting and any of the other mastering techniques discovered in this chapter that you think are appropriate.
- See if you can replicate the sound achieved in example 64 using your own settings and effects plug-ins.
- When you think you have achieved a quality mastered sound, compare your mastered version to Audio example 64 and see if you have managed to recreate something similar (if auditioning in the same DAW session, make sure your mastering plug-ins aren't also being applied to the reference track!).
- Keep tweaking your mastering until you are satisfied it sounds close to the provided mastered version, then bounce the track down to a new stereo file.
- Keep a note of what settings work for this audio track, but remember, every track will need bespoke mastering, there is no one setting which suits all audio!

As you may have noticed, the word listen has appeared many times throughout this chapter and indeed this book. How your finished track sounds is the most important factor, and it doesn't really matter which route you take to get to that point. Understanding how to use all of the tools at your disposal will give you the confidence to use them creatively to achieve your desired result. Ultimately, in a properly acoustically treated listening space, trust your ears!

Good luck with your music-making endeavours!
Simon Duggal

Glossary

A/D Analogue to digital conversion.
Active Speakers Speakers with amplifiers built into the cabinets.
Amplitude The maximum extent of a vibration or oscillation of sound measured from the position of zero amplitude.
Analogue All sounds in the natural world. Any sound that has not been converted to digital binary.
Arm To enable a track to be ready for recording.
Attenuate To reduce the level of.
Audio Interface A hardware device that connects to your computer via a USB, firewire or thunderbolt cable giving you better sound quality and connection capabilities than the computer's own sound card.
Bit Depth The number of bits of information in a single sample. Also known as word length.
Bounce Export all of the mixed tracks in your DAW into one interleaved or split stereo audio file.
Coaxial Speakers (Dual Concentric Speakers) Speakers with a single woofer with the tweeter placed in the centre of it.
Compressor Hardware or software plug-in devices which are used to obtain a more consistent level by reducing loud parts of the recording without limiting peaks.
Consolidate Join different audio or midi files together to form one new file.
Controller Keyboard MIDI or USB keyboard for playing virtual instruments in DAW software.
CPU A computer's central processing unit.
Crossover The circuitry in a speaker cabinet that prevents low frequencies being fed to, and causing damage to the tweeter.
D/A Digital to Analogue conversion.
Data Information stored on the computer's hard drive or temporarily held in the RAM of the computer.

DAW Digital audio workstation, e.g. Pro Tools, Logic, Ableton Live, Reaper, Reason, Cubase.

dB Abbreviation for decibels—a unit of measurement of the loudness of a sound.

dBm Decibels referenced to 1 milliwatt.

dBu and dBv Decibels referenced to 0.775 volts.

dBV Decibels referenced to 1 volt.

De-Esser Hardware or software plug-in devices which are used to reduce the loudness of unpleasant frequencies in vocal recordings when an "ess or shh" sound is made.

Digital Audio signals that have been converted to binary data in order to be processed inside a computer.

Dispersion How sound radiates outwards from a speaker.

Dither The process of adding low-level white noise (hiss) to digital audio, when the bit depth is reduced.

Downsample Reducing the sample rate of the source material.

DSP Digital signal processor that can perform processes in real time. Usually built into audio interfaces that handle plugin processes onboard without causing latency.

Dual Concentric Speakers (Coaxial Speakers) Speakers with a single woofer with the tweeter placed in the centre of it.

Expander Hardware or software plug-in devices used to increase the difference in loudness between quieter and louder sections of audio, making quiet sounds quieter and loud sounds louder.

Export Bounce all of the mixed tracks in your DAW into one interleaved or split stereo audio file.

Equaliser (Eq) Hardware or plugin device used to change the tone of a signal across the frequency spectrum.

Formants Resonances in the vocal tract that occur at intervals of roughly 1000 Hz giving voices the character that is unique to each person.

Freeze Bounce a track and its inserts to audio in place on the timeline. Inserts are then disabled to free the CPU.

Frequency The number of wave cycle recurrences for any given tone.

Frequency Drift The signal is sampled at precise and regular intervals but not in time with the word clock.

Fundamental The lowest audible frequency of a sound.

Gain Control over the increase or decrease in decibels (dB) of the input level of an audio signal.

Gain Staging Setting the correct input and output levels for each piece of equipment or plugin in a recording chain.

Harmonics A frequency above the lowest audible fundamental of the sound.

Hertz Unit of measurement for frequencies. Expressed as Hz or kHz.

In the Box Recorded and mixed entirely inside a computer.

Import Add audio or MIDI files to a DAW project.

Interleaved A single file contains left and right stereo or dual mono audio material.

Interpolation Adding samples to the original signal.

ISRC International Standard Recording Code—system for the identification of recorded music and music videos. Each ISRC is a unique identifier that can be permanently encoded into an audio recording or music video.

Jitter Audio samples recorded and played back at irregular intervals in relation to required word clock instances.

Kilohertz Unit of measurement for frequencies of 1000 Hz and above. Also expressed as kHz.

Level The loudness or volume of a sound.

Limiter Hardware or software plug-in devices which are used to reduce the peaks of an audio signal without affecting the rest of the sound.

Masking When frequencies that are not needed on one instrument, obscure the same frequencies that are required on another instrument.

MIDI Musical Instrument Digital Interface—protocol for connecting devices such as controller keyboards, electronic drum trigger pads or anything that supports MIDI, to your computer.

MIDI Notes Visual display on your computer of inputted MIDI data.

Mix A tonal and level balance of instruments, voices and effects.

Monitors Speakers used for critical listening in studios.

Mono An identical signal is fed to the left and right speakers creating a phantom centre image.

Native Plugins Plugin processing is handled by the computer.

Nearfield The listener sits close to the monitors. Usually within one or two metres.

Noise Gate Hardware or software plug-in devices that can be set to automatically mute the signal during parts of the audio track where the instrument is not being played.

Oversample Increase the sample rate for processing within a plugin. The plugin output is then downsampled back to the session sample rate.

PA Version A PA or personal appearance version is an export of a song with the lead vocal muted. The artist can then use this version for live appearances where it is not possible for the whole band to perform.

Panning Panoramic placement of sounds in the stereo field from left to right.

Passive Speakers Speakers that require an external amplifier.

PCM Pulse Code Modulation—the most common digital audio file format. AIFF and WAV files use pulse code modulation format.

Peak The highest momentary level of an audio signal.

Phantom Power Voltage sent from an audio interface or separate dedicated power supply through the microphone cable to power the microphone. Usually +48v on professional audio equipment.

Plugin Software equalisers, virtual instruments and effects for inserting on tracks in a DAW.

Polarity The position of an electrical signal above or below the median line. Reversing polarity will swap a positive voltage to a negative voltage position and vice versa.

Q Bandwidth on an equaliser. The amount by which frequencies are altered either side of a chosen frequency.

Quantise Snap the position of notes on the timeline to a predetermined location relative to the grid.

RAM Random access memory. Computer memory used to temporarily store data.

RFZ A reflection-free zone in a room.

RMS (Root Mean Square) The effective average output level of the whole waveform.

Room Mode Resonances in a room that exist when excited by a sound source.

Sample Rate The number of samples taken per second of an incoming audio signal.

SBIR Speaker Boundary Interference Response. Sound waves reflected off the room's boundaries interfering with the direct sound from the speakers.

SPL Sound pressure level.

Stems Sub mixes of your drums, bass, keyboards, vocals and other parts.

Stereo The source signal information differs on the left and right channels.

Subwoofer A single speaker that plays frequencies lower than the cut-off frequency of the satellite speakers.

Summing Multiple audio outputs are routed to the input of a single mono or stereo channel.

Timeline Tracks and grid of a DAW on which audio and MIDI information is recorded.

Tone The character of the sound, changeable by using an equaliser, amplifier or effects.

Transient The initial non-tonal part of a sound.

Tweeter Treble speaker.

Unfreeze Restore a bounced track and its inserts that was previously frozen to audio.

Upsampling The process of increasing the sampling rate of an audio file.

USB Universal Serial Bus. A protocol for connecting peripheral devices to a computer.

Velocity Intensity of a note or sound. Simulates the behaviour of piano keys, whereby there are differences in tone depending on how hard or soft the note is struck.

Volume The loudness of a sound.

Woofer Bass speaker.

Word Clock Digital time keeper that determines precisely when a sample is recorded and played back.

Word Length Another way of describing bit depth—the number of bits of information in a single sample.

X Abbreviation for crossfade.

X/Y Stereo microphone placement technique for minimising phase. Mics are placed close together facing opposite directions.

Z Abbreviation for Impedance. Hi-Z = high impedance—signals are more prone to interference and noise, and should be connected to Hi-Z inputs. Lo Z = low impedance—means the current is stronger therefore giving a better signal-to-noise ratio.

Zero Amplitude The point from which the signal level either rises or falls in amplitude.

Zero Filling Adding zeros to an audio file when upsampling.

Index

Numbers and Symbols
+4 dBu, 92
−10 dBV, 92
38% trick, 18
48v, 83
+48v, 63

A
AAC, 42, 57
Active, 83, 91, 92
Active crossover, 12
Active speakers, 12, 66
ADAT, 60
Additive equalising, 135
AES/EBU, 65
Algorithms, 145
Aliasing, 44, 47–49
Amplifier, 75
Amplitude, 3, 5, 6, 9, 197, 204, 209–212
Analog, 41, 42, 47, 48, 50, 57, 59, 60, 65, 75, 76, 78, 141, 145, 232
Analog Gain Staging, 75
Analog to digital converter (A/D), 41, 45, 47, 48, 50–52
Anti-aliasing filter, 44, 48, 49
Arrange window, 30–33
Attack, 141, 149, 150, 153, 155, 156, 158, 160, 162–166, 197–199
Audio, 7–9, 29–31, 33–35, 40, 105, 111
Audio interchangeable file format (AIFF), 57, 231
Audio interface, 41–43, 45, 47, 48, 51, 54, 55, 59–60, 62, 66–68, 71
Audio signal, 243
Automate, 205, 220, 222, 223

Automatic delay compensation (ADC), 56
Automation, 31, 33, 35, 160, 167
Auto release, 151
Auxiliary, 31, 33, 40
Auxiliary channel, 185, 187
Average loudness, 243–246
Axial modes, 105

B
Baffle step filter, 14
Balance, 185–187, 189, 190, 203, 229
Balanced cable, 60, 62, 63, 66
Balanced XLR, 12
Band-pass filter, 138
Bandwidth (Q), 134, 136, 137, 140, 142, 218, 219, 222
Baritone, 206
Bass, 7
Baxandall curve, 142, 143
Bell (or peak) filter, 137
Bidirectional pattern, 87
Binary, 239
Binary sequence, 41
Bit depth, 41, 45–47, 57, 239–241, 251
Boost, 193
Bounce, 231, 233
Brain, 189
Brickwall limiters, 164
Broadband absorption, 22
Broadband bass absorption, 107–108, 110
Broadband bass traps, 107–110, 113–121
Broadcast wave format (BWF), 57
Buffer, 53–57
Bus, 186, 187
Bus compression, 231

C

Calibrated measurement microphone, 111, 112
Calibration software, 72
Capacitor microphones, 82
Cardioid, 124, 125
Cardioid pattern, 84–86, 94
CD, 42, 57, 246
Centre, 201–204
Chamber, 174
Chorus, 123, 179, 183
Clarity, 229
Clipping, 123, 199, 229, 231, 237–238
Clips, 212
Club, 230
Coaxial, 64
Comb filtering, 21–24, 99, 103
Commercial recordings, 217
Compress, 197
Compressing, 193
Compression, 72, 217, 219, 220, 223, 225, 235–238, 248–251
Compressor/compressors, 75, 76, 149–163
Computer, 59–60, 65–67
Condenser microphone/condenser microphones, 82, 83, 93, 98, 124–128
Constructive interference, 102, 106, 107
Consumer playback devices, 215
Controller keyboard, 66, 69–70
Converters, 232
Convolution, 173
Convolution reverb, 236
Corrective equalisation, 237, 250
Counter, 32
Critical listening environments, 105, 121
Crossfade, 209–213
Cue mix, 71
Cut, 193

D

DC offset, 52–53
Decay, 149, 165, 175, 176, 197–199
Decibels (dB), 5
Decimation, 44, 45
Decoupling, 24
De-essers, 166–171
Degrees, 101
Delay, 101, 175, 177–179, 181, 217, 224
Destructive interference, 102, 103, 106, 107
DI Box, 41, 91–93
Diffusers, 110
Digital, 41–57, 59, 60, 64, 65, 232
Digital algorithms, 173
Digital audio, 209, 231, 239
Digital audio workstation (DAW), 29–41, 47, 49, 52–57, 76, 78, 80, 101, 103, 126–128, 183, 190, 191, 201, 202, 204
Digital gain staging, 76–79
DI input, 68
Direct injection, 92, 126
Direct input, 92, 126
Dispersion, 6, 9, 11
Distortion, 14, 180–181, 183, 199, 221, 237, 250
Dither, 229, 239–241, 251
Dithering, 239, 241
Double track, 224
Downsampling, 44–45, 49
Drum kit, 124, 125
Dual concentric speakers, 14
Dynamic compression, 229
Dynamic/dynamics, 37, 149–171, 217, 220, 222, 248, 249
Dynamic equalisation, 168
Dynamic equalisers, 141, 250
Dynamic microphone/dynamic microphones, 81–82, 124–127
Dynamic range, 45–47, 155, 165, 235, 244–246
Dynamic sensitivity, 89

E

Echoes, 173, 177–178, 183
Edit, 212, 213
Edit point, 211
Effect/effects, 72, 215–217, 220, 221, 224, 225
Effecting, 193
Effect returns, 222
Electro, 150
Envelope, 149
Equalisation, 229, 236, 238
Equalise, 189
Equaliser/equalisers, 72, 75, 133, 217–220, 222, 231
Equalising, 193
Equal loudness contours, 7
Even harmonics, 180
Expanders, 165
Export, 231–233

F

Fader, 31, 33, 185–187
Fades, 212
Feedback, 154–155
Feedforward, 154–155

FET, 153
FET compressors, 153
Figure 8 pattern, 87, 89
FireWire, 59
FLAC, 42
Flangers, 123, 179, 221
Fletcher–Munson curve, 7
Frequency drift, 50–51
Frequency/frequencies, 3–9, 12–18, 20–22, 24, 27, 28, 133–147, 189, 191, 205, 206, 235, 236, 247–249
Frequency range, 133, 143, 147, 246
Frequency response, 99, 100, 105–107, 109, 111, 112
Fricatives, 95

G
Gain reduction, 150–155, 163, 164, 170
Gain staging, 75–80
Glue, 249
Graphic equalisers, 134
Grid, 30, 32–33, 35, 37
Groove quantise, 36, 37
Guitar, 123, 126–127

H
Hall, 174
Hard knee, 152
Hard left, 201–204
Hard right, 201, 202, 204
Hardware, 75, 141, 145
Harmonic, 197
Harmonic enhancement, 250
Harmonic excitement, 229
Harmonic exciter, 236
Harmonic overtones, 221
Headphones, 59, 60, 66, 70–74, 124, 125, 129, 219, 223
Headroom, 76–80, 123, 231–233
Hertz (Hz), 3–5, 42
Hi-Fi, 239
High-pass filters (HPF),), 95–96, 136, 142, 176, 205, 206, 218, 225
High-shelf filter, 138
Hiss, 216, 239
Hi-Z, 69, 90
Hypercardioid pattern, 86, 89

I
Impedance/impedances, 65, 69, 71, 90, 92
Impulse responses, 173

Input/inputs, 60, 62, 66, 68, 69, 75, 76, 78–80
Input signal, 76, 78
Insert, 33
Inserting effects, 181
Insert sends, 187
Instrumental, 232, 233
Instrument/instruments, 59, 60, 62, 65, 66, 68, 69, 123, 124, 126, 127, 149, 155, 158, 159, 162, 163, 166, 193, 201, 203, 204
Instrument level, 91, 92
Interleaved, 231
International Standard Recording Code (ISRC), 229
Interpolation, 44
Inter-sample peaks, 76, 78, 232, 233

J
Jitter, 50–51

K
Kilohertz (kHz), 3, 4, 7, 42–45, 47–49, 55, 57
Knee, 152
The K-System, 24

L
Latency, 53–56, 141, 142
Left and right, 193
Limiter, 151, 163, 164, 171, 239
Limiting, 229, 231, 237–238, 250, 251
Linear phase, 142
Line level, 60, 66, 68, 90–92
Listen, 217, 220, 221, 224
Listening spot, 105, 107, 112
Loop, 210
Loud, 229, 230
Loudness, 7, 133, 134, 215, 237, 248, 249
Loudness Units Full Scale (LUFS), 230, 243–246
Low frequency, 219
Low-pass filter (LPF), 135, 136, 147
Low-shelf filter, 139
Low Z, 69
Lo-Z, 90

M
MAC, 65
Master, 215, 223
Mastering, 78, 195, 215, 229–230, 235–239, 241, 247–252

Mastering chain, 238, 249–251
Mastering engineer, 231, 247–249
Mastering studios, 247
Mastering tools, 235–238
Maximiser, 239
Metadata, 229
Metering, 230, 243–246
Microphone/microphones, 59, 60, 62, 66, 68–71, 75, 76, 80–101, 123–129, 205–207
Microphone polar patterns, 83, 84, 124
Microphone position, 123, 124, 126, 127
Mid/side processing, 193–195, 250
MIDI, 29–31, 34–40, 59, 60, 66, 69, 70
Midi edit window, 35–39
Minimum phase, 141
Mix, 78, 193, 195, 201–204, 229–233, 248–251
Mix channel, 33
Mix engineer, 215, 219, 221, 222
Mixing, 123, 173, 215–225
Modulation, 49, 52, 217
Modulation effects, 181
Monitor, 216, 217
Monitoring, 189, 190, 247
Monitoring in mono, 189–191
Monitor in mono, 216
Mono, 30, 31, 33, 40, 123, 186, 189–191, 249
Mono audio signal, 204
MP3, 42, 52, 57, 239
Multiband, 235, 238
Multiband compression, 249
Multiband compressors, 162–163
Music, 247, 251
Mute, 33, 35

N
New York compression, 160
Noise, 60, 62, 67, 69–71, 216
Noise floor, 77
Noise gates, 165, 166
Normalise, 231
Notch filter, 136, 137
Note length, 37, 38
Nyquist, 48, 49
Nyquist frequency, 44, 47–49

O
Oblique modes, 105
Odd harmonics, 180
Ohms, 71
Omnidirectional, 124, 189

Omnidirectional pattern, 88
Optical, 60, 64, 65
Optical compressors, 153
Opto, 150
Output/outputs, 59, 60, 62, 66, 68, 69, 75, 76, 78–80
Overlap, 212
Oversample, 44, 49
Oversampling, 44, 47–49

P
Pan, 33, 37, 220, 221
Pan law, 204
Panning, 201–204
Panoramic, 201
Panoramic position, 215
Parallel compression, 160–163
Parametric equalisers, 134
Passive, 83, 91–93
Passive crossover, 13
Passive speakers, 12, 13
PA version, 233
PC, 65
Peak, 243–246
Peak Program Meter (PPM), 244
Perceived loudness, 245
Phantom centre, 193
Phantom power, 63, 68, 82, 83, 90, 92
Phase, 9, 14, 99, 189
Phasers, 123, 176, 179, 183, 221
Phase shift, 101
Phono, 62, 64
Piano display, 146–147
Pitch bend, 37
Pitch correction, 182–183
Plate, 183
Playhead, 30, 31, 33
Plosives, 95, 205–207
Pluck, 197
Plugin/plugins, 31, 33, 44, 49, 53–56, 76, 78, 79, 141, 145, 193, 238
Polarity, 61, 62, 101, 103
Polar pattern, 83, 84, 89, 90, 94, 98
Pop shield, 95, 98
Portamento, 37
Port noise, 16
POW-r#1, 241
POW-r#2, 241
POW-r#3, 241
Preamp/preamps, 41, 60, 62, 68–69, 74, 75, 99, 101
Pre-masters, 232, 233
Processing, 229

Index

Pro Tools, 30–38
Proximity effect, 81, 89–90, 96, 98
Pulse code modulation (PCM), 57
Pultec low end trick, 219

Q
Quantisation, 46
Quantisation error, 239
Quantise, 35, 37
Quarter wavelength, 106, 107

R
Radio, 230
Ratio, 141, 219
RCA, 62, 64, 92
Record, 31, 33
Recording, 99–101, 103, 123–129, 133, 147, 173, 180, 183
Reference track, 248, 251
Reflection-free zone (RFZ), 107
Release, 141, 149–151, 153, 155, 156, 158, 160, 162–166, 197–199
Resonance, 169–171
Reverb, 123, 173–176, 181, 183, 185, 187, 217, 220, 222, 224, 225, 236, 238
Reverberation, 173–177, 183
Ribbon microphones, 83–84
Room, 173, 175, 183
Room acoustic treatment, 105–113
Room modes, 105, 106, 108
Room sound, 124, 125, 129
Root mean square (RMS), 230, 237, 243–246
Rotary pan knob, 201
Routing, 186–187

S
Safety copy, 233
Sample rate, 41–47, 49, 50, 55, 57, 251
Sample/samples, 42–45, 47, 49, 50, 53–55, 218
Satellite speakers, 15, 16, 27, 28
Saturation, 180–181, 183, 221, 224, 250
Send, 33
Sheen, 236
Shelving filter, 12
Shock mount, 95
Sibilance, 166–169, 206
Sibilants, 95
Sidechain compression, 158–159, 168–169
Signal, 99–101, 103
Silence, 231, 233

Sine waves, 101–103
Small diaphragm condenser microphones, 83
Soft clipping, 237
Soft knee, 152
Solo, 33, 35
Sound, 3–9, 99, 101, 103, 105–108, 110, 111, 121, 133, 135, 136, 141–147, 197–199
Sound dispersion, 189
Sparkle, 236
SPDIF, 60
Speaker, 3, 6–9, 105–110, 112, 121
Speaker boundary interference response (SBIR), 17, 72, 105, 110, 112, 247
Speaker placement, 11, 17–24, 28, 103
Spectrum analyser, 248
Speed of sound, 106
Squared low-pass filter, 48, 49
Spring, 174
Standing waves, 107
Stem mastering, 251–252
Stems, 231, 232
Stereo, 30, 31, 33, 40, 123, 125, 126, 128, 185, 186, 248, 251
Stereo audio file, 193, 215
Stereo enhancement, 236
Stereo field, 72, 74, 189, 193, 201, 203, 204
Stereo image, 21, 28, 72, 73
Stereo imaging, 229
Stereophonic, 203
Streaming, 230
Streaming service/streaming services, 245
Studio, 11–13, 15–17, 21, 27
Studio speakers, 12–14
Sub mixes, 231
Subgroup, 185–187
Subtractive equalising, 135
Subwoofer, 15, 27–28
Sustain, 149, 197–199
Sweet spot, 18–21, 27, 28
Synchronisation, 232

T
Tangential modes, 105
Tape saturation, 199
Television, 230
Threshold, 141, 149–152, 154–156, 158, 160, 162–168
Thunderbolt, 59
Tilt Eq Filter, 139
Timeline, 30, 31, 210
Tone, 37, 133, 135, 139, 146, 215, 219, 222
Tone Shaping, 250

Toslink, 64, 65
Track freeze, 33
Transient shaper, 197–199
Transient/transients, 197, 223
Transition, 211, 212
Transport, 31–32
Treble, 7
TRS, 92
TRS jack, 60, 62, 63
Turntable, 246
Tweeter, 12–14, 20

U
Unbalanced, 62–64, 66, 68
Unbalanced cables, 62, 63
Upsampling, 44
USB, 59, 65, 66, 68–70

V
Vacuum tube, 153
Variable MU, 153
VCA compressors, 153, 163
Velocity, 37, 38
Vibration, 16
Virtual instruments, 30, 31, 33, 35, 39, 40
Vocalist, 205, 217
Vocal/vocals, 93–98, 133, 136, 145, 193, 195
Voice/voices, 149, 155, 167, 201

Voltage-controlled amplifier (VCA), 153, 154, 185–187
Volume, 204
VU meters, 244

W
WAV, 57, 231
Wavelength, 3–5
White noise, 239
Width, 229
Woofer, 12–14, 19
Word clock, 50–51

X
XLR, 62, 63, 65, 69, 81, 82, 92
XLR cables, 63, 65
X/Y configuration, 127

Y
Yamaha NS-10M, 13

Z
Zero crossing, 209–213
Zero decibels full scale (0 dBFS), 24, 25, 76, 77, 79, 231, 232
Zero latency, 55

Printed by Printforce, the Netherlands